FESTIVAL GOLD

FORTY YEARS OF CHELTENHAM RACING

FESTIVAL GOLD

FORTY YEARS OF CHELTENHAM RACING

Stewart Peters

TEMPUS

frontispiece: Best Mate – winner of the Gold Cup in 2002 and 2003.

First published 2003

Tempus Publishing Ltd
The Mill, Brimscombe Port
Stroud, Gloucestershire GL5 2QG
www.tempus-publishing.com

British Library Cataloguing in Publication Data.
A catalogue record for this book is available from the British Library.

ISBN 0 7524 2817 9

Typesetting and origination by Tempus Publishing.
Printed in Great Britain

INTRODUCTION

For three magical days in the middle of March, a beautifully crafted sporting arena, carved within the picturesque Cotswold Hills in Gloucestershire, plays host to the most passionate, important and often mystical meeting the National Hunt Racing game has to offer. For seventy-two hours, this cauldron of drama and excitement grips its viewers similar to a hawk with a mouse. The heaving, multi-national masses that descend upon this event lend huge colour and atmosphere to the tense and competitive battles that lie in wait. They come for profit, for fun, for tradition, for history. They come because it is what the whole jumping season has been geared around. They come because it is Cheltenham, the one and only Festival.

Since its origin in 1902, the Cheltenham Festival has emerged emphatically as the centrepiece of the jump-racing season. It offers the chance for the best in the business to compete at championship level, and that level of competition has risen to immense new heights as racing has entered the twenty-first century.

Cheltenham is unique, unlike any other racecourse that its equine contestants encounter. Undulating and stamina-sapping, the sting in the tail regularly comes at the end of each contest in the form of the supremely challenging 'Cheltenham Hill', an ever-upward climbing passage runners must scale from the last obstacle to the winning line. It is a far cry from flat courses like Kempton Park and Newbury. Here, every weapon in a competitor's arsenal is needed for victory to be obtained.

Aside from those involved with the actual races, each Festival draws an influx of the keenest racegoers around. This is the meeting where the true followers of the National Hunt game can be found. They bring with them an enthusiasm for the sport they so admire that simply cannot be found at any other racing event. Of course, the vast band of visitors from the Emerald Isle adds a huge spice of rivalry to the mixture, and a feature of every Festival is just how many races the Irish will purge from their English hosts.

A figure synonymous with the Festival, the Queen Mother samples the pre-race paddock in 1984.

Confident too, any Irishman at the Festival will not hesitate in revealing their banker bet of the week, and if one of their team comes home in front, the receptions given can be nothing short of thunderous.

The three-day extravaganza, to date, plays host to twenty spellbinding races, including the three principal championship contests; the Gold Cup, the Champion Hurdle, and the Queen Mother Champion Chase. Other enchanting races at the meeting include the two-mile Triumph Hurdle for four-year-olds, the Royal & SunAlliance Chase – a novice version of the Gold Cup, the three-mile Stayers' Hurdle, the amateur's Gold Cup – the Foxhunter Chase, the Champion Bumper – run totally on the flat, and the race named after perhaps the most famous horse of them all – the Arkle Chase, a two-mile speed journey for novices.

Of the three main races, the Champion Hurdle over two miles was first run in 1927 and was won by a horse named Blaris. The race, more than any other at the Festival, has seen horses return year after year to prove themselves. Among those to taste glory and imbed their names in history were multiple winners Persian War, Night Nurse, See You Then and Istabraq, to select but a few, each bringing their own style to Cheltenham that made them great champions.

The hell-raising Two Mile Champion Chase – renamed in 1980 in honour of a figure synonymous with Cheltenham, the Queen Mother – was first run in 1959 and won by Quita Que. Royal Relief, Badsworth Boy, Pearlyman and Viking Flagship, among others, demonstrated their craft to mesmerising effect in this breakneck event.

But of course, it is the Gold Cup that will always be the jewel in the crown of the Cheltenham Festival. The 'Blue Riband' of chasing, run over the most taxing of three-and-a-quarter-mile trips, annually captures the hearts of the racing world with its ability to blend romance and skill with heartache and endeavour. First run in 1924 and won by Red Splash, the Gold Cup has undeniably become the most important, classiest jumping race in the world. From a mere £685 that Red Splash earned back in 1924, the most recent champion – the ever-blossoming titan Best Mate – enabled his connections to pocket a huge £203,000. The race itself is steeped in history and tradition, with countless names of horses, jockeys, trainers and owners that will forever be associated with the event. Not surprisingly, the triple-champion of the sixties, the mighty Arkle, remains the kingpin of the equine behemoths that have graced the race, though many have tried to snatch his mantle. Memories will never stop burning for the likes of the dual Irish winner L'Escargot, the freak-of-nature mare Dawn Run, and the nation's grey wonder, Desert Orchid, who all delivered lasting tales to the Gold Cup archives. Maybe in a few years from now, those same tales will be reserved for Best Mate, already a two-time winner at the tender age of eight and the sort of horse the racing world has waited an age for.

Emotion runs high when each Festival rolls around. Success and disappointment, triumph and tragedy go hand in hand at Cheltenham. It is the pinnacle of the jumping season. It is an occasion where its chief race summarises what it means to the racing world. It is Festival Gold.

Winners are greeted in style at Cheltenham, especially Irish ones.

THE AUTHOR

Stewart Peters is a freelance sports writer who lives in Cornwall. Having studied journalism at university in America, a lifelong passion for National Hunt Racing has seen Stewart write books on Aintree's Grand National, as well as this one about the Cheltenham Festival. He has attended every Gold Cup meeting since the age of sixteen, recounting Master Oats' year of 1995 as his fondest memory.

THE PHOTOGRAPHER

Bernard Parkin was established as Official Photographer to The Steeplechase Company (Cheltenham) Ltd in 1972 and still holds office. He was born in Cheltenham and has lived near the racecourse all his life. A professional artist, Bernard took up racecourse photography at the age of eighteen and began providing Her Majesty Queen Elizabeth The Queen Mother with photographs of her horses, eventually being granted a Royal Warrant. Since the death of the Queen Mother, Bernard has been appointed Racing Photographer to Her Majesty The Queen and granted his second Royal Warrant.

1963

MILL HOUSE

The big question surrounding the 1963 Cheltenham Festival revolved around Lambourn trainer Fulke Walwyn. The maestro from Saxon House stables in Berkshire had already achieved greatness by capturing two previous Gold Cups, with Mont Tremblent in 1952 and in the previous year's race with his fine chaser Mandarin. Now, what everybody wanted to know was: could Walwyn conjure a third win with arguably his best horse of the lot, the equine-machine known as 'the Big Horse', the six-year-old Mill House.

One of the major problems that Mill House and the rest of the runners at the 1963 Festival would have to overcome was the distinct lack of racing that had taken place in Britain during the winter. Endless droves of bad weather, including ice and snow, had wreaked havoc with the plans of trainers as countless meetings were lost due to the elements, and no doubt there was a horse or two short of full fitness by the time Cheltenham arrived.

Even so, plenty of runners descended on the Cotswolds for the three-day meeting, with the Irish confident of putting behind them the previous year's disappointing haul of just two winners.

Indeed, it was the Irish that were expected to dominate the opening day's events with a strong hand of challengers. None was more fancied than an extremely exciting six-year-old trained by Tom Dreaper for Anne, Duchess of Westminster. This horse, unbeaten in his four races during the season and considered one of the best and brightest prospects in training, was Arkle, and on the day he was simply awesome, as he crushed his rivals by twenty lengths under jockey Pat Taafe in the three-mile Broadway Chase for novices. Such was the manner of his victory, Arkle was soon being talked about as a red-hot contender for the 1964 Gold Cup itself.

Arkle aside, the Irish failed to notch another triumph on Tuesday, although they were represented by four seconds and a third. Team Spirit, whose finest hour was still to come in the 1964 Grand National, was among the winners on the

A future Grand National winner, little Team Spirit won the 1963 National Hunt Handicap Chase.

Gold Cup fancy Frenchman's Cove, the big-race disappointment.

So it came to Thursday, Gold Cup day, and the day 'the Big Horse' put his reputation on the line. It was no secret that Fulke Walwyn rated Mill House – an imposing horse at over seventeen hands high – as an extremely high-class animal. He had won two of his three races during the season, both at Sandown, and on one of those occasions in December, had easily accounted for his stablemate Team Spirit, who of course had significantly franked the form in competitive style on the Tuesday. Not surprisingly, Mill House was sent off the 7/2 favourite, with Willie Robinson on board.

The main rival to Mill House appeared to be the Tom Dreaper-trained Irish challenger Fortria. The horse, an eleven-year-old, had enjoyed a highly successful career. Twice winning the Two Mile Champion Chase, he had also won an Irish Grand National and had been runner-up to Mandarin in the 1962 Gold Cup. Jockey Pat Taafe was seeking his first winning Gold Cup ride having been second on the same horse the previous year and second on Mariner's Log in 1954.

Both Neville Crump's improving nine-year-old Rough Tweed, who had been second in the season's Hennessy Gold Cup, and Tom Jones' Frenchman's Cove – ante-post favourite for the Grand National – attracted their fair share of support, but many of the twelve-strong Gold Cup field lined up with poor form behind them. These included the mare Olympia, who had suffered from leg trouble, the grey horse Nicolaus Silver, who had won the 1961 Grand National but had been unplaced on his last five runs, and Pride Of Ivanhoe, who had generally struggled since stepping up from hunter-chasing.

On the first circuit, Stan Mellor sent Frenchman's Cove into the lead, where he was accompanied by Pride Of Ivanhoe and the rank outsider, Cannobie Lee, while just behind these came Mill House, Terry Biddlecombe's mount King's Nephew and another outsider in the shape of Longtail.

opening day; the stablemate of Mill House displayed brave battling qualities – a necessity for any Aintree aspirant – to win the National Hunt Handicap Chase from Brown Diamond.

The fifth year of the Two Mile Champion Chase produced an eventful finish as Sandy Abbot very nearly threw away a three-length lead up the finishing hill, eventually holding on to beat the race favourite, Scottish Memories, in a fantastic duel.

Having roared home Arkle at odds-on the day before, Irish eyes were smiling again as they celebrated a one-two in the Champion Hurdle on Wednesday. Successful aboard Winning Fair, Alan Lillingston became the first amateur to win the race since 1938 after conquering the challenge of Farrney Fox.

The 'Big Horse', Mill House and jockey Willie Robinson before their Gold Cup win.

Although he remained with the leaders for a long way, Frenchman's Cove was never jumping fluently and he made numerous mistakes, particularly at the ditches, which did little to suggest he could be a force jumping round the Grand National course, and with a mile to go, he was beaten. Jumping even worse was Nicolaus Silver, who had become detached from the remainder with a full circuit to travel.

None of this was of any concern to Mill House however, and the favourite was jumping superbly. By the time the field reached the fourteenth fence, Robinson and 'the Big Horse' took command, and although Fortria had jumped through to be second at this point, it was soon obvious he was no match for Mill House.

It mattered little to the outcome when King's Nephew fell three from home when in third position, and jumping with the power of a giant, Mill House cruised home under Robinson to win by a very comfortable twelve lengths from Fortria, with Duke Of York coming home late to claim third place, to go along with his fourth in the 1962 running.

The beaten horses had no excuses. Fortria's trainer Tom Dreaper conceded that they had been beaten by a superior horse, while Frenchman's Cove, who would go on to finish a disappointing twentieth in the Grand National, had ruined his round with careless jumping – in stark contrast to the winner.

As for Mill House, the sky now seemed the limit for this impressive bay gelding, who in winning landed a huge gamble for his owner Mr Bill Gollings, as well as giving Walwyn his third Gold Cup as a trainer. The legendary Golden Miller, who had won five Gold Cups during the thirties, had won the first of his titles as a five-year-old, and naturally, with Mill House being only six, comparisons were drawn which paid the new champion an enormous

1963 GOLD CUP RESULT

FATE – HORSE	AGE/WEIGHT	JOCKEY	ODDS
1st – MILL HOUSE	6-12-0	G.W. ROBINSON	7/2*
2nd – FORTRIA	11-12-0	P. TAAFE	4/1
3rd – DUKE OF YORK	11-12-0	F. WINTER	7/1
4th – Longtail	8-12-0	J. Leech	20/1
5th – Pride Of Ivanhoe	8-12-0	Mr P. Hewitt	25-1
6th – Caduval	8-12-0	Mr L. Morgan	10/1
7th – Frenchman's Cove	8-12-0	S. Mellor	11/2
Fell – Olympia	9-12-0	L. McLoughlin	100/8
Fell – King's Nephew	9-12-0	T.W. Biddlecombe	100/8
Fell – Nicolaus Silver	11-12-0	H. Beasley	33/1
Pulled Up – Cannobie Lee	12-12-0	D. Nicholson	100/1
Pulled Up – Rough Tweed	9-12-0	G. Scott	100/9

Weight is in stone & pounds

Race favourite denoted by *

14 March 1963

Going – Soft

Winner – £5,958

Time – 7mins 7 2/5secs

12 Ran

Mill House	Bay gelding by King Hal – Nas Na Riogh	
Fortria	Bay gelding by Fotrina – Senria	
Duke Of York	Bay gelding by Flush Royal – Queen Of The Dandies	

Winner bred by Mrs B.M. Lawlor

Winner trained by F. Walwyn at Lambourn, Berkshire.

OTHER 1963 FESTIVAL RESULTS

(Race, winner, jockey, odds)

Glos Hurdle (Div. I)	Honour Bound	T.W. Biddlecombe	3/1
Two Mile Champion Chase	Sandy Abbot	S. Mellor	5/1
National Hunt Chase	Time	Mr I. Balding	8/1
National Hunt Hcap Chase	Team Spirit	G.W. Robinson	100/8
Glous Hurdle (Div. II)	Buona Notte	J. Haine	7/2
Broadway Chase	Arkle	P. Taafe	4/9
Glos Hurdle (Div. III)	Deetease	C. Chapman	9/1
Cotswold Chase	Ben Stack	P. Taafe	13/8
United Hunts Challenge Cup	Baulking Green	Mr G. Small	5/2
Champion Hurdle Ch Cup	Winning Fair	Mr A. Lillingston	100/9
Kim Muir Mem Ch Cup	Centre Circle	Mr B. Ancil	6/1
Grand Annual Chase	Anner Loch	D. Nicholson	7/1
George Duller Hcap Hurdle	Happy Arthur	T. Brookshaw	4/1
Spa Hurdle	Beau Normand	W. Rees	5/1
Cathcart Challenge Cup	Some Alibi	G.W. Robinson	9/4
Foxhunters' Challenge Cup	Grand Morn II	Mr R.A. Bloomfield	15/2
County Handicap Hurdle	Bahrain	T. Carberry	11/2
Mildmay Of Flete Ch Cup	Milo	J. Gifford	11/2

compliment indeed. Certainly none of the current crop of seasoned chasers appeared likely to threaten his crown. If he was to be challenged for supremacy, it looked as though a member of the novice group would have to raise their game to meet the substantial level that the now mighty Mill House had set.

Fulke Walwyn trained four Gold Cup winners, the third being Mill House.

1964

ARKLE

One of the highlights of the 1963 Cheltenham Festival had been the emergence of a young pretender from the Emerald Isle. Such was the ease and convincing manner of his win in the Broadway Chase that Arkle was instantly projected as a leading player for the 1964 Gold Cup. In his first campaign out of novice company, Arkle's reputation had grown considerably, particularly in his native Ireland. The 1964 Festival would feature the first Gold Cup meeting between the young challenger and 'England's champion', the title-holder and seemingly unbeatable Mill House. They had met once already during the season in the Hennessy Gold Cup at Newbury, with England winning round one on points. The rematch in the big one at Cheltenham had racing fans everywhere drooling with anticipation.

Before the big guns could have their moment, there were the opening two days of the Festival to get through. Opening day on this occasion was actually on the Thursday, with the meeting climaxing on Saturday. Tom Dreaper, in addition to Arkle in Saturday's Gold Cup, sent a powerful team to Cheltenham, and Flyingbolt – a five-year-old that had won all his three races during the season – got the Irish trainer

off to a flying start by winning the very first race, the Gloucestershire Hurdle Division I. Dreaper then followed up when his Ben Stack, a horse that had won at the 1963 Festival, took the Two Mile Champion Chase. Ireland claimed a third victory on the opening day when Dorimont won the National Hunt Chase for amateur riders.

In the midst of all the Irish jubilation, a new chasing star was confirmed in the Totalisator Champion Novice Chase, formerly the Broadway Chase, as the exciting and bold-jumping Buona Notte, trained by Bob Turnell, reaped his sixth win in a row by holding off another Dreaper inmate in the form of Fort Leney in a magnificent finish. Although not entirely convincing on the day, Buona Notte's progression through the season to the top of the novice tree had been well noted, and the horse was certainly considered as one who could threaten the Gold Cup hierarchy in future seasons.

In a wide open Champion Hurdle on Friday, a record number of runners, twenty-four, went to post, and it was Magic Court for trainer Tommy Robson, that emerged victorious, taking the title back to the north of the country for the first time since Doorknocker in 1956.

Both Mill House and Arkle had won their respective races at the 1963 Festival very easily, so it was with great interest when the two clashed for the first time in the Hennessy in November. On that occasion, Arkle was right in contention at the third last, when an error left him sprawling on landing, gifting the race to Mill House who consequently sauntered home. Since then, Mill House had bolstered his reputation with thumping successes in the King George VI Chase at Kempton and the Gainsborough Chase at Sandown, while Arkle had licked his wounds on the other side of the Irish Sea, picking up three-mile chase wins at Leopardstown (twice) and Gowran Park. Although there remained an air of inconclusivity surrounding the Hennessy result, most people

– hoards of Irish punters excluded – expected the current champion to confirm the Newbury places and become the first horse since the Vincent O'Brien-trained Cottage Rake in 1949 to retain his crown. Certainly his starting price of 8/13 indicated rock-solid confidence in Mill House, confidence that was eagerly backed up by his trainer Fulke Walwyn.

Only two other runners dared to take on the big two, although one happened to be a former Gold Cup winner, the eleven-year-old Pas Seul. The horse had triumphed in 1960 and had been runner-up a year later but was now out of form and started at a price of 50/1, while the fourth horse in the race was King's Nephew, a faller in the 1963 renewal but a horse that could proudly claim to be the last to have taken the scalp of Mill House, albeit at the beginning of the 1963 season.

Flutters of snow filled the Cheltenham air shortly before the start of the Gold Cup, but as the horses ran down to the start, the sun appeared to grace the race with its presence.

The champion set the pace on the first circuit with a steady gallop, and the opening lap passed without incident, with Pat Taafe on Arkle prepared to stalk the galloping machine.

There was a brief moment of worry for the favourite as he made a mistake at the ditch early on the second circuit, but he made up for it with a spectacular leap a fence later. As Mill House came to the water jump for the second time, he was four lengths clear and travelling strongly, and with Pas Seul and King's Nephew both starting to struggle, it appeared he only had Arkle to beat to retain his crown. This, however, would be as good as it got for Mill House – his reign as King of Cheltenham was about to be blown into a thousand pieces.

Pat Taafe had Arkle beautifully poised just over a length down at the third last and even though Mill House served up a huge leap to double his lead, Arkle casually cruised up to

Arkle stunned Mill House to capture the Gold Cup for Ireland.

join the leader in a matter of seconds, with Taafe sitting motionless. It now became obvious that Mill House was in serious trouble. Jumping the second last together, Willie Robinson went for his whip on his horse while Arkle sailed into the lead at the last and Taafe then let Arkle unleash his finishing speed and the combination sprinted clear to leave a trailing and stunned Mill House beaten by five lengths.

Unsurprisingly, the Irish contingent exploded with joy at Arkle's success, one that had given trainer Dreaper revenge over Walwyn, having sent out Fortria to be second to his rival's horses in the last two Gold Cups. Dreaper had bought Arkle as a yearling on behalf of Anne, Duchess Of Westminster, and the horse's only defeat in two campaigns of chasing had been in the season's Hennessy.

There was almost disbelief in the Mill House camp over the total destruction of their hero, although both Walwyn and Robinson were gracious in defeat. It could well have been

1964 GOLD CUP RESULT

FATE – HORSE	AGE/WEIGHT	JOCKEY	ODDS
1st – ARKLE	7-12-0	P. TAAFE	7/4
2nd – MILL HOUSE	7-12-0	G.W. ROBINSON	8/13*
3rd – PAS SEUL	11-12-0	D.V. DICK	50/1
4th – King's Nephew	10-12-0	S. Mellor	20/1

7 March 1964
Going – Good
Winner – £8,004
Time – 6mins 45. 6secs
4 Ran

Arkle	Bay gelding by Archive – Bright Cherry
Mill House	Bay gelding by King Hal – Nas Na Riogh
Pas Seul	Bay gelding by Erin's Pride – Pas De Quatre

Winner bred by Mrs M.K. Baker
Winner trained by T.W. Dreaper at Kilsallaghan, Ireland.

OTHER 1964 FESTIVAL RESULTS

Glos Hurdle (Div. I)	Flyingbolt	P. Taafe	4/9
National Hunt Hcap Chase	Prudent Barney	T.W. Biddlecombe	10/1
Totalisator Cha N Chase	Buona Notte	J. Haine	11/8
Two Mile Champion Chase	Ben Stack	P. Taafe	2/1
National Hunt Chase	Dorimont	Mr C. Vaughn	4/1
Glos Hurdle (Div. II)	Elan	D.V. Dick	9/2
Cotswold Chase	Greektown	M. Scudamore	13/2
United Hunts Challenge Cup	Baulking Green	Mr A. Frank	11/8
Champion Hurdle Ch Cup	Magic Court	P. McCarron	100/6
Kim Muir Memorial Ch Cup	Jim's Tavern	Mr G. Pitman	10/1
George Duller Hcap Hurdle	Do Or Die	T. Norman	25/1
Grand Annual Chase	Richard Of Bordx	G.W. Robinson	9/1
Spa Hurdle	Nosey	H. Beasley	100/30
Foxhunters' Challenge Cup	Freddie	Mr A. MacTaggart	1/3
County Handicap Hurdle	Icy Wonder	J. King	11/2
Mildmay Of Flete Ch Cup	Take Plenty	R. Vibert	100/9
Cathcart Challenge Cup	Panisse	M. Scudamore	7/2

that Mill House – a giant of a horse who would become increasingly dogged by injury as his career progressed – may not have been the same horse as the one that stormed away with the title in 1963, but the fact remained that Arkle had come to Cheltenham as the underdog, displayed impeccable jumping skills and ultimately showed no mercy to his opponents as he displayed the killer instinct of a champion in victory. With his authority on the chasing world now resoundingly stamped, Arkle, only a seven-year-old, had the potential to go on and become one of the great ones.

1965

ARKLE

By the time of the 1965 Cheltenham Festival, the star novice chaser from the previous year had been tragically killed in action. Buona Notte, normally a fine jumper, had cruelly had his life taken at Doncaster in January after smashing into a fence during the Great Yorkshire Chase, a race that also claimed the life of a leading Grand National contender in Red Thorn. It was a sad loss to racing, particularly since Buona Notte was one of a small handful of chasers that may have given the imperious Arkle something to think about in the Gold Cup itself. The dearth of worthy challengers to the champion in the Gold Cup became magnified even more when Fort Leney, Arkle's stablemate, was selected by Tom Dreaper to run instead in the National Hunt Handicap Chase. Fort Leney had looked a promising Gold Cup contender when being outlasted by Buona Notte in the Champion Novice Chase the previous year, and for his 1965 Festival target he would have to shoulder a huge 12st 7lb.

Snow made an unwanted appearance on the course in the days leading up to the Festival, so bulldozers and a good deal of manpower were used from the preceding Friday in an attempt to have the track ready.

Ready it was, and not for the first time in recent years, many Irish horses were fancied, led of course by Arkle. Despite running bravely under his huge burden, Fort Leney could only finish second to Rondetto in the National Hunt Handicap Chase on the opening day, while another of Dreaper's stars, Ben Stack, finished back in fourth in his attempt at landing back-to-back Two Mile Champion Chase titles. A new star had surfaced in this race, however, as Dunkirk, ridden by Dave Dick, jumped from fence to fence in a scintillating display of front-running to win, although he almost ruined his performance by clouting the last.

The successor to Buona Notte in the Totalisator Champion Novice Chase was another warrior from the seemingly endless stream of Dreaper stars, as Arkloin prevailed.

On the Wednesday, hot odds-on favourite Flyingbolt was given a supreme challenge by Acrophel in the two-mile

The stylish Dunkirk landed the Champion Chase.

above: Flyingbolt, one of the highest rated chasers of all time, was the winner of the Cotswold Chase.

left: Kirriemuir, a Champion Hurdle surprise at 50/1.

Cotswold Chase for novices. Acrophel was in the lead and travelling strongly when capsizing three out, gifting the favourite the race. There was no doubt that Flyingbolt was a magnificent horse – in fact he would go down as one of the best chasers of all time – but he certainly received his share of luck on this occasion.

Fulke Walwyn's Kirriemuir had won seven times in the previous season and had been well fancied for the 1964 Champion Hurdle, in which he finished third. Now, having suffered a tough time in handicap races during the current season, he attempted another crack at the race at starting odds of 50/1. This was to be his day however, as he came back to form to produce a shock but not undeserved win under Willie Robinson.

For the second straight year, only four runners contested the Gold Cup. Arkle arrived at Cheltenham as one of the hottest favourites for the race in years. The horse had won three of his four races during the season, with the one shock defeat coming in the Massey-Ferguson Gold Cup at Cheltenham, although on that occasion, Arkle had been giving huge chunks of weight away as he finished third behind the talented grey horse Flying Wild and the ill-fated Buona Notte.

Mill House was back to run in the Gold Cup for the third consecutive year, although the horse was considered a pale imitation of the monster that roared away to win in 1963. Still, he had won his last two races and had given weight away to decent horses in the process, and the horse seemed to have retained much of his courage and jumping power. Whether he could prove a match for Arkle remained to be seen.

The other two horses in the line-up, the ten-year-old Caduval, and amateur Mr W. Roycroft's mount Stoney Crossing, were huge outsiders. Stoney Crossing was at least an interesting contestant. The horse had never even run over hurdles, never mind chase fences, and although the horse had run competitively on the flat, his only competitive jumping experience was through three-day eventing, having been part of the Australian team that competed in the Tokyo Olympic Games.

Despite the snow of the previous week, a frosty wind had blown steadily on Prestbury Park leaving good jumping conditions. Even though the pace was just steady on the first circuit, Caduval tailed off after just half a mile.

Mr Roycroft, who also happened to be the owner of Stoney Crossing, was able to keep in touch for the first half of the race, but then the big two began to pull clear.

For much of the first two miles, Arkle had led, rarely threatened for his place, but Mill House put in a mighty leap

1965 GOLD CUP RESULT

FATE – HORSE	AGE/WEIGHT	JOCKEY	ODDS
1st – ARKLE	8-12-0	P. TAAFE	30/100*
2nd – MILL HOUSE	8-12-0	G.W. ROBINSON	100/30
3rd – STONEY CROSSING	10-12-0	MR W. ROYCROFT	100/1
4th – Caduval	10-12-0	O. McNally	33/1

11 March 1965
Going – Good
Winner – £7,986
Time – 6mins 41 1/5secs
4 Ran

Arkle	Bay gelding by Archive – Bright Cherry
Mill House	Bay gelding by King Hal – Nas Na Riogh
Stoney Crossing	Brown gelding by North Riding – Sunlit Stream

Winner bred by Mrs M.K. Baker
Winner trained by T.W. Dreaper at Kilsallaghan, Co. Dublin.

OTHER 1965 FESTIVAL RESULTS

Glos Hurdle (Div. I)	Red Tears	S. Mellor	7/1
National Hunt Hcap Chase	Rondetto	P. Taafe	100/30
Totalisator Champ N Chase	Arkloin	L. McCloughlin	100/7
Two Mile Champion Chase	Dunkirk	D.V. Dick	8/1
National Hunt Chase	Red Vale	Mr G. Small	100/8
Glos Hurdle (Div. II)	Havago	H. Beasley	11/8
Cotswold Chase	Flyingbolt	P. Taafe	4/9
Kim Muir Memorial Ch Cup	Burton Tan	Maj. R. Collie	10/1
Champion Hurdle Ch Cup	Kirriemuir	G.W. Robinson	50/1
United Hunts Challenge Cup	Baulking Green	Mr G. Small	15/8
George Duller Hcap Hurdle	Coral Cluster	T.W. Biddlecombe	8/1
Grand Annual Chase	Fort Rouge	G. Milburn	13/2
Spa Hurdle	Antiar	D. V. Dick	6/1
Foxhunters' Challenge Cup	Woodside Terrace	Mr R.H. Woodhouse	33/1
County Handicap Hurdle	Mayfair Bill	A. Turnell	100/7
Mildmay Of Flete Ch Cup	Snaigow	J. Lehane	100/6
Cathcart Challenge Cup	Scottish Memories	H. Beasley	4/9

four from home, a jump that gave his followers a glimmer of hope. But after his beautiful leap at the last open ditch, Mill House then put in an untidy jump three out, and from here on in it was Arkle's race. The champion led by two lengths at the second last, and an enormous jump at the final fence put the icing on the cake, as he and Pat Taafe shot up the finishing hill to win by twenty lengths from a demoralised Mill House, with Stoney Crossing and his fifty-one-year-old jockey back in third and getting a fine reception from the crowd.

The win merely confirmed Arkle's superiority and he had become the first horse since Cottage Rake in 1949 to retain his title. Taafe even went as far as to say that Arkle was better now than twelve months previously. With that in mind, and with such an easy win to his name, many wondered just how good this superb horse would eventually become.

The incomparable Arkle won the Gold Cup with ease.

1966

ARKLE

The 1966 Cheltenham Gold Cup gave Arkle the opportunity to join an elite band of great modern-day chasers. Cottage Rake had won three Gold Cups from 1948 to 1950, while the legendary Golden Miller remained, at this stage, as the horse that every other Gold Cup contender would be compared to, having won a record five crowns between 1932 and 1936. No other horses in the history of the race had won three or more times. Now Arkle, an easy winner in 1964 and an even easier one in 1965, attempted his third win in the race. Certainly Arkle could not have handpicked an easier looking field if he had tried, with his chief competition either sidelined through injury or attempting other races. His great rival, Mill House, had won at Cheltenham in January, and despite suffering from a bruised foot, was declared by trainer Fulke Walwyn as on course for both the Gold Cup and the Grand National. But when Mill House strained a tendon during exercise a week before the Gold Cup, Walwyn's horse was forced to miss both engagements. With Fort Leney also injured and two other Tom Dreaper stars – the magnificent Flyingbolt and the 1965 Totalisator Champion Novice Chase winner Arkloin – both attempting

alternative Festival races, the Gold Cup looked at Arkle's mercy.

The most enthralling finish on Tuesday came in the Totalisator Champion Novice Chase where the six-year-old Different Class just beat Jomsviking by a whisker on the line. Different Class was owned by film star Gregory Peck.

The brilliant chestnut Flyingbolt had won the Gloucestershire Hurdle Division I at the 1964 Festival and the Cotswold Chase at the 1965 Festival. This time around he was attempting an audacious double, one that got off to a super start on the Tuesday with an inspired win in the Two Mile Champion Chase under Pat Taafe. But despite a brave effort, Flyingbolt went down to Salmon Spray, also a chestnut, in Wednesday's Champion Hurdle, eventually finishing third.

The top two-mile novice chasers in England and Ireland met in the Cotswold Chase on Wednesday, and on this occasion England came out on top, with Arctic Sunset delivering a bold show of jumping to see off the Irish favourite, the Dreaper-trained Thorn Gate. Both horses were considered two fine young chasers for the future.

By the time Thursday's Gold Cup came around, support for Arkle was unwavering. Impossible to back at odds of 1/10, it appeared the horse merely had to stand up to record his third straight victory. The support was well justified. Arkle had won all four of his races during the season, including a Hennessy Gold Cup, and on his latest start had won a third consecutive Leopardstown Chase on heavy ground. The Leopardstown win was his first race in Ireland for over twelve months, and his loyal supporters then followed the wonder-horse to Cheltenham for a St Patrick's Day showdown and a place in history.

Opposition to the great horse was pitiful. Only Snaigow offered any sort of recent form, having won his last two races. At the previous two Cheltenham Festivals, Snaigow

Salmon Spray (far left) was the hero in the Champion Hurdle.

had won a Mildmay Of Flete Chase and been runner-up in a Cotswold Chase. Here, he would be ridden by David Nicholson, and at 100/7, was the closest in the betting to Arkle. The other three runners, Dormant, Sartorius and Hunch had not won a race between them for a considerable amount of time.

As an expectant crowd settled down to watch the race, fully prepared to greet a three-time Gold Cup winner back in the winner's enclosure, it was Dormant and jockey Michael Scudamore that set a moderate early pace.

Having toyed with his opponents for long enough, Arkle, equipped with a sprig of shamrock in his brow-band, took command as they jumped the eighth fence, taking it, like the seven beforehand in fast, accurate style.

So well was he jumping that what happened at the eleventh sent shockwaves around the course. Arkle had

begun to draw clear when he appeared simply to not take off at the fence, clouting it with his chest. Certainly most horses would have come down as a result of such a blunder, but the unrivalled balance of Arkle, together with the coolness of Taafe, meant the horse simply surged on without breaking stride. Arkle may well have been laughing at those who had gasped at the fence before as he soared the twelfth in majestic fashion.

As the champion sailed onwards, it was left to Snaigow and Dormant to endure their own private battle for second place, but when the former made a complete mess of the third last, that honour was reserved for Dormant. At the same fence, the race sadly witnessed a fatality with the demise of Hunch.

By this time, Arkle had come well clear and to a thoroughly deserved standing ovation, he crossed the line a

1966 GOLD CUP RESULT

FATE – HORSE	AGE/WEIGHT	JOCKEY	ODDS
1st – ARKLE	9-12-0	P. TAAFE	1/10*
2nd – DORMANT	9-12-0	M. SCUDAMORE	20/1
3rd – SNAIGOW	7-12-0	D. NICHOLSON	100/7
4th – Sartorius	11-12-0	T.W. Biddlecombe	50/1
Fell – Hunch	9-12-0	S. Mellor	33/1

17 March 1966
Going – Good
Winner – £7,674
Time – 6mins 54 2/5secs
5 Ran

Arkle	Bay gelding by Archive – Bright Cherry
Dormant	Chestnut gelding by Domaha – Miss Victoria
Snaigow	Bay gelding by Vulgan – Nicotania

Winner bred by Mrs M.K. Baker
Winner trained by T.W. Dreaper at Kilsallaghan, Ireland.

OTHER 1966 FESTIVAL RESULTS

Race	Horse	Jockey	Odds
Glos Hurdle (Div. I)	Beau Caprice	T. Jennings	6/1
National Hunt Hcap Chase	Arkloin	P. Taafe	5/2
Totalisator Champ N Chase	Different Class	D. Mould	10/1
Two Mile Champion Chase	Flyingbolt	P. Taafe	1/5
National Hunt Chase	Polaris Missile	Mr M.J. Thorne	100/6
Glos Hurdle (Div. II)	Fosco	D. Moore	7/2
Cotswold Chase	Artic Sunset	G. Milburn	3/1
Kim Muir Memorial Ch Cup	Jimmy Scot	Mr J. Lawrence	6/1
Champion Hurdle Ch Cup	Salmon Spray	J. Haine	4/1
United Hunts Challenge Cup	Snowdra Queen	Mr H. Oliver	5/2
George Duller Hcap Hurdle	Harvest Gold	J. Fitzgerald	5/1
Grand Annual Chase	Well Packed	Mr T. Stack	100/7
Spa Hurdle	Trelawny	T.W. Biddlecombe	11/4
Foxhunters' Challenge Cup	Straight Lady	Mr R. Shepherd	100/8
County Handicap Hurdle	Roaring Twenties	G. Milburn	10/1
Mildmay Of Flete Ch Cup	Tibidabo	J. King	7/1
Cathcart Cha Cup Chase	Flying Wild	T. Carberry	5/4

thirty-length victor. Neither Taafe nor Dreaper had been unduly worried by the horse's gaffe at the eleventh, displaying further their total faith in the horse.

Arkle could now proudly take his place in the record books as only the third horse to win the race three times, and he now surely had the great Golden Miller's total of five wins – injury permitting – firmly in his sights. He certainly appeared unstoppable on this kind of form, and as the celebrations commenced in the winner's enclosure, few expected the scene to be any different in twelve months time.

To top off Arkle's success on Thursday, Ireland rounded off another Festival with a win for the classy grey mare Flying Wild in the Cathcart Chase. The horse was trained by Dan Moore and ridden by Tommy Carberry. This was a combination that had to be noted as the decade wore on.

Pat Taafe rode four Gold Cup winners, including in 1966 on Arkle.

1967

WOODLAND VENTURE

As Arkle embarked on his quest for a fourth consecutive Gold Cup win, there appeared little to suggest that his reign as champion would come to an end. Although the horse began his season by just failing to give two and a half stone to the talented grey Stalbridge Colonist in the Hennessy Gold Cup, he was soon back on track with an effortless success at Ascot. His next engagement came in the King George VI Chase at Kempton, where his opponents included the Gold Cup runner-up Dormant and Fred Rimell's useful bay, Woodland Venture. Mysteriously, Arkle never looked settled in the race and he consequently made a mistake at the open ditch on the second circuit. The three-times Gold Cup winner was under heavy pressure from Terry Biddlecombe on Woodland Venture at the second last, but when the latter came to grief, there appeared no reason why Arkle should not have gone on and won. But after a howler at the last fence and then faltering badly on the run-in, Dormant was able to steam through and almost embarrassingly overturn the great horse. In the aftermath of the race, it emerged that Arkle had indeed broken down badly and had been seriously injured. Surgery was ultimately required for a cracked pedal bone in his hoof and although he came through the operation well enough, his racing career hung in the balance.

Sadly, in autumn 1968, Anne, Duchess of Westminster announced the horse's retirement from racing, and he spent his remaining days on the Duchess' farm in Co. Kildare. Come the spring of 1970, with rheumatism in his leg leaving him a virtual cripple, the grave decision was taken to have Arkle put down. Here was one horse that, even now he had gone, would truly stand the test of time. To this day, bright, up and coming prospects are continually described as 'the next Arkle', not 'the next Golden Miller or Cottage Rake', which, while possibly being unfair on those horses, is surely the ultimate compliment as to how highly Arkle was, and still is, regarded. As an honour to the horse, Cheltenham have a statue of him erected in the complex, while the old Cotswold Chase has been known, since 1969, as the Arkle Challenge Trophy. Arkle, and his accomplishments, will never be forgotten.

The first Festival since 1962 without Arkle would be one where Irish trainer Tom Dreaper would be missing much of his ammunition. Flyingbolt, who had won the Irish Grand National at the end of the previous season, had developed a viral infection and would be absent on this occasion, while his stablemate Baby Snatcher – considered Ireland's best novice chaser – had been ruled out since February with injury. In addition, Dreaper's stable jockey Pat Taafe was sidelined with a broken leg suffered from a fall from the good Thorn Gate in the season's Great Yorkshire Chase.

In Flyingbolt's absence, the Two Mile Champion Chase crown on the Tuesday went to the rangy American-bred challenger Drinny's Double. The horse had only been in third place at the last fence, but powered up the hill to overhaul Pawnbroker and the previous Festival's Cotswold Chase winner Arctic Sunset.

Terry Biddlecombe won the Gold Cup aboard Woodland Venture.

Earlier in the day, Different Class had added to his success in the 1966 Totalisator Champion Novice Chase by winning the National Hunt Handicap Chase under David Mould. The win propelled Different Class to prominence for the upcoming Grand National, where he would be involved in the most bizarre running of that particular race.

On the Wednesday, twenty-three runners – the second biggest field since the inaugural running in 1927 – lined up for the Champion Hurdle. Plenty were in with a chance at the last, and it was the six-year-old Saucy Kit that emerged to win by four lengths under Roy Edwards from the Queen Mother's horse, Makalder.

For the first time since 1962, the Gold Cup featured a favourite other than Mill House or Arkle. The honour went to another Dreaper star, Fort Leney. Runner-up in his races at the 1964 and 1965 Festivals, Fort Leney had missed the 1966 Festival altogether as part of a long lay-off from a heart ailment, a problem that was first diagnosed when the horse flopped in the 1965 Scottish Grand National. The horse had displayed class and bravery when securing an all-the-way win in the season's Leopardstown Chase under top weight, and had been favourite for the Gold Cup since. Standing in to ride Fort Leney for Taafe was youngster Peter McCloughlin, who would be having his first experience of Cheltenham.

Among the opposition to the favourite were Mill House, Woodland Venture, Stalbridge Colonist and What A Myth. Mill House had missed the infamous King George race through lameness but had bounced back with an encouraging third in Doncaster's Great Yorkshire Chase. No horse had ever regained its Gold Cup crown, and even though Mill House had won his latest start at Sandown in February, it was clear he would have to improve again to recapture his glory days.

Woodland Venture, trained by Fred Rimell, had been bitterly unlucky not to have won the King George, but was somewhat overlooked in the betting market having been beaten twice since. What A Myth had enjoyed a consistent season, Ryan Price's charge winning the Mandarin Chase having come home a fast finishing third to Stalbridge Colonist in the Hennessy at Newbury. Stalbridge Colonist had gone on from his Newbury success to run a useful third to the up and coming youngster The Laird in the Massey-Ferguson Chase, before falling on his latest start at Haydock.

With the fortunate King George winner Dormant also in the line-up, the 1967 Gold Cup certainly had a competitive edge to it, an edge missing from the Arkle-dominated years, and it was the rank outsider Foinavon that took them along for much of the first half of the race, albeit at a patient pace.

Going well for David Nicholson – standing in for the injured Willie Robinson – was Mill House, and he disputed the lead as they approached the sixth from home. But he crashed through the top of the fence and came down, ruining his hopes of regaining the title.

This left Woodland Venture, who was travelling sweetly, on his own in front, leading from What A Myth and Stalbridge Colonist, then slightly further back came outsider Dicky May. At this stage Fort Leney, who had not been travelling well on ground too quick for him, was clearly beaten as the leaders raced on.

As the contest entered its closing stages, it came down to a match between Woodland Venture and the plucky little grey Stalbridge Colonist. The grey horse had delayed the start of the race by spreading a plate, but once the action had started he had jumped beautifully, and over the last two flights he had matched the much bigger horse with some fine leaps.

1967 GOLD CUP RESULT

FATE – HORSE	AGE/WEIGHT	JOCKEY	ODDS
1st – WOODLAND VENTURE	7-12-0	T.W.BIDDLECOMBE	100/8
2nd – STALBRIDGE CNIST	8-12-0	S. MELLOR	11/2
3rd – WHAT A MYTH	10-12-0	P. KELLEWAY	3/1
4th – Dormant	10-12-0	J. King	10/1
5th – Dicky May	8-12-0	P. McCarron	25/1
6th – Fort Leney	9-12-0	P. McCloughlin	11/4*
7th – Foinavon	9-12-0	J. Kempton	500/1
Fell – Mill House	10-12-0	D. Nicholson	4/1

16 March 1967
Going – Good to Soft
Winner – £7,999
Time – 6mins 58 1/5secs
8 Ran

Woodland Venture	Bay gelding by Eastern Venture – Woodlander
Stalbridge Colonist	Grey gelding by Colonist II – Eesofud
What A Myth	Chestnut gelding by Coup de Myth – What A Din

Winner bred by Mr H. Collins
Winner trained by T.F. Rimell at Kinnersley, Severn Stoke, Worcs.

OTHER 1967 FESTIVAL RESULTS

Glos Hurdle (Div. I)	Chorus	J. Haine	15/2
National Hunt Hcap Chase	Different Class	D. Mould	13/2
Totalisator Champion N Chase	Border Jet	J. Gifford	4/1
Two Mile Champion Chase	Drinny's Double	F. Nash	7/2
National Hunt Chase	Master Tammy	Capt. B. Fanshawe	100/7
Glos Hurdle (Div. II)	Early To Rise	J. King	11/2
Cotswold Chase	Artic Stream	B. Hannon	8/1
Kim Muir Memorial Ch Cup	Chu-Teh	Mr N. Gaselee	9/2
Champion Hurdle Ch Cup	Saucy Kit	Roy Edwards	100/6
United Hunts Challenge Cup	Baulking Green	Mr G. Small	5/4
George Duller Hcap Hurdle	Stepherion	N. Bampton	100/9
Cheltenham Grand A Chase	San Angelo	J. Buckingham	10/1
Spa Hurdle	Beau Normand	J. King	6/1
Foxhunters' Challenge Cup	Mulbarton	Mr N. Gaselee	Evens
County Handicap Hurdle	Cool Alibi	R. Reid	20/1
Mildmay Of Flete Ch Cup	French March	Mr B. Hanbury	25/1
Cathcart Ch Cup Chase	Prince Blarney	R. Barry	100/8

But as they ran up the final hill, it was Biddlecombe on Woodland Venture that proved just the stronger, holding on in a driving finish for a three-quarters-of-a-length win. Doing his best work late, on quicker than ideal ground, was What A Myth, who finished third ahead of Dormant. The favourite Fort Leney trailed in a disappointing sixth.

Woodland Venture provided the first Gold Cup winner for trainer Fred Rimell and champion jockey Terry Biddlecombe. The nearest Rimell had got to winning as a jockey was second to Prince Regent aboard Poor Flame in 1946, and Woodland Venture's performance saluted a fine training performance from him. Woodland Venture had won three of seven races as a novice the previous season but had then suffered badly from ringworm prior to the current season. After his near miss in the King George, the horse had suffered from teeth trouble, so the speculative Rimell had been purposely easy on the horse with the Gold Cup in mind.

Woodland Venture's dam, Woodlander, was a half-sister to Green Drill, who had been third to Mr What in the 1958 Grand National. In that same race a month later Foinavon, a remote last in this edition of the Gold Cup, would go on to become the biggest-shock winner of all time when winning at 100/1 after virtually every horse was put out of the race following a pile-up at the twenty-third fence.

1968

FORT LENEY

The infectious livestock disease foot and mouth had reared its ugly head in the country in October 1967, and this had resulted in the cancellation of all racing for a six-week period. One of the races lost to the outbreak was the King George VI Chase at Kempton. While the situation had come under control by the time of the 1968 Cheltenham Festival, the watch on movement of horses that fell within the infected areas had only been lifted just days before the three-day meeting. Obviously, many horses had missed out on preparatory races and others would be arriving at Prestbury Park below peak-fitness.

Ireland, as usual, had their banker for the meeting, and on this occasion the honour fell to the promising French Tan in Tuesday's Gloucestershire Hurdle Division I. Considered by the Irish as a future Gold Cup winner and already being compared to Arkle in some quarters, French Tan was backed as though defeat was unimaginable, but defeated he was when, under heavy pressure from the eventual winner King Cutler, he fell two out.

The Irish gained compensation though in the very next race, the Totalisator Champion Novice Chase, when the six-year-old chestnut Herring Gull got the better of Gay Trip – a future Grand National winner.

The Two Mile Champion Chase looked like being one of the races of the meeting, and it featured a hot favourite in Ronan, a horse that was a half-brother to Mill House. But Tom Dreaper's charge could only manage third, as Border Grace appeared to have the race in the bag when approaching the last three lengths clear. However, a bad mistake there allowed reigning champion Drinny's Double, under Frankie Nash, to come through and steal the victory.

The opening day's crowd had been somewhat disappointing in terms of numbers, but those that stayed until the last race saw a fine all-the-way performance by another promising chestnut, L'Escargot, in the Gloucestershire Hurdle Division II. L'Escargot was ridden by Tommy Carberry.

Wednesday's Champion Hurdle saw a high-class field turn out on firm ground. Le Vermontois had been heavily backed for weeks and still attracted strong support despite finishing an unpleasing seventh in the Eastleigh Hurdle at Newbury two weeks before the Festival. But on the day, it was Persian War at odds of 4/1 that came out on top, delivering one of the best performances in the race for many years.

The 1967 Gold Cup winner Woodland Venture was missing, as he had been for the whole season, through injury when the 1968 renewal came round on Thursday. Despite overnight rain loosening up the firm ground, conditions were considered not to the liking of the 1967 third What A Myth, and he was a late withdrawal from the contest, leaving a small but select group of five to face the starter.

Despite now being eleven and a faller in the previous year's race, Mill House was back for a fifth attempt. The horse had only run once during the season, when second at Sandown in the Gainsborough Chase, and had missed vital warm-up runs because of recent firm ground. Discarding

The grey Stalbridge Colonist was third in the Gold Cup having been runner-up in 1967.

those negative factors, Mill House was made favourite, probably on the strength of a win in the Whitbread Gold Cup at Sandown at the back end of the previous season, a performance where the old horse had rolled back the years.

Fort Leney and Stalbridge Colonist were both back to renew acquaintances. The rain had come just in time to save Fort Leney from being withdrawn, as connections – remembering the gelding's flop performance the year before – realised that the softened ground had lost much of its jar. Fort Leney came into the race in winning form, having won his latest start at Leopardstown. Stalbridge Colonist had been his usual consistent self during the season, winning twice and finishing second to one of his opponents here,

Bassnet, most recently at Windsor. Terry Biddlecombe took the mount on the grey.

A highly promising newcomer to the race was The Laird, a seven-year-old trained by Bob Turnell, who had won with Pas Seul in 1960. The horse had plenty of speed, having won both the Massey-Ferguson Chase and the Stones Ginger Wine Chase – races over two and a half miles – earlier in the season, while he had also proven himself over three miles when winning at Sandown in February. However, his backers had to be wary of his jumping, as The Laird had fallen twice in his last four runs.

It was just like old times for Mill House, as he happily led the field along for the best part of a circuit and a half, until,

1968 GOLD CUP RESULT

FATE – HORSE	AGE/WEIGHT	JOCKEY	ODDS
1st – FORT LENEY	11-12-0	P. TAAFE	11/2
2nd – THE LAIRD	7-12-0	J. KING	3/1
3rd – STALBRIDGE COLONIST	9-12-0	T. W. BIDDLECOMBE	7/2
4th – Bassnet	9-12-0	D. Nicholson	9/1
Fell – Mill House	11-12-0	G.W. Robinson	2/1*

21 March 1968
Going – Firm
Winner – £7,713
Time – 6mins 51secs
5 Ran

Fort Leney	Bay gelding by Fortina – Leney Princess
The Laird	Brown gelding by Border Chief – Pre Fleuri
Stalbridge Colonist	Grey gelding by Colonist II – Eesofud

Winner bred by Col. J. Thomson
Winner trained by T.W. Dreaper at Kilsallaghan, Ireland.

OTHER 1968 FESTIVAL RESULTS

Gloucestershire Hurdle (Div. I)	King Cutler	B. Fletcher	85/40
Totalisator Champion Novice Chase	Herring Gull	J. Crowley	9/1
National Hunt Handicap Chase	Battledore	C. Stobbs	3/1
Two Mile Champion Chase	Drinny's Double	F. Nash	6/1
National Hunt Chase	Fascinating Forties	Mr M. Dickinson	9/1
Gloucestershire Hurdle (Div. II)	L'Escargot	T. Carberry	13/2
Cotswold Chase	The Hustler	B. Brogan	20/1
Cheltenham Grand Annual Chase	Hal's Farewell	J. King	5/1
Champion Hurdle Challenge Cup	Persian War	J. Uttley	4/1
United Hunts Challenge Cup	Snowdra Queen	Mr D. Edmunds	13/2
George Duller Handicap Hurdle	The Spaniard	B. Brogan	8/1
Kim Muir Memorial Challenge Cup	Chu-Teh	Mr D. Crossley-Cooke	3/1
Mildmay Of Flete Handicap Chase	Merrycourt	J. Gifford	20/1
Foxhunters' Challenge Cup Chase	Bright Beach	Mr C. Macmillan	5/1
Daily Express Triumph Hurdle	England's Glory	J. Uttley	9/2
County Handicap Hurdle	Jolly Signal	J. Uttley	6/1
Cathcart Challenge Cup Chase	Muir	P. Taafe	10/11

just as in the 1967 Gold Cup, he made a mistake that would cost him the race. Going easily at the time, the 1963 champion did not get high enough at the fence after the second water jump, coming down in frustrating fashion just as the race was starting to get interesting.

Fort Leney had been left two lengths in front of The Laird, followed by Stalbridge Colonist and Bassnet, but as the leader rounded the final bend, first The Laird and then the grey horse came to challenge him.

A blunder cost Stalbridge Colonist valuable ground two out and this left Fort Leney and The Laird to approach the last fence together, neck and neck, with the latter seemingly travelling the stronger.

Almost diving at the last, The Laird lost momentum, allowing Pat Taafe on Fort Leney to march in to a commanding three-length lead. But Jeff King on The Laird had not given up and roused his horse for one last effort. The grey Stalbridge Colonist had also displayed his tenacious fighting spirit to be close up with the two leaders on the run-in, but as the line loomed, it was Fort Leney, showing the utmost courage, that held on to take the crown, giving his jockey a fourth win in the race.

Fort Leney's marvellous win had given his remarkable trainer Tom Dreaper his fifth Gold Cup win, following Prince Regent way back in 1946 and then the glory years of Arkle. This victory was down to a great deal of patience, as the horse had missed lots of time in his career due to a heart ailment, but heart was one element that Fort Leney showed on the day, fully deserving his battling win.

Sadly, this was one Gold Cup hero that had now had his finest hour. In November 1968, Fort Leney broke down badly at Fairyhouse. He never raced again.

1969

WHAT A MYTH

An extremely wet winter had presented contestants with a different sort of problem in the build up to the 1969 Cheltenham Festival. Whereas the program leading up to the 1968 Festival had been badly interrupted by the foot-and-mouth crisis, this time around, many preceding meetings had unfortunately succumbed to typical English weather. On the other side of the coin, the mudlarks – denied their chance to shine at the firm-ground Festival of the year before – would be in their element, as the official going at Cheltenham on this occasion was heavy.

Irish hopes were not as high as they had been at previous Festivals, and although they had a potential star of the future in Leap Frog in the first race on Tuesday – the Gloucestershire Hurdle Division I – the opener went to Terry Biddlecombe on Normandy. The win set up a fine meeting for Biddlecombe, who ultimately rode three winners and three other placed horses.

The Totalisator Champion Novice Chase threw forward a horse that would become a major player in all the big chases for years to come. Spanish Steps, a six-year-old trained by Edward Courage, relished the conditions and showed excellent stamina in recording a fifteen-length win. The horse

would go on to be a regular in races like the Gold Cup and the Grand National.

Tom Dreaper had already trained two winners of the National Hunt Handicap Chase in his time, Sentina and Arkloin, but on this particular Tuesday he was out of luck, as his Vulture could only manage fifth place behind Pat McCarron's mount Chancer. Vulture, a nephew to Arkle, would perhaps run his finest race in the following season's Grand National, where he finished second to Gay Trip having looked the likely winner for a long way.

Muir, who had capped a fine 1968 Festival for Dreaper when winning the Cathcart Chase shortly after Fort Leney's Gold Cup success, returned on this occasion to get the better of the flamboyant young star Even Keel in the Two Mile Champion Chase.

All the talk surrounding Wednesday's Champion Hurdle was whether Persian War could become the fifth horse in the race's history to retain its title. The horse had been unwell in the run-up to the Festival and had only been cleared by the vet to run at the beginning of March. However, come the race, the versatile Persian War proved that he was extremely worthy of his title of Champion Hurdler, with a brave win on heavy ground, to go along with his win on firm ground the year before. The horse collared Drumikill at the last and then went on to record a four-length victory.

After Specify – a horse that would go on to win the 1971 Grand National – had opened Thursday's proceedings with a win in the Mildmay Of Flete Chase, a threat emerged to Persian War's future bid for a third Champion Hurdle crown when Coral Diver, under Biddlecombe, proved himself the very best four-year-old when courageously winning the Triumph Hurdle.

So the stage was set for the 1969 Cheltenham Gold Cup. After missing the previous season through injury, hopes were

high that Woodland Venture could return to scale the heights he reached in 1967. The horse's season had produced a confusing mixture of results, with one win from four runs, but it was his latest run – the Castle Trial Chase at Warwick – that had connections most perplexed. Starting a warm favourite against weak opposition, the horse ran a miserable race, and it seemed that all was not well with the 1967 hero. Even though he had been as low as 8/1 in the betting, Woodland Venture was pulled out on the eve of the Gold Cup, and later that year, while in the paddock of his owner Mr Harry Collins, the horse died from internal haemorrhaging. This was a tragic end to a wonderful racehorse.

One of the horses expected to love the heavy ground in 1969 was the Ryan Price-trained What A Myth. Third in 1967 and a late withdrawal in 1968, What A Myth had also run in three Grand Nationals, the most successful of which

left: Chatham's win in the Arkle Chase was part of a fine Festival for Terry Biddlecombe.

below: Specify wins the Mildmay Of Flete Handicap Chase, two years before his finest hour in the Grand National.

What A Myth soars the last before winning the Gold Cup.

was a ninth place in the chaotic Foinavon race of 1967. After a fall in the 1968 National, it was decided that rather than let the horse carry impossible weights in handicap races, he would be better suited to a spell hunter-chasing. The ploy clearly worked, as the twelve-year-old won both his starts during the season.

Two horses, The Laird and Domacorn, headed the betting market. The Laird, owned by Mr Jim Joel, had won two of his three races during the season and his only defeat had been to Stalbridge Colonist in Sandown's Gainsborough Chase. On his latest start, The Laird had been most impressive when giving weight and a beating to Fearless Fred – a one time Gold Cup hope himself – at Windsor. Domacorn, trained by Fred Rimell, was perhaps the most interesting horse in the field, and was considered a fine replacement for Woodland Venture. The fast-improving seven-year-old had not been out of the first two positions in his last five runs, and Rimell was extremely confident of his charge's chance.

Another young challenger appearing in his first Gold Cup was the Gordon Richards-trained Playlord. The northern hope had won three of his four races during the season, and

had been most impressive when taking the Great Yorkshire Chase, accounting for Domacorn in the process.

It was the Gold Cup veteran Stalbridge Colonist that proudly led the biggest field since 1963 – eleven runners – and the race was beginning to warm up nicely as the field approached the eighth fence. Here, the outsider Dicky May came crashing down, and The Laird had no chance of avoiding the faller and he was frustratingly brought down.

Two fences later, the grey also tumbled out of the reckoning, leaving the youngest horse in the race, the six-year-old King Cutler, to take command from outsiders Kellsboro' Wood and Arab Gold. At this stage, the three most fancied horses left in the race, Domacorn, Playlord and What A Myth, settled nicely just behind the leaders.

As the second circuit progressed, it was obvious the heavy going was now starting to become a major factor, and five fences from home and clearly enjoying himself, What A Myth and jockey Paul Kelleway began to take control.

The only horse that appeared ready to battle the leader was Domacorn, and as the two horses came down the hill, it was the younger soldier that appeared ready to unleash a menacing bid for glory. However, Domacorn was rudely stopped in his tracks as he battered the second last so badly that Biddlecombe did well to stay aboard. The horse had lost momentum and ground, and his jockey had lost his whip.

Seizing his chance, Kelleway rode What A Myth strongly over the final flight and up the finishing hill and, despite a brave fightback from Domacorn, the twelve-year-old held on with the mud flying to record a memorable win. The conditions had clearly got the better of Playlord, who came home very tired in third with Arab Gold fourth. After his unfortunate exit at the eighth, Bob Turnell's hope The Laird was found to have punctured a shoulder, and although the situation was well retrievable, an attempted assault on the Grand National was thwarted.

1969 GOLD CUP RESULT

FATE – HORSE	AGE / WEIGHT	JOCKEY	ODDS
1st – WHAT A MYTH	12-12-0	P. KELLEWAY	8/1
2nd – DOMACORN	7-12-0	T. W. BIDDLECOMBE	7/2*
3rd – PLAYLORD	8-12-0	R. BARRY	4/1
4th – Arab Gold	8-12-0	P. Buckley	25/1
5th – King Cutler	6-12-0	B. Fletcher	22/1
Fell – Stalbridge Colonist	10-12-0	S. Mellor	9/2
Fell – Dicky May	10-12-0	P. McCarron	22/1
Pulled Up – Castle Arbour	9-12-0	F. Dever	100/1
Pulled Up – Kellsboro' Wood	9-12-0	A. Turnell	50/1
Pulled Up – Furtive	10-12-0	Mr J. Roycroft	100/1
Brought Down – The Laird	8-12-0	J. King	7/2*

20 March 1969
Going – Heavy
Winner – £8,129
Time – 7mins 27 1/5secs
11 Ran

What A Myth	Chestnut gelding by Coup de Myth – What A Din
Domacorn	Brown gelding by Domaha – Spring Corn
Playlord	Bay gelding by Lord Of Verona – Playwell

Winner bred by D. J. Muir
Winner trained by Ryan Price at Findon, Sussex.

OTHER 1969 FESTIVAL RESULTS

Glos Hurdle (Div. I)	Normandy	T.W. Biddlecombe	10/1
Totalisator C Novice Chase	Spanish Steps	J. Cook	100/8
National Hunt Hcap Chase	Chancer	P. McCarron	6/1
Two Mile Champion Chase	Muir	B. Hannon	15/2
National Hunt Chase	Lizzy The Lizard	Mr G. Cann	10/1
Glos Hurdle (Div. II)	Private Room	G.W. Robinson	10/1
United Hunts Challenge Cup	Bright Willow	Mr R. Chugg	7/2
Grand Annual Chase	All Glory	Mr A. Robinson	10/1
Champion Hurdle Ch Cup	Persian War	J. Uttley	6/4
Arkle Ch Trophy Chase	Chatham	T.W. Biddlecombe	10/1
George Duller Hcap H (Div. I)	Parlour Moor	M. Gifford	100/7
George Duller Hcap H (Div. II)	Boonah	R. Quinn	100/8
Kim Muir Memorial Ch Cup	Pride Of Kentucky	Mr R. Charlton	100/8
Mildmay Of Flete Hcap Chase	Specify	B.R. Davies	5/1
Daily Express Triumph Hurdle	Coral Diver	T.W. Biddlecombe	3/1
Cathcart Challenge Cup Chase	Kinloch Brae	T.E. Hyde	3/1
County Handicap Hurdle	Gay Knight	A. Branford	100/7
Foxhunters' Ch Cup Chase	Queen's Guide	Mr G. Wade	10/1

What A Myth, on his ground, had proved himself a top performer and had presented Ryan Price with his first Gold Cup winner. Price had bought What A Myth as a three-year-old and among the horse's twenty-one wins was a Whitbread Gold Cup. Having become the oldest horse to win for eighteen years, the newest Gold Cup winner was promptly retired as a champion.

While it was immediately guaranteed there would be a new champion come 1970, one horse had leapt into the thoughts of many with a superb display on the same day. As the current Gold Cup winner was still receiving his well-earned post-race congratulations, it was just possible that connections of Kinloch Brae – a spectacular winner of the Cathcart Chase – were dreaming of similar scenes in twelve months time.

Lady Weir, owner of What A Myth, holds the Gold Cup next to the Queen Mother.

1970

L'ESCARGOT

The 1970 Cheltenham Festival saw a much-welcomed upswing in attendance over recent years. Over the course of the three-day meeting, 60,100 spectators passed through the gates, and although these numbers are chicken-feed compared to twenty-first century Festival crowds, they were, in 1970, a thirty per cent increase on the 1969 turn-out.

Many of the opening day crowd expected to see Royal Relief – who together with Spanish Steps in the Gold Cup gave trainer Edward Courage some strong ammunition – win the first race on the card, the Two Mile Champion Chase. This would start an amazing sequence of appearances in the race for Royal Relief, who would run in an incredible eight editions of the event, the last being in 1977. On this occasion though, the horse would have to be content with the runner-up spot, as veteran rider Pat Taafe galvanised Straight Fort to win, while in the last race on Tuesday, the Gloucestershire Hurdle Division II, an exciting novice staked his claim as one to watch in the future, as Bula triumphed under Gold Cup-winning jockey Paul Kelleway.

All eyes on Wednesday were on Persian War and his attempt to win three straight Champion Hurdles. Only

Hatton's Grace (1949-1951) and Sir Ken (1952-1954) had ever achieved such a feat. The horse had been having trouble with his wind throughout the season, but as he had shown on both extremes of ground at the last two Festivals, Persian War was a real fighter, and on this occasion, he overcame Josh Gifford on Major Rose to take his place in history. It was Persian War's only victory of the season, and all present at Cheltenham rightly saluted a wonderful champion.

The 1970 Gold Cup had a fresh feel about it. Of the twelve runners, only The Laird had competed in the race before. This factor brought a whole new level of excitement and anticipation to the contest, while a number of fancied Irish runners also provided a strong element of rivalry for the race.

Completing the hat-trick, the great Persian War draws away in the Champion Hurdle.

The hot favourite Kinloch Brae at the start of the Gold Cup.

Owned by Mr Raymond Guest, a former American ambassador to Ireland, L'Escargot was the least fancied of the Irish challenge. L'Escargot had been Horse of the Year in America following a win in the country's Meadowbank Chase at Belmont Park, while his biggest success in England during the season had been the Wills Premier Chase at Haydock Park. A useful hurdler with a fair amount of speed, the big chestnut was trained by Dan Moore, who had actually wanted to run L'Escargot in the Two Mile Champion Chase, but had relented at Mr Guest's request, giving the owner his first runner in the Gold Cup.

Heading the English challenge was Spanish Steps. The horse had numerous qualities, including stamina, jumping, and the ability to handle all ground conditions. Even more striking was his hat-trick of wins leading up to the Gold Cup, which featured impressive successes in the Hennessy Gold Cup, the Benson and Hedges Gold Cup at Ascot and Sandown's Gainsborough Chase. Of course, the horse had annihilated the Totalisator Champion Novice Chase field on heavy going at the 1969 Festival, while his win in the Hennessy during the current season came on contrasting firm ground. The horse, ridden by John Cook, seemed sure to be in the shake-up.

With a field that also included the season's King George winner Titus Oates, a Mackeson Gold Cup winner in Gay Trip, the 1968 Champion Novice Chase winner Herring Gull, and former Gold Cup favourite The Laird, the 1970 edition of the race had real strength in depth.

Right from the off, Titus Oates, under Stan Mellor, set a strong pace, followed by outsiders Larbawn, Arcturus and Freddie Boy, then came the fancied pair of Kinloch Brae and Spanish Steps.

The first casualty of the race was Arcturus, who bowed out at the sixth fence, while the tough, young giant from

Favourite was the Willie O'Grady-trained seven-year-old Kinloch Brae, a horse that was owned by Anne, Duchess of Westminster, and therefore ran in the famous yellow and black Arkle colours. A worthy favourite he was. The horse had been most impressive when winning the 1969 Cathcart Chase, and he had now racked up seven wins from his last eight runs, including an unbeaten streak of four coming in to the Gold Cup. At times a breathtaking jumper, Kinloch Brae was partnered by Timmy Hyde.

A strong contender from Northern Ireland and a year older than Kinloch Brae was French Tan. A powerfully-built brown gelding, French Tan was trained in Armagh by Archie Watson. The horse had been hobdayed the season previously, and this seemed to have improved him beyond recognition. French Tan had taken his last three races, including the Whitbread Trial Chase at Ascot, and his followers were extremely confident of their charge giving Pat Taafe a fifth success in the race.

1970 GOLD CUP RESULT

FATE – HORSE	AGE / WEIGHT	JOCKEY	ODDS
1st – L'ESCARGOT	7-12-0	T. CARBERRY	33/1
2nd – FRENCH TAN	8-12-0	P. TAAFE	8/1
3rd – SPANISH STEPS	7-12-0	J. COOK	9/4
4th – Freddie Boy	9-12-0	R. Pitman	40/1
5th – The Laird	9-12-0	J. King	40/1
6th – Gay Trip	8-12-0	K.B. White	50/1
7th – Larbawn	11-12-0	M. Gifford	25/1
Fell – The Dikler	7-12-0	G.W. Robinson	10/1
Fell – Titus Oates	8-12-0	S. Mellor	10/1
Fell – Arcturus	9-12-0	P. Buckley	50/1
Fell – Kinloch Brae	7-12-0	T. Hyde	15/8*
Brought Down – Herring Gull	8-12-0	J. Crowley	33/1

19 March 1970
Going – Good to Soft
Winner – £8,103
Time – 6mins 47 3/5secs
12 Ran

L'Escargot	Chestnut gelding by Escart III – What A Daisy
French Tan	Brown gelding by Trouville – Kilted Angel
Spanish Steps	Bay gelding by Flush Royal – Tiberetta

Winner bred by Mrs B. O'Neill
Winner trained by D. Moore at Co. Kildare, Ireland.

OTHER 1970 FESTIVAL RESULTS

Two Mile Champion Chase	Straight Fort	P. Taafe	7/4
National Hunt Chase	Domason	Mr R. Alner	10/1
Totalisator C Novice Chase	Proud Tarquin	P. Taafe	100/7
Glos Hurdle (Div. I)	Ballywilliam Boy	R. Coonan	4/1
National Hunt Hcap Chase	Charter Flight	A. Turnell	100/8
Glos Hurdle (Div. II)	Bula	P. Kelleway	3/1
United Hunts Ch Cup	Grey Sombrero	Mr C. Candy	33/1
Grand Annual Chase	Fortina's Palace	P. Jones	10/1
Champion Hurdle Ch Cup	Persian War	J. Uttley	5/4
Arkle Challenge Trophy Chase	Soloning	P. Kelleway	4/1
George Duller Hcap Hurdle	Vulmegan	S. Mellor	100/8
Kim Muir Memorial Ch Cup	Rainbow Valley	Mr M. Dickinson	10/1
Mildmay Of Flete Hcap Chase	Verona Forest	G. Scott	25/1
Daily Express Triumph Hurdle	Varma	B. Barker	100/7
Foxhunters' Ch Cup Chase	Highworth	Mr R. Woodhouse	15/2
County Handicap Hurdle	Khan	Lord Petersham	100/8
Cathcart Challenge Cup Chase	Garrynagree	P. Taafe	2/1

Fulke Walwyn's yard, The Dikler, was next to depart at the eleventh.

Kinloch Brae was a horse that loved to dictate from the head of affairs, and it was not long before Hyde sent the favourite up to join Titus Oates in the lead, and the pair led out for the second circuit from Freddie Boy, Larbawn and Spanish Steps.

The first signs of worry for Spanish Steps followers came at the fence before the second water jump, when the horse was given reminders by Cook, and it was here that Kinloch Brae took the race by the throat, with the hills dwarfing the beautiful racing theatre seemingly urging the favourite into a daring winning raid.

Running up the hill, Kinloch Brae now led French Tan, with L'Escargot staying on strongly and passing the weakening Spanish Steps. But the notorious third last fence, where the horses meet it on a downhill stride, was still lying in wait. Travelling sweetly in the style of a winner, although being shadowed at the time by French Tan, Kinloch Brae struck the underpart of the fence and could not recover on the landing side, cruelly crashing to the floor. Herring Gull was brought down by the stricken favourite, while independantly, Titus Oates also plunged out of the race, giving Mellor a most uncomfortable fall in the process.

The whole complexion of the race had now altered, and it was French Tan and L'Escargot that settled down to battle out the remainder of the race, with Spanish Steps under heavy pressure in third.

Surely now, the perceived superior stamina of French Tan would win the day, after all, Dan Moore had wanted to go for a shorter trip with his warrior. But surprisingly, half way up the run-in, it was L'Escargot – far from going at a snail's pace – that began to wear down his rival and pulled out a length-and-a-half win after the pair had been neck and neck as they flew the last. Spanish Steps came home a slightly disappointing third ahead of Freddie Boy. The Laird, who had turned in an up and down season, had been last for a long way and came home fifth of seven finishers, one of which was Gay Trip, who would soon enjoy glory at Aintree in the Grand National.

At 33/1, L'Escargot had become the joint-longest priced winner of the race ever, sharing the honour with the 1955 champion Gay Donald, and at the same time became the eleventh Irish-trained winner since the war. Whether L'Escargot would have got the better of Kinloch Brae in a finish remained to be seen; certainly Mr Guest did not think there was a horse in the race to match the favourite. The fact was though that L'Escargot had jumped, stayed, battled and ultimately won, and in doing so registered Mr Guest's second phase of a plan to win the Derby, the Gold Cup and the Grand National. Larkspur in 1962 and Sir Ivor in 1968 had done the business in the Derby, and now L'Escargot had triumphed in a fantastically entertaining Gold Cup. All that remained now was the National.

L'Escargot (nearside) about to out-battle French Tan in the Gold Cup.

1971

L'ESCARGOT

Rain had left the going for the 1971 Cheltenham Festival on the soft side. These were conditions that neither of two defending champions – Persian War in the Champion Hurdle and L'Escargot in the Gold Cup – particularly minded, and much of the excitement surrounding this edition of the Festival was whether these two great horses could retain their crowns. For L'Escargot, it would mean becoming only the fifth horse in the history of the race to pull off the feat, the others being Easter Hero, Golden Miller, Cottage Rake and Arkle. For Persian War, a win would carry even greater meaning, as no horse had ever won more than three Champion Hurdles.

The Irish banker of the meeting came in the Totalisator Champion Novice Chase on the Tuesday, as the promising Argent started a heavy favourite. But as is often the case in this fiercely competitive and hectic three mile chase, the favourite came unstuck, as Argent fell, allowing David Nicholson to win aboard 14/1 chance Tantalum.

The next race on Tuesday's card was the Two Mile Champion Chase. A fall by the 1970 winner Straight Fort gave the edge to the Australian-bred chaser Crisp, and the horse delivered in grand style to win under jockey Paul Kelleway. Indeed, so impressive was Crisp's victory that many wondered whether here could be a Gold Cup contender in the making.

Later on in the day, ten-year-old Lord Jim advertised his claims as a very real contender for the upcoming Grand National with a win in the National Hunt Handicap Chase, where he made virtually all the running.

Hopes were high on Wednesday that Persian War could register his record-breaking fourth win in the Champion Hurdle, despite having looked past his best during the course of the season. However, it was not to be for the old warrior, as on the day, it was clear there was now a new hurdling star, as young Bula easily won the race. Bula was an excellent successor to Persian War, and to his credit, the

The stunning Australian-bred chaser Crisp winning the Champion Chase.

Heavily fancied, Into View
disappointed in the Gold Cup.

three-time winner ran very bravely to be second, eclipsing his old rival Major Rose.

Numerous stars were missing from Thursday's long-awaited Gold Cup. The previous year's favourite, Kinloch Brae, had finished lame when winning the John Bull Chase at Wincanton the week before the Gold Cup and was forced to miss the race, while the 1970 runner-up French Tan was also absent through injury. The useful Titus Oates, because of the ground – which had become increasingly soft thanks to fifteen hours of continuous rain – had been a late withdrawal, while Spanish Steps was denied a run due to a mistake with his entry, and this left a field of eight to face the starter.

There was no doubt that Ireland had a particularly strong hand this time around, and two of their hopefuls, L'Escargot and Leap Frog, began the race as co-favourites of three. The reigning champion L'Escargot, perhaps unfairly seen as a lucky winner in 1970 following the fall of Kinloch Brae, had endured a disappointing season. The chestnut had not won a race, although a third place at Leopardstown in February had given some cause for encouragement for trainer Dan Moore.

L'Escargot would, however, have to be at his best to fend off the two promising Irish seven-year-olds, Leap Frog and Glencaraig Lady. Trained by Tom Dreaper and ridden by Val

L'Escargot's trainer Dan Moore chats to the Queen Mother following the horse's Gold Cup triumph.

the race, a challenge that also included Fulke Walwyn's horse The Dikler, who had three recent wins to his name.

The state of the ground led to a change of starting place. The horses would begin between the fourth and fifth fences and would jump twenty-three obstacles as opposed to the usual twenty-two.

The early leader in the race was the 10/1 chance Royal Toss and he lead the field at a steady pace in the boggy conditions, until Glencaraig Lady took hold of proceedings at the seventh fence, tracked by L'Escargot. Even at this early stage, it was obvious that Into View was not appreciating the ground and he trailed the field.

There was not too much change in the order as the race progressed at an extremely slow pace. Glencaraig Lady was jumping very well and was going easily, with L'Escargot well in touch. Leap Frog was plugging away but was giving the impression the whole affair may be too much for him, while Into View continued to struggle.

O'Brien, the fast-improving Leap Frog had won the season's Embassy Premier Chase Final at Haydock, while the mare Glencaraig Lady was trained by Francis Flood and had been runner-up in the previous season's Irish Grand National.

Trying to repel the Irish trio was the third horse that would start as joint favourite, Into View. Trained by Fred Winter, the horse had yet to run over the full Gold Cup distance, so his stamina, especially on soft ground, was highly questionable. However, he had enjoyed a fruitful season, and trying a trip of three miles at Windsor in February, he came home an easy winner. Further aiding his cause would be the assistance from Paul Kelleway in the saddle. Kelleway was having a fine Festival, having already secured the Two Mile Champion Chase and the Champion Hurdle, and Into View certainly appeared the strongest of the English challenge for

Winning owner Raymond Guest with the Gold Cup.

1971 GOLD CUP RESULT

FATE – HORSE	AGE / WEIGHT	JOCKEY	ODDS
1st – L'ESCARGOT	8-12-0	T. CARBERRY	7/2*
2nd – LEAP FROG	7-12-0	V. O'BRIEN	7/2*
3rd – THE DIKLER	8-12-0	BARRY BROGAN	15/2
4th – Into View	8-12-0	P. Kelleway	7/2*
5th – Fortina's Palace	8-12-0	P. Jones	33/1
6th – Herring Gull	9-12-0	H. Beasley	33/1
Fell – Glencaraig Lady	7-12-0	R. Coonan	7/1
Fell – Royal Toss	9-12-0	E. P. Harty	10/1

18 March 1971
Going – Soft
Winner – £7,995
Time – 8mins 1 3/5secs
8 Ran

L'Escargot	Chestnut gelding by Escart III – What A Daisy
Leap Frog	Bay gelding by Trouville – Maggie's Leap
The Dikler	Bay gelding by Vulgan – Coronation Day

Winner bred by Mrs B. O'Neill
Winner trained by D. Moore at Co. Kildare, Ireland.

OTHER 1971 FESTIVAL RESULTS

Gloucestershire Hurdle (Div. I)	Persian Majesty	T.W. Biddlecombe	13/2
Aldsworth Hurdle	Midsprite	M. Gifford	7/1
Totalisator Champion Novice Chase	Tantalum	D. Nicholson	14/1
Two Mile Champion Chase	Crisp	P. Kelleway	3/1
National Hunt Chase	Deblin's Green	Mr J. Edmunds	9/2
National Hunt Handicap Chase	Lord Jim	J. Haine	8/1
Gloucestershire Hurdle (Div. II)	Barnard	J. Haine	4/1
Grand Annual Chase	Khan	F. Carroll	2/1
Sun Alliance and London Foxhunters'	Hope Again	Mr R. Smith	16/1
Champion Hurdle Challenge Cup	Bula	P. Kelleway	15/8
Arkle Challenge Trophy Chase	Alpheus	E. Wright	15/1
Spa Hurdle	Clever Scot	B.R. Davies	11/4
Kim Muir Memorial Challenge Cup	Black Baize	Mr J. Lawrence	13/8
Mildmay Of Flete Handicap Chase	Hound Tor	M. C. Gifford	14/1
Daily Express Triumph Hurdle	Boxer	J. Uttley	100/30
County Handicap Hurdle	Carry Off	D. Goulding	25/1
United Hunts Challenge Cup	Sally Furlong	Mr T. Holland-Martin	6/4
Cathcart Challenge Cup Chase	The Laird	J. King	2/1

As the field came to the third last, having lost the fallen Royal Toss at the fence before, Glencaraig Lady was still travelling smoothly. But just like Kinloch Brae the year before, the fence found the leader out. Hitting it hard, Glencaraig Lady was unable to maintain her balance on landing and knuckled over in agonising fashion. It was too far out to tell if she would have won, but she had been going very well and certainly was not ready to give in without a fight.

This all left L'Escargot in front, with Leap Frog moving past The Dikler into second place. It looked like it may turn into a real scrap, but try as he might, Leap Frog could not match the excellent stamina and finishing power that L'Escargot displayed. Ploughing up the hill in impressive fashion,

L'Escargot came home ten lengths clear of his compatriot to huge Irish cheers, deservedly taking his place in the record books as only the fifth horse to retain his crown. The Dikler had run a solid race in his second Gold Cup and came home third, ahead of the disappointing Into View.

There was no doubt that Glencaraig Lady was running a brave race when she fell, but winning jockey Tommy Carberry was adamant that his horse would have won whatever had happened, so strongly was the winner going. L'Escargot was a fine champion, and it was soon announced that the dual winner had big plans for 1972. As well as bidding for a third straight Gold Cup success, L'Escargot would also be targeted at none other than the Grand National.

1972

GLENCARAIG LADY

The big question that needed answering in 1972 was whether L'Escargot could win a third Gold Cup. Golden Miller, Cottage Rake and Arkle had all successfully completed their hat-tricks in the race, meaning no horse had ever failed when going for a third win in succession.

The opening day of the 1972 Festival on Tuesday saw the customary Irish banker put forward, and not for the first time in a short span of years, saw a horse compared to Arkle. The latest to wear the mantle was Sea Brief, trained by Tom Dreaper's son Jim, and the horse had won all four of his novice chases in impressive style. However, despite carrying the legendary yellow and black colours made famous by the three-time Gold Cup winner, Sea Brief could only manage fourth place in the Totalisator Champion Chase for novices, with victory going to Clever Scot, who made all the running. Clever Scot was a fine horse in his own right. Owned by American Milton Ritzenberg, he had won the Spa Hurdle at the 1971 Festival. An interesting horse filled third place in the form of the massive Charlie Potheen. Here was a horse that would go on to figure prominently in future Gold Cups.

Earlier in the day, the Edward Courage-trained Royal Relief had won the Two Mile Champion Chase at the third attempt, while in the last race on Tuesday, a horse that was to prove a powerhouse in the hurdling division in upcoming years, Comedy Of Errors, finished runner-up to Noble Life and jockey Thomas Murphy in the Gloucestershire Hurdle.

Wednesday was all about two Rolls-Royces from former champion jockey Fred Winter's stable. Both were much hyped and started as odds-on favourites in their respective races. Neither horse disappointed. First, ridden by Richard Pitman, Pendil simply crushed a useful field in the Arkle Chase, hinting that here could be a Gold Cup contender for 1973. So good was Pendil's performance that Winter was quick to label him as the best in Europe over two miles. Still buzzing from Pendil's blistering show, the Cheltenham crowd were then treated to Bula, under Paul Kelleway, destroying the field to win his second Champion Hurdle. The horse had now

Royal Relief (far side) wins the Champion Chase from Jabeg. The winner ran in the race eight times.

Bula and Paul Kelleway – Champion Hurdle victors.

renew acquaintances. Leap Frog, who had beaten both Crisp and The Dikler in the Massey-Ferguson Gold Cup, was perhaps slightly the more fancied this time around, although he shared second place in the betting with L'Escargot. Leap Frog had gone through the season unbeaten, and had been ante-post favourite for the Gold Cup at one point.

L'Escargot carried the usual confidence from his trainer Dan Moore, despite again arriving for the Gold Cup without a win during the season. Even so, the chestnut had experience on his side as well as stamina and the ability to cope with the soft going.

Glencaraig Lady came to the Gold Cup in winning form, having scored recently at Thurles. The little mare was looking to make it third time lucky at the Festival, having fallen on her two previous chase appearances when both times in winning positions. Young Frank Berry was given the chance to guide the mare round on this occasion.

won fifteen of his sixteen races and received an immediate quote of 2/1 for the 1973 Champion Hurdle from Ladbrokes.

With such glorious performances from his stable stars on Wednesday, Winter had every reason to be confident of success in Thursday's Gold Cup; after all, he housed the favourite for the race in the powerful Australian-bred chaser Crisp. The horse had excelled himself in both Australia and America before arriving in Britain, where in 1971, he had taken the Festival's Two Mile Champion Chase in exciting fashion. Having flopped due to having a temperature in the Massey-Ferguson Gold Cup earlier in the season, Crisp had then rebounded by winning over three miles at both Sandown and Kempton. Despite these victories and the fact the horse was favourite, doubts remained surrounding Crisp's stamina and how the bold front runner would cope with the prevailing soft ground.

The three Irish principals from the previous year, L'Escargot, Leap Frog and Glencaraig Lady, were back to

Pendil leads Avondhu on his way to victory in the Arkle Chase.

Bula (left) is poised to win his second
Champion Hurdle title.

The remainder of the field for the 1972 Gold Cup was none too shabby either, with the contenders including The Dikler, who had won the King George earlier in the season, the 1970 Grand National winner Gay Trip, one of the ante-post favourites for the current season's Grand National in Dim Wit, and big-race regular Spanish Steps, whose build-up had been hampered by a hock injury.

The early pace was set by Terry Biddlecombe on Gay Trip, who took the field along from Glencaraig Lady, L'Escargot, Royal Toss and Spanish Steps, and for much of the first circuit, the leading group remained unaltered. Crisp, a horse that loved to cut out the running, was being held up to preserve his stamina, a tactic the big Australian chaser seemed to be far from pleased with.

It was Glencaraig Lady that made the first move on the second circuit, as she went up to join Gay Trip, chased by the improving big, white face of The Dikler, then came L'Escargot, Royal Toss, Spanish Steps and Crisp.

Five fences from home and with the pressure mounting, the race changed again. The Irish horse Leap Frog plunged out of contention, and Fulke Walwyn's enormous challenger The Dikler strode on, turning up the hill in menacing fashion pressed by Glencaraig Lady, the smooth-travelling L'Escargot and then Crisp. The winner was sure to come from this group.

As they cleared three out, the crowd began to believe that L'Escargot might just be ready to join the Gold Cup greats, so well was he going, but a slow jump at the second last had the champion cooked, as the race outlook changed once more.

The outsider Royal Toss was creeping ever closer, ridden by Nigel Wakley, and he began to loom large as the King George winner The Dikler jumped the last fence with a fractional lead from Glencaraig Lady. Crisp had now faded badly, and the three leaders then locked together for a supreme battle to the line. The finish was an enthralling spectacle, and in the end, it was the brave Glencaraig Lady on the far side that edged home in one of the closest finishes of all time. The mare battled her heart out to win by three-quarters of a length from the fast-finishing Royal Toss, with The Dikler a head back in third. L'Escargot had to be content with fourth place, while the ground seriously hampered the fifth-placed Crisp. There was a long steward's enquiry involving the three leading horses, but Glencaraig Lady eventually kept the race as the places remained unchanged.

Glencaraig Lady – who like the 1968 hero Fort Leney, was sired by the 1947 Gold Cup winner Fortina – triumphantly became the third Irish winner in a row and the thirteenth in total since the war. In addition, she had become the first mare to win since Kerstin in 1958. Not

1972 GOLD CUP RESULT

FATE – HORSE	AGE/WEIGHT	JOCKEY	ODDS
1st – GLENCARAIG LADY	8-12-0	F. BERRY	6/1
2nd – ROYAL TOSS	10-12-0	N. WAKLEY	22/1
3rd – THE DIKLER	9-12-0	BARRY BROGAN	11/1
4th – L'Escargot	9-12-0	T. Carberry	4/1
5th – Crisp	9-12-0	R. Pitman	3/1*
6th – Spanish Steps	9-12-0	W. Smith	10/1
7th – Bighorn	8-12-0	D. Cartwright	33/1
8th – Gay Trip	10-12-0	T.W. Biddlecombe	35/1
9th – Titus Oates	10-12-0	R. Barry	40/1
Fell – Leap Frog	8-12-0	V. O'Brien	4/1
Pulled Up – Young Ash Leaf	8-12-0	T. Stack	40/1
Pulled Up – Dim Wit	8-12-0	D. Mould	66/1

16 March 1972
Going – Soft
Winner – £15,255
Time – 7mins 17 4/5sces
12 Ran

Glencaraig Lady	Chestnut mare by Fortina – Luckibash
Royal Toss	Brown gelding by Royal Challenger – Spinning Coin II
The Dikler	Bay gelding by Vulgan – Coronation Day

Winner bred by J.F. Hogan
Winner trained by F. Flood in Ireland.

OTHER 1972 FESTIVAL RESULTS

Aldsworth Hurdle	Even Dawn	R. Hyett	40/1
Two Mile Champion Chase	Royal Relief	W. Smith	15/8
Totalisator C Novice Chase	Clever Scot	D. Mould	11/1
National Hunt Hcap Chase	Jomon	D. Mould	8/1
National Hunt Chase	Charley Winking	Mr D. Scott	20/1
Gloucestershire Hurdle	Noble Life	Thomas Murphy	16/1
Arkle Ch Trophy Chase	Pendil	R. Pitman	10/11
Lloyds Bank Hurdle	Parlour Moor	M. Gifford	13/2
Champion Hurdle Ch Cup	Bula	P. Kelleway	8/11
Sun A & London Foxhunters'	Credit Call	Mr C. Collins	7/4
Grand Annual Chase	Tudor Dance	J. King	4/1
Kim Muir Mem Ch Cup	The Ghost	Mr J. Mead	5/2
George Duller Hcap Hurdle	Drake's Gold	G. Howey	28/1
Mildmay Of Flete Hcap Chase	Mocharabuice	G. Thorner	11/2
Daily Express Triumph Hurdle	Zarib	W. Smith	16/1
County Handicap Hurdle	Cold Day	R. Hyett	15/1
United Hunts Challenge Cup	Real Rascal	Mr G. Hyatt	11/4
Cathcart Ch Cup Chase	Soloning	R. Pitman	6/5

bad for a horse that cost a mere 800 guineas when owner Mr Patrick Doyle bought her from breeder Jim Hogan as a three-year-old.

The win had illustrated the training talents of Francis Flood, who had successfully overcome the mare's numerous injury problems in her career to get her to peak in such a race. Sadly, those injury problems had resurfaced again in the titanic finish, and it transpired that Glencaraig Lady had broken down, forcing her in to a premature retirement to the paddocks. Although her injury problems had ultimately got the better of her, Glencaraig Lady's luck had finally changed on the track in the hallowed surroundings of the Cotswold Hills at Cheltenham, and the gallant mare fittingly departed the racing game as a champion.

Glencaraig Lady made up for a fruitless bold run in 1971 by winning the 1972 Gold Cup.

1973

THE DIKLER

The 1973 Cheltenham Festival seemed to revolve around one man, Fred Winter. Most trainers would be happy to say they held the favourite for one race at the great meeting, but on this occasion Winter was responsible for the favourites in the three biggest races at the Festival – the Gold Cup, the Two Mile Champion Chase and the Champion Hurdle – as well as the favourite for the Totalisator Champion Chase, the novice's Gold Cup.

The first of the Winter hotpots was Crisp in Tuesday's Two Mile Champion Chase. Having fluffed his lines when favourite for the 1972 Gold Cup, he had roared to the head of the market for this event after destroying a high-class field at Newbury. With the ground good, everything looked in Crisp's favour, but this race was to signal the start of a largely disappointing sequence of events for Winter, not only at this Festival, but later at Aintree and Ascot as well. Crisp failed to sparkle and could only finish third behind the talented American horse Inkslinger and race-regular Royal Relief. Not content with upsetting the Winter bandwagon, Inkslinger reappeared on the Thursday to claim the Cathcart Chase. The American horse was ridden in both races by Tommy Carberry.

The next race on Tuesday was the Totalisator Champion Chase, where Winter was ready to play his next card. This time the ace came in the form of the strapping novice Killiney, a gifted horse unbeaten in seven races over fences. Starting a very warm odds-on chance, Killiney salvaged some pride for his trainer following the disappointment of Crisp, as he won his eighth chase in a row under Richard Pitman, despite appearing not to appreciate the left-handed track – all Killiney's other wins had been when going right-handed.

The next of the Winter big guns to step forward was the dual Champion Hurdle winner Bula on Wednesday, and a chance for the horse to join the race's great names such as Hatton's Grace, Sir Ken and Persian War. But there was to be another upset here, as Bula was always struggling and eventually trailed home fifth behind a rising star in the shape

One of a galaxy of Fred Winter-trained stars, the big novice Killiney took the Sun Alliance Chase.

The magnificent Pendil, favourite for the Gold Cup.

of Comedy Of Errors. There was no shame in being beaten by the winner, after all, Comedy Of Errors would go on to become a truly great champion, but Winter could be forgiven for thinking this was not going to be his year.

Even so, the Lambourn trainer still had the jewel in his crown to come. Surely Pendil would not suffer the same fate as Crisp and Bula? The brilliant eight-year-old Pendil, he

who had crushed the Arkle Trophy field in 1972, had now won all eleven of his chases, including a string of five during the current season which featured a fine success in the King George at Kempton. One of the main factors that made Pendil such a force was an ultra-quick turn of foot between fences, an asset that allowed him to dominate races at anywhere between two and three miles. A clever jumper as

1973 GOLD CUP RESULT

FATE – HORSE	AGE/WEIGHT	JOCKEY	ODDS
1st – THE DIKLER	10-12-0	R. BARRY	9/1
2nd – PENDIL	8-12-0	R. PITMAN	4/6*
3rd – CHARLIE POTHEEN	8-12-0	T.W. BIDDLECOMBE	9/2
4th – L'Escargot	10-12-0	T. Carberry	20/1
5th – Garoupe	9-12-0	F. Berry	50/1
6th – Spanish Steps	10-12-0	P. Blacker	10/1
7th – Red Candle	9-12-0	J. Fox	50/1
Fell – Clever Scot	8-12-0	D. Mould	22/1

15 March 1973
Going – Good
Winner – £15,125
Time – 6mins 38.6secs
8 Ran

The Dikler	Bay gelding by Vulgan – Coronation Day
Pendil	Bay gelding by Pendragon – Diliska
Charlie Potheen	Bay gelding by Spiritus – Irish Biddy

Winner bred by J.F. Moorhead
Winner trained by F. Walwyn at Lambourn, Berkshire

OTHER 1973 FESTIVAL RESULTS

Aldsworth Hurdle	Willie Wumpkins	P. Colville	11/1
Two Mile Champion Chase	Inkslinger	T. Carberry	6/1
Totalisator C Novice Chase	Killiney	R. Pitman	8/15
National Hunt Hcap Chase	The Chisler	M. Dickinson	6/1
National Hunt Chase	Foreman	Mr W. Shand Kydd	11/2
Gloucestershire Hurdle	King Pele	D. Nicholson	13/2
Arkle Challenge Trophy Chase	Denys Adventure	G. Thorner	8/1
Lloyds Bank Hurdle	Moyne Royal	D. Mould	10/1
Champion Hurdle Ch Cup	Comedy Of Errors	W. Smith	8/1
Sun Alli and London Fhunters'	Bullock's Horn	Lord Oaksey	5/1
Grand Annual Chase	Coolera Prince	N. Wakley	8/1
Kim Muir Memorial Ch Cup	Hinterland	Mr W. Foulkes	5/2
George Duller Hcap Hurdle	Parthenon	D. Mould	7/2
Mildmay Of Flete Hcap Chase	Vulgan Town	J. Haine	9/2
Daily Express Triumph Hurdle	Moonlight Bay	J. Haine	85/40
County Handicap Hurdle	Current Romance	D. Nicholson	20/1
United Hunts Challenge Cup	Lord Fortune	Mr J. Edmunds	5/1
Cathcart Challenge Cup Chase	Inkslinger	T. Carberry	21/20

well, any stamina doubts Pendil followers had were eased as the ground for the 1973 Gold Cup officially rode good.

It was a relatively new cast of Gold Cup players that lined up in 1973, and another first-timer in the race, the massive Charlie Potheen, held second place in the betting market at 9/2. A chancy jumper, but even so a horse with a large amount of talent, Charlie Potheen had won both his starts during the season, the Hennessy Cognac Gold Cup and the Great Yorkshire Chase. Charlie Potheen was one of two runners for Fulke Walwyn; the other was The Dikler, who would be running in his fourth Gold Cup, having finished third in the previous two editions. The Dikler's regular jockey, Barry Brogan, had been forced to miss the race with injury, and his place went to top northern-based rider Ron Barry, who had previously ridden Playlord to be third in the 1969 Gold Cup.

Running at his sixth Festival and in his fourth straight Gold Cup was L'Escargot, who was the main hope from a weak Irish challenge that also featured 50/1 outsider Garoupe, while the previous year's Totalisator Champion Chase winner Clever Scot, trained by Tom Jones, also made the line-up.

The early running was made by Charlie Potheen, who thundered over the first few fences at a terrific pace, and it was soon clear that this was going to be a very fast run Gold Cup. Clever Scot, Spanish Steps and Pendil all chased the leader as they prepared to run past the stands.

At the twelfth fence, the race lost Clever Scot, who crashed out of the action leaving Charlie Potheen three lengths to the good from Spanish Steps, Pendil and The Dikler, and as the leading group began to bunch together for the second circuit, the Irish challengers L'Escargot and Garoupe were not too far behind.

As the second lap wore on, it became obvious that Pendil was looking increasingly like winning, as he was cruising under Pitman, and at the third last, with most of the field in trouble, he swept past Spanish Steps and began to loom large on the leader Charlie Potheen.

It looked nailed on that the favourite was going to win at the second last as he jumped past the long time leader and into a clear lead, a lead that was almost three lengths at the final fence. Meanwhile, The Dikler had been done no favours by his stablemate Charlie Potheen, who had hung to his left and interfered with Ron Barry's mount as he dropped back out of contention. Nevertheless, Barry conjured The Dikler into a huge effort at the last fence, and the horse did not let him down, flying the obstacle and meeting the ground at full speed with Pendil in his sights.

Pendil had looked unbeatable at the last fence, but all of a sudden the favourite started to idle and stare about. This gave the chasing Barry and The Dikler the incentive they needed. Using his big stride, The Dikler unbelievably caught Pendil yards from the winning line, and although Pitman worked furiously to get his horse back up, the damage was done and The Dikler had won the Gold Cup.

The Cheltenham hill had undone Pendil, and afterwards, Pitman blamed himself for the horse's defeat, believing he had gone to the front too soon on the favourite. It was little consolation to Pitman that he had helped to smash the course record time for the Gold Cup, with The Dikler beating Fort Leney's 1968 time by 12.4 seconds.

Ron Barry had snatched victory from defeat on his gallant partner, a notoriously hard ride and extremely headstrong, while at his fourth attempt, The Dikler had given his genial trainer Fulke Walwyn his fourth Gold Cup success. The stable's other runner, Charlie Potheen, had run with credit to finish third, one place ahead of L'Escargot. The great Irish horse had run in his final Gold Cup, but had an Aintree Grand National victory in his future – a 1975 win in which The Dikler finished fifth – which finally fulfilled the dream of his owner Mr Raymond Guest.

For Fred Winter, the former jockey to Walwyn, this had been a wretched Festival. Crisp and Bula aside, Pendil's defeat seemed hardest to fathom. Sometimes it is just not meant to be. Sadly, Winter's luck did not improve in the following weeks. In the Grand National at the end of March, Crisp ran the race of his life, capturing the hearts of the public by jumping with tremendous flair to lead all the way in the race only for a certain Red Rum to steal victory in the dying strides. Even worse, his star novice Killiney was tragically killed at Ascot in April, denying Winter a possible Gold Cup winner of the future. At times, National Hunt racing can be a cruel game.

A giant of Gold Cups past, The Dikler (4) stole the 1973 Blue Riband under Ron Barry.

1974

CAPTAIN CHRISTY

As a pleasant surprise, racing received a relatively mild winter, greatly reducing the amount of meetings that fell to cancellation. However, when an inch of snow fell on Cheltenham the Sunday before the Festival, organisers of the meeting must have feared the worst. But to everyone's relief, the sun came out on Monday, melting the majority of the snow and meaning a precautionary inspection was passed. However, all this had left the going for Tuesday as heavy.

Delightfully, the sun kept shining as the Festival began, and immediately, it was the Irish who were off to a flyer, as Brown Lad, their splendid novice, won the opening SunAlliance Novices' Hurdle. This was followed by a very popular success for the evergreen Royal Relief, ridden by Bill Smith, in the Two Mile Champion Chase. It was the second time that Royal Relief had won the race, and on this occasion, he beat another very good two-miler and Sandown specialist, Tingle Creek.

Glanford Brigg entered the SunAlliance Chase, formerly the Totalisator Champion Novice Chase, as the season's outstanding novice chaser. The horse had run up a sequence of six straight wins, but not for the first time in the event in recent years, the favourite was undone. Victory went to an Irish raider in Ten Up, who won by three lengths for his owner Anne, Duchess of Westminster.

Wednesday featured a classic Champion Hurdle that saw exhilarating race-newcomer, Lanzarote dethrone Comedy Of Errors. The pair were locked together at the final hurdle, before Lanzarote displayed some awesome finishing power to storm up the hill for victory under Richard Pitman. Bula, the dual champion-hurdler, had begun a chasing career in impressive fashion. He was all set to miss the Champion Hurdle for an audacious crack at the Gold Cup, only for an injury, following a win at Newbury, to rule him out of the contest.

With sunshine having been a feature of this Festival, the ground for Gold Cup day had changed from heavy to soft.

Pendil, the horse that had long been favourite for the Gold Cup, had avoided a recent bout of coughing at his trainer Fred Winter's yard to take his place in the 1974 line-up. The horse's only chasing defeat remained the bitterly disappointing loss to The Dikler in the 1973 race, and he had marched

Tragically killed in the 1977 Gold Cup, Lanzarote won the 1974 Champion Hurdle under Richard Pitman.

left: Pictured in 1997, legendary commentator Sir Peter O'Sullevan owned the 1974 Triumph Hurdle winner Attivo.

far left: Attivo (nearside) leads Gleaming Silver in the Triumph Hurdle.

strongly towards redemption this time around with four wins from four races during the season. Pendil had slaughtered The Dikler twice in recent races, in the Massey-Ferguson Gold Cup at Cheltenham and the King George at Kempton, and if anything, it seemed even less likely he would be defeated on this occasion. Richard Pitman was again on board the favourite as he looked to bury the ghosts of 1973.

His two thrashings by Pendil aside, The Dikler had enjoyed another remarkably fruitful season. In this particular era of chasing, The Dikler really was a model of consistency, and although undeniably headstrong, the horse was tough and brave and rarely ran a bad race. Fulke Walwyn's soldier was in good heart to defend his crown, as recent victories at Wincanton and Newbury had proved.

The race had been denied one promising novice with the absence of Bula, but was presented with an equally intriguing prospect in the form of the risky-jumping but super-talented Irish representative Captain Christy. Trained by four-time winning rider Pat Taafe, the exciting seven-year-old had been an eyecatching third in the 1973 Champion

Hurdle, and the rangy bay horse had looked full of promise as a chaser. With a fall and an unseated rider in his recent form column, many questioned the decision to pitch the novice in at Gold Cup level, but Taafe obviously considered Captain Christy fully worthy of his place in the line-up, and the horse arrived at Cheltenham in winning form having won his last two races.

Fulke Walwyn's second and third runners, Charlie Potheen and Game Spirit – the latter of which was owned by the Queen Mother and gave Terry Biddlecombe a final ride in the race – and the outsider High Ken, were also in the line-up, while the seven-runner field was completed by the 1973 dual-Festival winner Inkslinger, who had warmed up for the challenge of tackling a distance further than he normally encountered with a good third to the improving horse Lean Forward at Leopardstown. The American-bred and owned Inkslinger was the mount of Tommy Carberry.

With Peter O'Sullevan's horse Attivo warming up the crowd with a popular win in the Triumph Hurdle, the Gold Cup field were ready. Just like the year before, it was Charlie

above: Halfway in the Gold Cup, Game Spirit leads Pendil, The Dikler and eventual winner Captain Christy.

left: Beaten but happy, Terry Biddlecombe chats to the Queen Mother, owner of Gold Cup third Game Spirit.

Potheen – who had not raced since November – that cut out the early running, and he led from Inkslinger, Pendil and Game Spirit. It was interesting to see that the novice Captain Christy was settled by Bobby Beasley at the back of the field during the early stages.

Inkslinger, whose only run at a comparable distance had been in the previous season's Irish Grand National, was the first to depart the race as he came down at the tenth fence. He had been travelling well enough and was in second place when he fell.

Charlie Potheen still led on the second circuit, but it was High Ken, the 100/1 shot, that went into the lead seven fences from home. Pendil, travelling sweetly once more for Pitman, tracked the leader, with Game Spirit and The Dikler not for away. Captain Christy remained last.

Churning along as the field reached the top of the hill, High Ken approached the third last fence in the lead from Pendil and Game Spirit. Cheltenham's most hazardous fence was about to make its mark on the 1974 Gold Cup story, as High Ken failed to negotiate the obstacle and came to grief. In a cruel twist of fate, Pendil, directly behind the leader, toppled over High Ken and out of the race. Ironically, the favourite had jumped the fence beautifully, but the gods had not written his name on the Gold Cup this time – and they never would.

Leaving the frustrated favourite behind, it was now The Dikler that steamed on, Ron Barry sensing another victory on Walwyn's giant, and from being last much of the way, the novice Captain Christy had moved stylishly through to be the danger.

1974 GOLD CUP RESULT

FATE – HORSE	AGE/WEIGHT	JOCKEY	ODDS
1st – CAPTAIN CHRISTY	7-12-0	H. BEASLEY	7/1
2nd – THE DIKLER	11-12-0	R. BARRY	5/1
3rd – GAME SPIRIT	8-12-0	T.W. BIDDLECOMBE	20/1
4th – Charlie Potheen	9-12-0	W. Smith	33/1
Fell – Inkslinger	7-12-0	T. Carberry	11/1
Fell – High Ken	8-12-0	B.R. Davies	100/1
Brought Down – Pendil	9-12-0	R. Pitman	8/13*

14 March 1974
Going – Soft
Winner – £14,572
Time – 7mins 5.8secs
7 Ran

Captain Christy	Bay gelding by Mon Capitaine – Christy's Bow
The Dikler	Bay gelding by Vulgan – Coronation Day
Game Spirit	Chestnut gelding by Game Rights – Castile

Winner bred by George Williams
Winner trained by P. Taafe in Ireland.

OTHER 1974 FESTIVAL RESULTS

Race	Horse	Jockey	Odds
Sun Alliance Novices' Hurdle	Brown Lad	R. Barry	2/1
Two Mile Champion Chase	Royal Relief	W. Smith	6/1
Joe Coral Golden Hurdle Final	Kastrup	G. Thorner	10/1
Sun Alliance Chase	Ten Up	T. Carberry	7/2
National Hunt Chase	Mr Midland	Mr M. Morris	7/2
Grand Annual Chase	Dulwich	M. Salaman	100/30
Lloyds Bank C Novice Hurdle	Avec Moi	R. Rowell	5/4
Arkle Challenge Trophy Chase	Canasta Lad	J. King	2/1
Champion Hurdle Ch Cup	Lanzarote	R. Pitman	7/4
Lloyds Bank Hurdle	Highland Abbe	R. Smith	15/2
Foxhunter Ch Cup Chase	Corrie Burn	Mr I. Williams	20/1
Mildmay Of Flete Hcap Chase	Garnishee	D. Mould	6/1
Kim Muir Memorial Ch Cup	Castleruddery	Mr T.M. Walsh	14/1
Daily Express Triumph Hurdle	Attivo	R.G. Hughes	4/5
National Hunt Hcap Chase	Cuckolder	A. Turnell	6/1
County Handicap Hurdle	True Song	G. Old	14/1
Cathcart Challenge Cup Chase	Soothsayer	R. Pitman	11/8

The pair were almost inseparable until the Irish horse nudged in front as they came to the last fence. But the drama was not over yet, and it was here that Captain Christy made his first real error, as he smacked the fence hard and landed awkwardly, giving The Dikler a real advantage.

But now was the time for everyone to see how right Taafe had been in electing this race for his star, and having quickly drawn level, Beasley unleashed Captain Christy up the hill to storm home by five lengths from the brave defending champion, sparking huge Irish celebrations among the spectators.

Game Spirit had been third and Charlie Potheen fourth, but although Winter remained modest in defeat, Pitman could hardly believe he had not won chasing's Blue Riband, admitting Pendil was going beautifully when he made his exit. Pendil would go down as one of the best horses never to have won a Gold Cup. He never ran in the race again.

Captain Christy though had staked his claim as chasing's new star, and at seven, his future looked extremely rosy, after all, the horse had seemed to improve with every chase he ran in, and there was surely more improvement still to come. Captain Christy had been bought privately by Pat Taafe for owner Mrs Jane Samuel in 1972, and Bobby Beasley, for whom Captain Christy was a second Gold Cup win after Roddy Owen in 1959, had carried out Taafe's waiting instructions perfectly in the race. Irish support erupted in the winner's enclosure, and with four wins in the last five Gold Cups on the back of wins for the likes of Arkle and Fort Leney in the 1960s, the Emerald Isle had plenty of reason to celebrate.

1975

TEN UP

After the snow that had threatened to wreak havoc with the 1974 Cheltenham Festival, the hazard that faced the 1975 meeting also came from the skies. The weekend before the Festival, there was a mass downpour of heavy rain, and on the preceding Sunday, Cheltenham Racecourse was waterlogged. Similar to the previous year, an inspection was called for Monday and the unfortunate outcome was that Tuesday had to be abandoned. With one vital day lost, Wednesday's programme was restructured to include eight races, although the conditions were atrocious and extremely heavy.

However, after passing an inspection on Wednesday morning, race they did – the day's highlight being a rematch between Lanzarote and Comedy Of Errors in the Champion Hurdle. The defending champion Lanzarote struggled in the conditions and this allowed his rival to become the first horse to regain his title, having initially won in 1973.

Comedy Of Errors' gritty performance aside, it was Ireland that stole the opening day with three victories. Lough Inagh won the Two Mile Champion Chase, beating Royal Relief. The amazing Royal Relief, ridden on this occasion by Lord Oaksey, had now finished in the frame in the last six

runnings of the race, including victories in 1972 and 1974, and the horse's next stop was at Aintree in the Grand National where, despite being well fancied, he would fall for the second year in succession.

The Irish joy continued when Bannow Rambler took the Lloyds Bank Champion Novice Hurdle, and the treble was completed when Brown Lad, who had developed into an exceptional novice chaser, won the Lloyds Bank Hurdle. Brown Lad had been due to run in the SunAlliance Novice Chase, but was rerouted when that race was claimed by the weather.

Conditions were like a bog come Gold Cup day, and very few of the horses in the seven-runner big race field were expected to appreciate the ground.

With ante-post favourite Pendil sustaining a tendon injury two weeks before the Gold Cup, the mantle of market leader went to the excellent winner of the previous year, Captain Christy, even though there were serious doubts about the

Comedy Of Errors on his way to regaining the Champion Hurdle crown he first won in 1973.

above: Lough Inagh returns from victory in the Champion Chase.

above right: Gold Cup stars of the future; Tied Cottage leads from Brown Lad in the Lloyds Bank Hurdle.

horse acting on the ground. The champion's finest moment of the season had come in the King George, a race in which Pendil had been deemed unbeatable. Captain Christy won the Kempton race from Pendil by eight lengths, but then slumped badly in the Thyestes Chase at Gowran Park and also in the Leopardstown Chase (the latter coming on swamp-like ground similar to the Gold Cup going). Captain Christy then dead-heated with the subsequent Two Mile Champion Chase winner Lough Inagh in a two-and-a-half-mile chase at Thurles, leaving Pat Taafe to describe his horse as being in grand shape for a bid to retain his crown.

The betting market indicated that the main challenger to Captain Christy would come from Jim Dreaper's promising Ten Up. The horse, equipped with the famous Arkle colours, had won the SunAlliance Chase at the 1974 Festival and had illustrated his love of mud when winning the Whitbread Trial Chase at Ascot in February in gruelling conditions. The Irish handicapper rated Ten Up a full 10lbs inferior to Captain Christy, but, such was Ten Up's appetite for testing conditions, that this gap appeared almost irrelevant.

1975 GOLD CUP RESULT

FATE – HORSE	AGE/WEIGHT	JOCKEY	ODDS
1st – TEN UP	8-12-0	T. CARBERRY	2/1
2nd – SOOTHSAYER	8-12-0	R. PITMAN	28/1
3rd – BULA	10-12-0	J. FRANCOME	5/1
4th – Glanford Brigg	9-12-0	S. Holland	25/1
5th – High Ken	9-12-0	Barry Brogan (Remounted)	33/1
Pulled Up – Bruslee	9-12-0	A. Turnell	12/1
Pulled Up – The Dikler	12-12-0	R. Barry	20/1
Pulled Up – Captain Christy	8-12-0	R. Coonan	7/4*

13 March 1975
Going – Heavy
Winner – £17,757.50
Time – 7mins 53secs
8 Ran

Ten Up	Brown gelding by Raise You Then – Irish Harp
Soothsayer	Bay or Brown gelding by Mystic II – Sagoma
Bula	Brown gelding by Raincheck – Pongo's Fancy

Winner bred by Joe Osborne
Winner trained by J. Dreaper at Kilsallaghan, Ireland.

OTHER 1975 FESTIVAL RESULTS
Tuesday of meeting cancelled due to weather, as well as last three races on Thursday

Arkle Challenge Trophy Chase	Broncho II	C. Tinkler	8/1
Two Mile Champion Chase	Lough Inagh	S. Barker	100/30
Joe Coral Golden Hurdle Final	Saffron Cake	E. Wright	13/1
Lloyds Bank C Novice Hurdle	Bannow Rambler	F. Berry	9/2
Champion Hurdle Ch Cup	Comedy Of Errors	K.B. White	11/8
Lloyds Bank Hurdle	Brown Lad	T. Carberry	7/4
Foxhunter Ch Cup Chase	Real Rascal	Mr G. Hyatt	8/1
Mildmay Of Flete Hcap Chase	Summerville	A. Turnell	4/1
National Hunt Hcap Chase	King Flame	J. Francome	12/1
Kim Muir Memorial Ch Cup	Quick Reply	Mr R. Lamb	15/2
Sun Alliance Novices' Hurdle	Davy Lad	D.T. Hughes	5/2
Daily Express Triumph Hurdle	Royal Epic	F. McKenna	20/1

With Pendil absent, Fred Winter relied on two newcomers to the race. Bula, ridden by John Francome, was trying to become the first horse to pull off the Champion Hurdle/Gold Cup double, and the horse clearly had an affection for Cheltenham. Bula's first attempt at a three-mile trip had gone well recently at Windsor in the Fairlawne Chase, but many believed the horse really wanted good ground to be at his best. Bula's stablemate, Soothsayer, had won the Cathcart Chase at the 1974 Festival, and the American horse was the mount of Richard Pitman.

High Ken, newcomers Glanford Brigg and Bruslee, and The Dikler – who had suffered from training problems during the season and appeared past his best – concluded the line-up for 1975, and the race would be omitting three of the fences, such was the state of the ground.

Glanford Brigg, runner-up to Ten Up in the 1974 SunAlliance Chase, and High Ken were the first to show as the field sloshed through the ground, and at the fourth fence it was the mud-loving Ten Up that jumped into the lead.

Even before the halfway point, much of the field seemed to be struggling as Ten Up marched on. It was not long before Bruslee, who entered the race in fair form with jockey Andy Turnell on board, cried enough, clearly hating the conditions, and was pulled up before the eleventh fence. The Dikler, running in his sixth Gold Cup, was pulled up a fence later, then Captain Christy – who had been in touch early on – gradually began to lose his position and faded rapidly soon after, his reign finally coming to an end when he was pulled up at the fourteenth.

As the remainder continued to struggle, it was left to the Winter pair of Bula and Soothsayer to chase Ten Up. Bula had run with credit and held every chance at the second last, but he quickly tired thereafter; Tommy Carberry got a fine leap out of Ten Up at the last fence, and from there on

above: Anne, Duchess of Westminster greets her horse Ten Up after his Gold Cup win.

left: Suited to the gruelling conditions, Ten Up saw off Bula to win the Gold Cup.

in it was game over. Ten Up powered up the hill with the mud flying and eventually won by six lengths from the physically drained duo of Soothsayer and Bula. Glanford Brigg and the remounted High Ken were the only others to complete the course.

There was no doubting that everything had been in Ten Up's favour and that on the day he was the only horse to truly act on the ground. It would be unfair to downgrade Ten Up's win – after all, he had won the SunAlliance Chase in better conditions the year before and had proved throughout the season that he was an improving horse with a good deal of scope.

It was a result that further increased some impressive Gold Cup tallies. The win confirmed the Dreaper legacy in the race, with Jim becoming the first second generation to ever train the Gold Cup winner, following his father Tom's five glorious successes. It was a third winning ride in the race for Tommy Carberry and the fourth win for owner Anne, Duchess of Westminster, who had paid 5,500 guineas for the horse at Goffs Sales as a three-year-old. The real hero of the day though was Ten Up, who had conquered the most testing of conditions to take his place in the record books. Ireland had won the Gold Cup again – was there any home-team horse on the horizon capable of bucking the trend?

ROYAL FROLIC

The defending Gold Cup champion Ten Up was the focus of attention at the 1976 Cheltenham Festival. The horse had won his latest start and was expected to put up a bold show on this occasion as he attempted to emulate (most recently) L'Escargot, by winning back-to-back titles. Then the bomb went off. The horse had developed an unwanted knack of breaking blood vessels, and as a cure for this in his native Ireland, trainer Jim Dreaper had been giving Ten Up a preventative injection before his races. While this was not a problem in Ireland, the Cheltenham stewards warned Dreaper that the horse faced disqualification if traces of the injection were found in a dope test if finishing in the first four. It was revealed Dreaper had used similar injections on Lough Inagh before that horse had won the 1975 Two Mile Champion Chase and also on former Gold Cup runner Leap Frog. Following a discussion with the horse's owner, Anne, Duchess of Westminster, and concluding that the cons of running outweighed the pros, Dreaper withdrew Ten Up on the day of the race, much to his annoyance. Consequently, Dreaper was fined £125 for taking Ten Up out – surely an excellent example of a 'no win situation'?

There were plenty of interesting results as the 1976 Festival got underway on the Tuesday. Skymas, winner of the 1973 Mackeson Gold Cup, rolled back the years in the Two Mile Champion Chase to win the race as an eleven-year-old. The annual sighting in the event of Royal Relief got no further than the fourth fence on this occasion, as the horse was brought down.

The SunAlliance Chase turned out to be, as proved over time, a very strong renewal. The line-up included Forest King, winner of nine chases at a wide range of distances and owned and trained by Ken Hogg, and Davy Lad, who had won the SunAlliance Novices' Hurdle the previous year and would go on to have great future success at Cheltenham. However, both horses were eclipsed by an Irish horse called Tied Cottage, who jumped superbly for jockey Tommy

Six-time contestant Bird's Nest gives chase, but Night Nurse has flown in the Champion Hurdle.

The magnificent Champion Hurdle winner Night Nurse.

Carberry to beat the outsider No Gypsy. Tied Cottage's bold, front-running style would be a feature of Gold Cups in the future.

One of the performances of the opening day came in the National Hunt Chase for amateur riders, where Sage Merlin, a future Grand National participant, put in a fine display under jockey Peter Greenall to win from Romany Bay and Pacify.

Undoubtedly, however, the clash of the day on Wednesday came in the Champion Hurdle. This was a vintage edition of the race, and signalled a new era in the hurdling sphere. Former champions Comedy Of Errors and Lanzarote were back, but it was newcomers that were to purge this race as Night Nurse led all the way to win by two-and-a-half lengths from Bird's Nest. Night Nurse and Bird's

Nest would form part of a quartet of hurdlers that would dominate the race – and the hurdling scene – for a considerable number of years. Night Nurse and Bird's Nest pillaged this edition, but on the horizon lurked two other fine hurdlers in waiting, Monksfield and Sea Pigeon.

In contrast to the Champion Hurdle, Thursday's Gold Cup was viewed as a sub-standard renewal of the race, with Captain Christy sidelined through injury and now Ten Up unable to compete. The focus of attention switched to Fred Winter's Bula, who was now eleven and was expected to appreciate the fast going on this occasion. The mount of John Francome, it was well documented the horse was trying to become the first ever to complete the Champion Hurdle/Gold Cup double. If Bula was going to achieve this, he needed to avoid the curse of being favourite that had

Royal Frolic jumps the last clear of Colebridge in the Gold Cup.

snared recent Winter runners in the race. Into View, Crisp and Pendil had all been beaten in recent Gold Cups, but Bula's form seemed solid, having won three of his five races during the season, including Sandown's Gainsborough Chase and Windsor's Fairlawne Chase on his last two starts.

Despite the disappointment of Ten Up, Jim Dreaper still had two useful weapons to go to war with. Brown Lad had been an exceptional novice chaser the previous season and his wins had included the Irish Grand National. The horse had stuck to handicaps during the current season and had won three times – including a thumping of the useful Grand National hope Ball Hopper at Punchestown. However, the feeling was that Brown Lad needed soft ground to be at his best, although he remained well backed in the market and started at a price of 13/8. The second Dreaper runner was the consistent Colebridge, ridden by Frank Berry.

Royal Frolic (who at seven-years-old was, along with Roman Bar, the youngest horse in the race) was trained by Fred Rimell, who had handled the 1967 winner Woodland Venture. After a win in the Greenall Whitley Breweries

Chase a fortnight prior to the Gold Cup, Rimell had persuaded Royal Frolic's owner, Sir Edward Hamner, to run the improving horse in the Blue Riband, despite the owner's fear that the animal may be too young. Rimell's reasoning was that (undeniably) nobody connected with the horse was getting any younger, and that this was certainly a year where an outsider could win.

The ground was riding good-to-firm as the runners were sent on their way, and a useful pair of staying chasers in Money Market and What A Buck were the first to show, followed by Glanford Brigg and veteran The Dikler. The pace was moderate and the first circuit was remarkably incident free, with little change in the running order until John Burke sent Royal Frolic ahead of The Dikler in fourth place.

The field lost the fallen Flashy Boy as they ran up the hill for the final time, and then Glanford Brigg took over from Colebridge, Royal Frolic, What A Buck and The Dikler, although Royal Frolic was travelling really well and out-jumped the leader at the third last. It was here that Bula, who had been creeping ever closer, made a mistake that severely interrupted his progress. Now the race was on in earnest, and Brown Lad, who clearly disliked the going, and Colebridge chased frantically after Royal Frolic.

Try as they might, the Dreaper pair simply could not catch the leader; when Royal Frolic jumped the last in grand style, the race was as good as over. Rimell's horse subsequently strode up the run-in to win by five lengths. Brown Lad had run extremely bravely to finish second on ground that was far from ideal, while Colebridge came in third ahead of the Grand National-bound Money Market. The Dikler, running in his record seventh and final Gold Cup, came home safely in eighth place. The big disappointment of the race was the 6/4 favourite Bula, and both Winter and Francome were bemused by the horse's poor showing.

1976 PIPER CHAMPAGNE GOLD CUP RESULT

FATE – HORSE	AGE/WEIGHT	JOCKEY	ODDS
1st – ROYAL FROLIC	7-12-0	J. BURKE	14/1
2nd – BROWN LAD	10-12-0	T. CARBERRY	13/8
3rd – COLEBRIDGE	12-12-0	F. BERRY	12/1
4th – Money Market	9-12-0	R. Barry	33/1
5th – Glanford Brigg	10-12-0	M. Blackshaw	50/1
6th – Bula	11-12-0	J. Francome	6/4*
7th – Otter Way	8-12-0	G. Thorner	50/1
8th – The Dikler	13-12-0	A. Branford	33/1
9th – Roman Bar	7-12-0	P. Kiely	50/1
Fell – Flashy Boy	8-12-0	D.T. Hughes	16/1
Pulled Up – What A Buck	9-12-0	J. King	16/1

18 March 1976
Going – Good to Firm
Winner – £18,134.50
Time – 6mins 40.1secs
11 Ran

Royal Frolic	Bay gelding by Royal Buck – Forward Miss
Brown Lad	Brown gelding by Sayajirao – Caicos
Colebridge	Brown gelding by Vulgan – Cherry Bud

Winner bred by John Seymour
Winner trained by T.F. Rimell at Kinnersley, Severn Stoke, Worcs.

OTHER 1976 FESTIVAL RESULTS

Sun Alliance Novices' Hurdle	Parkhill	D.T. Hughes	4/1
Two Mile Champion Chase	Skymas	M. Morris	8/1
Joe Coral Golden Hurdle Final	Good Prospect	R.R. Evans	10/1
Sun Alliance Chase	Tied Cottage	T. Carberry	12/1
National Hunt Chase	Sage Merlin	Mr P. Greenall	5/2
Grand Annual Chase	Dulwich	B.R. Davies	9/4
Lloyds Bank C Novice Hurdle	Beacon Light	A. Turnell	14/1
Arkle Challenge Trophy Chase	Roaring Wind	R. Crank	11/1
Champion Hurdle Ch Cup	Night Nurse	P. Broderick	2/1
Lloyds Bank Hurdle	Bit Of A Jig	D.T. Hughes	2/1
Foxhunter Ch Cup Chase	False Note	Mr B. Smart	11/4
Mildmay Of Flete Hcap Chase	Broncho II	M. Dickinson	7/2
Kim Muir Memorial Ch Cup	Prolan	Mr T.M. Walsh	3/1
Daily Express Triumph Hurdle	Peterhof	J.J. O'Neill	10/1
National Hunt Hcap Chase	Barmer	J. McNaught	20/1
County Handicap Hurdle	Java Fox	Mr G. Jones	16/1
Cathcart Ch Hunters' Chase	Mickley Seabright	Mr P. Brookshaw	6/4

A surprise winner he may have been, but Royal Frolic had jumped extremely well for John Burke, winning the day in handy fashion and continuing a trend set by Captain Christy and Ten Up of young, first-time runners to win the Gold Cup. Things would continue to roll sweetly for Rimell, as the very next month he captured the Grand National for an amazing fourth time, courtesy of Rag Trade.

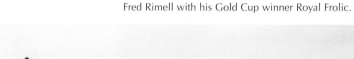

Fred Rimell with his Gold Cup winner Royal Frolic.

DAVY LAD

Since the war, the Irish had made the annual journey to Cheltenham full of hopes and dreams. They had collected a grand total of 114 victories and had dominated the Gold Cup in recent times, winning nine of the previous thirteen runnings. At the 1977 Cheltenham Festival, the Irish arrived with their largest squad yet, with an excess of forty runners ready to pillage the top prizes. The Gold Cup in particular had a distinctly Irish flavour this time around, with four of the thirteen runners hailing from the Emerald Isle, and all with very fair chances.

As usual, there was an Irish banker: on this occasion the horse in question was the eight-year-old Mount Prague, trained by Mick O'Toole and ridden by top amateur Ted Walsh. The horse was running in the four-mile National Hunt Chase, where his stamina was expected to come into play. This race was, however, to prove a momentary blip at the 1977 Festival for O'Toole, as Mount Prague fell at the sixteenth, with victory going to Alpenstock and jockey Dick Saunders. (Saunders would in the future achieve an even greater success aboard Grittar in the 1982 Grand National.)

The Two Mile Champion Chase certainly appeared to be a hot renewal in 1977, with two-time Champion Hurdler Bula running in the race after disappointing in previous Gold Cups. Opposition included an excellent two-miler, the front-running Tingle Creek, Royal Relief – unbelievably having what would be his eighth and final run in the race – and the previous year's winner, Skymas. Bula's luck did not improve in this race, as both he and Royal Relief fell at the fourth, with Bula's fall seeing him damage muscles in his shoulder. At the business end, the race went again to the evergreen Skymas, who touched off Grangewood Girl by a neck.

Even though Comedy Of Errors ran in the Lloyds Bank Hurdle over three miles instead, Wednesday featured another classic Champion Hurdle battle involving Bird's Nest, Night Nurse, Monksfield and Sea Pigeon. In contrast to the previous year, the ground was riding soft, so it illustrated just how good a horse Night Nurse was when he was able to battle through the conditions to win his second consecutive Champion Hurdle, beating the Irish challenger Monksfield. Night Nurse was a charismatic and worthy champion, and everyone now wanted to know if the horse could join Hatton's Grace, Sir Ken and Persian War in the 'hat-trick club'.

Skymas and jockey Mouse Morris just have the Cheltenham hill to climb to achieve Champion Chase glory.

60

It had not been a good Festival for Fred Winter as Gold Cup day arrived. First he had seen Bula fall heavily on Tuesday, and then Thursday started off with his fancied Rathconrath losing fifteen lengths at the start of the Triumph Hurdle, costing the horse any chance of winning the race. Now though, he had a fantastic chance of erasing all the bad memories of Gold Cups past with his wonderful young chaser Lanzarote in the Blue Riband. Although the horse was worryingly inexperienced – only Mont Tremblant in 1952 with four previous outings had won the Gold Cup with the same amount of chase experience – both Winter and jockey John Francome were remarkably confident about Lanzarote's chances. Of his four chases, Lanzarote had won his last three with ease, exhibiting fast jumping and superb finishing speed. If he could handle jumping under Gold Cup pressure, then Francome believed there would be nothing to stop Lanzarote becoming the first horse to win both the Champion Hurdle and the Gold Cup.

The Irish challenge was strong and deep. Their top hope and the race favourite was Bannow Rambler, who came into the event following three straight wins, including an impress-ive weight-giving performance in the Leopardstown Chase. Also representing Ireland were the soft ground-loving Davy Lad, the 1976 SunAlliance Chase winner Tied Cottage, and Frank Berry's mount Fort Fox, a very talented horse but one that was prone to jumping errors and had fallen on his last two starts.

All thirteen runners were Gold Cup virgins, and among those considered as possible winners were Fort Devon, Zarib and Tamalin. Fort Devon was looking to give Fulke Walwyn a fifth win in the race and had previously been a high-class chaser in America, winning both the Maryland Hunt Cup and the Maryland Grand National. The horse had run three times in England, with a good second to the useful Royal Marshal II in the King George. Fort Devon was another expected to love the soft going and a test of stamina.

Zarib, a nine-year-old novice that had missed the previous season through injury, was looking to follow up Royal Frolic's win in the 1976 race and give trainer Fred Rimell his third Gold Cup success, while Tamalin was the hope of northern trainer Gordon Richards: the horse had run very well behind the smart Zeta's Son in the season's Hennessy Gold Cup before registering a win in soft ground at Newcastle on his latest start.

As one of the most open-looking Gold Cups for years got underway, it was Tied Cottage and jockey Tommy Carberry that made the running at a good early pace, hacking along from Fort Devon, Banlieu, April Seventh, Davy Lad and Lanzarote. This was, however, to be an incident-packed race, and the first casualty came at the fifth fence, where Zarib crashed out. This was merely a meek prelude to the shocking episode that lay in wait at fence number nine.

Going very nicely, Lanzarote jumped the fence well, but on landing, the horse faltered before crumbling to the ground. Tragically, the horse had broken a near-hind leg and there was nothing that could be done to save him. Whether it was his inexperience or just bad luck was unclear, but one thing was certain, the Winter Gold Cup hoodoo had struck again, with this being the most bitter of pills to swallow.

Almost as an afterthought, the favourite Bannow Rambler had been brought down by Lanzarote's fall, and even though he was remounted by Michael Furlong, his hopes had vanished, and he was well adrift when ultimately pulled-up two fences from home.

Leaving behind the sad scenes at the ninth, Tied Cottage bounded on, and continued his lead on to the second circuit, chased closely by Fort Devon.

It was noticeable how well Fort Devon was going under Bill Smith and as they jumped the sixteenth, where outsider Banlieu was pulled up, he was challenging Tied Cottage for

1977 PIPER CHAMPAGNE GOLD CUP RESULT

FATE – HORSE	AGE/WEIGHT	JOCKEY	ODDS
1st – DAVY LAD	7-12-0	D.T. HUGHES	14/1
2nd – TIED COTTAGE	9-12-0	T. CARBERRY	20/1
3rd – SUMMERVILLE	11-12-0	J. KING	15/1
4th – April Seventh	11-12-0	S.C. Knight	66/1
5th – Fort Fox	8-12-0	F. Berry	10/1
6th – Tamalin	10-12-0	J.J. O'Neill	11/1
7th – Master H	8-12-0	Mrs J. Weston	66/1
Pulled Up – Banlieu	7-12-0	B.R. Davies	66/1
Pulled Up – Bannow Rambler	8-12-0	M. Furlong	11/4*
Pulled Up – Even Up	10-12-0	R. Champion	50/1
Fell – Fort Devon	11-12-0	W. Smith	5/1
Fell – Zarib	9-12-0	R.R. Evans	12/1
Slipped Up – Lanzarote	9-12-0	J. Francome	7/2

17 March 1977
Going – Soft
Winner – £21,990
Time – 7mins 13.6secs
13 Ran

Davy Lad	Bay gelding by David Jack – Chateau
Tied Cottage	Bay gelding by Honour Bound – Cottage Ray
Summerville	Chestnut gelding by Bowsprit – Stella d'Oro

Winner bred by Mrs K. Westropp-Bennett
Winner trained by M. O'Toole at Maddenstown, Kildare, Ireland.

OTHER 1977 FESTIVAL RESULTS

Race	Horse	Jockey	Odds
Sun Alliance Novices' Hurdle	Counsel Cottage	S. Treacy	6/1
Two Mile Champion Chase	Skymas	M. Morris	7/2
Joe Coral Hurdle Final	Outpoint	P. O'Brien	10/1
Sun Alliance Chase	Gay Spartan	M. Dickinson	13/2
National Hunt Chase	Alpenstock	Mr C. Saunders	14/1
Grand Annual Chase	Tom Morgan	T. Stack	9/4
Lloyds Bank C Novice Hurdle	Mac's Chariot	D.T. Hughes	7/1
Arkle Challenge Trophy Chase	Tip The Wink	D.T. Hughes	15/2
Champion Hurdle Ch Cup	Night Nurse	P. Broderick	15/2
Lloyds Bank Hurdle	Town Ship	T. Carberry	5/2
Foxhunter Ch Cup Chase	Long Lane	Mr R. Shepherd	9/4
Mildmay Of Flete Hcap Chase	Uncle Bing	J. Francome	9/2
Daily Express Triumph Hurdle	Meladon	T. Carberry	6/1
Kim Muir Memorial Ch Cup	Double Negative	Mr P. Brookshaw	11/2
National Hunt Hcap Chase	Gay Vulgan	W. Smith	4/1
County Handicap Hurdle	Kilcoleman	T. Kinane	14/1
Cathcart Ch Hunters' Chase	Rusty Tears	Mr N. Madden	7/4

the lead. But at the very next fence, the outlook of the race changed completely, as Fort Devon attempted to jump a rainbow, misjudged the obstacle, and came down. Now it was Summerville and jockey Jeff King that stormed through, and the pair appeared to have taken a winning initiative with just five fences to jump.

As Summerville bounded on from Tied Cottage, only Davy Lad seemed to be making any headway from the remainder, but significant headway it was as jockey Dessie Hughes urged his mount forward on his desired ground and, at the second last, the partnership became serious challengers.

Now Summerville, who had been travelling like the winner, inexplicably began to falter between the last two

Summerville was the unlucky horse of the 1977 Gold Cup.

Dessie Hughes timed Davy Lad's run to perfection as the pair saw off Tied Cottage in the Gold Cup.

Davy Lad's owner, Anne-Marie McGowan with trainer Mick O'Toole (centre).

fences, and both Davy Lad and Tied Cottage cruised past him going to the last. It was Dessie Hughes on Davy Lad who had timed his run to perfection and, soaring the last, the horse steamed on up the run-in to thwart a one-paced Tied Cottage by six lengths. Bravely, Summerville had plugged on for third place, despite the fact (as it later emerged) that the horse had broken down after the second last. Summerville's stablemate, April Seventh, came home in fourth place, with Fort Fox – who had never been a threat – eventually finishing fifth.

The tragic demise of Lanzarote had left Fred Winter speechless. Worse was still to come for the trainer, as three weeks after the Festival, Bula had to be put down after failing to recover from the shoulder injury sustained from his fall. Both Bula and Lanzarote were fine champions and the fact they were each cut down on the course where they had their finest moments imparted an ironic, sombre taste to the aftermath of the 1977 Festival.

For Mick O'Toole and Dessie Hughes though, it had been a glorious Gold Cup success. O'Toole revealed it had long been his ambition to win the Gold Cup, while the win crowned a fine Festival for Hughes, as he also won the Arkle Trophy on Tip The Wink and the Champion Novice Hurdle on Mac's Chariot.

Davy Lad, who had given O'Toole his first Festival success in the 1975 SunAlliance Novices' Hurdle, had been brought by his trainer for 5,000 guineas as a three-year-old and sold to owner Mrs Anne-Marie McGowan. Mrs McGowan's only other horse, Parkhill, had won the SunAlliance Novices' Hurdle in 1976.

So the Irish had claimed another Gold Cup, and Davy Lad had been the one to benefit from the misfortunes of others. This is not to say that he was merely a lucky winner though, as he had handled the ground imperiously and jumped superbly. However, his fortune was shortly to evaporate as he headed for Aintree in a bid for the near-impossible Gold Cup/Grand National double. Frustratingly, the newest Gold Cup champion fell at just the third fence, the big ditch. As Fred Winter would discover twelve months on, the racing game really does have its highs and lows.

MIDNIGHT COURT

The 1978 Cheltenham Festival was run in two parts. The Tuesday and Wednesday of the meeting were unscathed and run on their scheduled March dates; however, when early morning snow fell on Thursday 16 March, Cheltenham officials had no choice but to reschedule the Gold Cup – along with the Triumph Hurdle – for 12 April. Obviously, this move favoured some contestants more than others, with the ground destined to be in a considerably better state later in the year.

The Tuesday in March was a particularly happy day for Irish jockey Tommy Carmody. Riding at his first Festival, the jockey claimed the big race of the day, the Two Mile Champion Chase, aboard newcomer Hilly Way, beating, among others, the English hotpot Early Spring, who made numerous errors. Earlier in the day, Carmody had been successful on the hot favourite Mr Kildare in the SunAlliance Novices' Hurdle.

All the old favourites were back in Wednesday's Champion Hurdle as Night Nurse attempted his third straight win in the race. This time though, there was to be a new hero as Monksfield, ridden by forty-four-year-old jockey Tommy Kinane, took up the running two flights out from the

defending champion before holding off a late charge from Sea Pigeon. The Irish may have dominated the Gold Cup in recent times, but Monksfield's win was their first in the Champion Hurdle for fifteen years.

Earlier on Wednesday, a possible Champion Hurdler of the future was unearthed as the six-year-old Golden Cygnet, ridden by amateur Niall Madden, produced a sparkling performance to win the Waterford Crystal Supreme Novices' Hurdle. In the very next race, the gutsy northern challenger Alverton beat a strong field to win the Arkle Trophy under jockey Graham Thorner. Thorner was standing in for the injured Jonjo O'Neill and O'Neill's similarly injured under-study Ian Watkinson.

By the time April's Gold Cup rolled around, the field – and the going – had changed dramatically. Horses that were due to run in March but did not make the line-up in April were Bannow Rambler, Gay Spartan, Bunker Hill, Casamayor,

Hilly Way (far side) would emerge victorious in the Champion Chase.

left: A jubilant Tommy Kinane is congratulated having won the Champion Hurdle on Monksfield.

below: The electric youngster Golden Cygnet captured the Supreme Novices' Hurdle.

Master Spy, Precious Jem and Uncle Bing. Most notable of the absentees were the prolific but now injured Gay Spartan and the previous year's favourite Bannow Rambler. In addition, the defending champion Davy Lad was missing because of an injured foot.

The going was now much better than it had been in March, and officially rode good, much to the delight of trainer Fred Winter, whose big hope this time around – Midnight Court – appreciated such conditions. Midnight Court was undeniably the most progressive horse in the race and, at seven years of age, his potential was still untapped. The horse had won all six of his chases during the season, beginning with wins at Newbury and Doncaster. There then followed a pair of impressive victories at Ascot, the first a

65

John Francome and Midnight Court on their way to Gold Cup glory.

beating of the smart handicapper Ghost Writer in the Kirk and Kirk Chase, and then an easy win over Gold Cup withdrawal Master Spy in the SGB Chase. Wins at Newbury and Chepstow followed, and despite allegations of bribery and corruption hanging over the head of big-race jockey John Francome, Midnight Court was strongly fancied to give Winter a long-awaited Gold Cup triumph.

Despite Midnight Court's impressive season, the race favourite was Fort Devon, a faller in the 1977 renewal. Fulke Walwyn's runner had been prepared all season with the Gold Cup in mind, and the horse had won three of his four races, the sole defeat coming in the Hennessy Gold Cup where he was narrowly beaten by Bachelor's Hall.

Bachelor's Hall was perhaps the dark horse of the race, and his form during the season was very strong. The horse had won the Mackeson Gold Cup, Hennessy, King George and the Welsh Champion Chase. Despite these excellent results, Martin O'Halloran's mount was only third in the betting, starting at a generous 7/1.

The first two home in the 1976 Gold Cup were back, having missed the 1977 edition. Royal Frolic, again ridden

by John Burke, had endured an up-and-down campaign, but was not unfancied in an attempt to give Fred Rimell a third Gold Cup success. Brown Lad had been done no favours by the switch to April, as the Irish Grand National winner notably preferred soft ground. Still, the classy twelve-year-old had run above expectations when finishing second on unfavourable ground two years previously.

The early stages of the race were very non-committal and tedious. No runner seemed willing to set any kind of searching gallop, so it was Fort Devon and Bill Smith that found themselves in front from Forest King – fifth in the 1977 Grand National – Royal Frolic, Fort Fox, Midnight Court and Neville Crump's runner, Cancello.

As Royal Frolic went up to join Fort Devon on the second circuit, it was noticeable that the pace was starting to increase, and Fort Fox was the first victim of this new rhythm as, travelling just behind the leading pair, he blundered and unseated his jockey at the fifteenth.

As they made the climb up the hill, Fort Devon and Royal Frolic were cutting each other's throats, while in behind them, Midnight Court, Master H and Cancello were waiting to pounce, Francome's mount starting to look particularly ominous.

Having to cut out the running had not suited Fort Devon and at the third last he began to send out distress signals. This presented Francome with an invitation to unleash Midnight Court, who quickly shot through on the inside.

By the last fence, Midnight Court was going tremendously well and, even though Royal Frolic was in second, he was clearly beaten when he crashed out taking the final obstacle. Guided home in picturesque style, Midnight Court crossed the line a convincing winner by seven lengths from the staying-on Brown Lad, with Master H and Bachelor's Hall the next to finish. A disappointed Bill Smith came home fifth aboard the exhausted favourite Fort Devon.

1978 PIPER CHAMPAGNE GOLD CUP RESULT

FATE – HORSE	AGE/WEIGHT	JOCKEY	ODDS
1st – MIDNIGHT COURT	7-12-0	J. FRANCOME	5/2
2nd – BROWN LAD	12-12-0	T. CARBERRY	8/1
3rd – MASTER H	9-12-0	R. CRANK	18/1
4th – Bachelor's Hall	8-12-0	M. O'Halloran	7/1
5th – Fort Devon	12-12-0	W. Smith	2/1*
6th – Cancello	9-12-0	D. Atkins	45/1
Pulled Up – Forest King	9-12-0	R. Barry	80/1
Pulled Up – Otter Way	10-12-0	J. King	50/1
Unseated Rider– Fort Fox	9-12-0	T. McGivern	20/1
Fell – Royal Frolic	9-12-0	J. Burke	11/1

12 April 1978
Going – Good
Winner – £23,827.50
Time – 6mins 57.5secs
10 Ran

Midnight Court	Bay gelding by Twilight Alley – Strumpet
Brown Lad	Brown gelding by Sayajirao – Caicos
Master H	Chestnut gelding by Master Owen – Last Resort

Winner bred by Airlie Stud
Winner trained by F. Winter at Lambourn, Berks.

OTHER 1978 FESTIVAL RESULTS

Sun Alliance Novices' Hurdle	Mr Kildare	T. Carmody	8/11
Two Mile Champion Chase	Hilly Way	T. Carmody	7/1
Joe Coral Golden Hurdle	Water Colour	K. Whyte	11/1
Sun Alliance Chase	Sweet Joe	S. Smith-Eccles	12/1
National Hunt Chase	Gay Tie	Mr J. Fowler	10/1
Grand Annual Chase	Young Arthur	A. Webb	3/1
Waterford Crystal S N Hurdle	Golden Cygnet	Mr N. Madden	4/5
Arkle Challenge Trophy Chase	Alverton	G. Thorner	5/2
Waterford Crystal C Hurdle	Monksfield	T. Kinane	11/2
Waterford Crystal Stayers' H	Flame Gun	Mr N. Madden	14/1
Foxhunter Ch Hunters' Chase	Timmie's Battle	Mr P. Greenall	7/2
Mildmay Of Flete Hcap Chase	King Or Country	P. Leach	7/1
Daily Express Triumph Hurdle	Connaught Ranger	J. Burke	25/1

The Gold Cup and the Triumph Hurdle were run in April after the original Thursday in March was postponed due to weather. All other races were run in March.

The Gold Cup had been the only major race to elude Winter, and the ovation he received on Midnight Court's return to the winner's enclosure was both rapturous and deserving. Who could begrudge the man that had suffered such cruel luck with grand horses such as Bula and Lanzarote? Winter had also been extremely unlucky not to have already won the Blue Riband through Pendil. Winter had won the race as a jockey aboard Saffron Tartan in 1961 and a year later on Mandarin, but there was no doubting Midnight Court's victory meant a great deal to him. The horse, owned by Mrs Olive Jackson, was held in the highest regard by Winter, who went as far as to say that Midnight Court may have been the best he had ever trained. The bookmakers were also impressed, and Midnight Court swiftly received a miserly quote of 4/1 to retain his title in the following year's event.

After years of misfortune, Midnight Court's Gold Cup win was a fantastic, emotional moment for trainer Fred Winter.

hurdler Willie Wumpkins, ridden by amateur Jim Wilson. The race began an amazing sequence in the event for Willie Wumpkins, who would go on to win for the next two years, the last time at the grand old age of thirteen.

The SunAlliance Chase looked to be a very strong renewal, with the favourite being the Tony Dickinson-trained Silver Buck. Dickinson had contemplated running the highly impressive Silver Buck in the Gold Cup itself, but had eventually decided against it. In the race though, it was Master Smudge – wearing a sheepskin noseband to aid with some jumping problems – that led for most of the way before powering up the hill to win, with Silver Buck back in third. The ground had been heavy, and Master Smudge had jumped beautifully out of the testing conditions, proving he would be a match for any chaser in the future given similar going. Indeed, Tuesday was a very interesting day in terms of Gold Cups. The day had featured Little Owl, Master Smudge and Silver Buck, and all three would play key roles in the big race in upcoming years.

ALVERTON

The Cheltenham Gold Cup of 1979 was, on paper at least, a very open-looking event. The field contained an exciting blend of improving novices, tough and experienced veterans, a dual Champion Hurdle winner, a former Gold Cup winner and a horse that would go on to complete an incredible fairytale. Even so, this particular Gold Cup remained highlighted by a number of significant absentees. The ante-post favourite and the season's King George winner, Gay Spartan, had been pulled out only days before the race having gone lame after exercise, while the Irish horse Jack Of Trumps – who had then replaced Gay Spartan at the head of the betting market – was also forced to miss the race. With former winners Davy Lad and Midnight Court also on the easy-list, the time appeared right for a new jumping star to write their name into the Gold Cup history books.

Tuesday saw amateur Ted Walsh steer Hilly Way to a repeat victory in the Two Mile Champion Chase, becoming the fifth horse to win the race for a second time.

In the very next race, the Coral Golden Hurdle Final, five-year-old Little Owl, a prolific young winner ridden by Jonjo O'Neill, had to settle for second place behind veteran

Master Smudge (11) leads Silver Buck (nearside) in the SunAlliance Chase.

Peter Easterby, trainer of Gold Cup hero Alverton.

Monksfield and Sea Pigeon (9) battle out the finish to the Champion Hurdle. For the second year running, Monksfield won.

Trainer Mick O'Toole, whose Yellow Dean had been the beaten Irish banker in Tuesday's SunAlliance Novices' Hurdle, gained some glorious compensation on Wednesday when his Chinrullah, an odds-on chance, marked himself out as a star of the future by winning the Arkle Trophy.

For many, the Champion Hurdle had been diluted with the absence of the ill-fated Golden Cygnet. The brilliant youngster, a winner at the 1978 Festival, was in the process of destroying a good field in the Scottish Champion Hurdle at Ayr the previous April when he took an ultimately fatal fall. It was a huge loss for trainer Edward O'Grady and, to this day, Golden Cygnet is still considered one of the best (if not the best) hurdler never to have competed in the Champion Hurdle. In the race itself Monksfield, despite rumours surrounding the horse's wellbeing, battled superbly to collar Sea Pigeon on the run-in, repeating his win of the previous year. Monksfield on this occasion was ridden by Dessie Hughes and trained by Des McDonagh.

Thursday's Gold Cup began with joint favourites. The first of these was the now thirteen-year-old Brown Lad, twice a runner-up in the race. Jim Dreaper's charge had not won during the season, but was a three-time winner of the Irish Grand National, and on this occasion had the heavy ground he relished.

Sharing favouritism with Brown Lad was the ultra-tough and stamina-packed chestnut from the yard of Peter Easterby, Alverton. The horse had broken down very badly as a three-year-old and at one time it was debatable whether he would race again. But Alverton subsequently recovered to become a very good horse on the flat and became even better when switched to fences. The horse, partnered in the Gold Cup by Jonjo O'Neill, had won the Arkle Trophy the year before and entered the Gold Cup in winning form and with conditions underfoot in his favour.

Two young guns hoping to blast their way to Gold Cup stardom were Night Nurse and Gaffer. Night Nurse, twice a

1979 PIPER CHAMPAGNE GOLD CUP RESULT

FATE – HORSE	AGE/WEIGHT	JOCKEY	ODDS
1st – ALVERTON	9-12-0	J.J. O'NEILL	5/1*
2nd – ROYAL MAIL	9-12-0	P. BLACKER	7/1
3rd – ALDANITI	9-12-0	R. CHAMPION	40/1
4th – Casamayor	9-12-0	B.R. Davies	50/1
5th – Brown Lad	13-12-0	G. Dowd	5/1*
6th – Gaffer	7-12-0	W. Smith	6/1
7th – Night Nurse	8-12-0	G. Thorner	6/1
Pulled Up – Bawnogues	8-12-0	C. Smith	50/1
Pulled Up – Bit Of Manny	10-12-0	R. R. Evans	100/1
Pulled Up – Mighty's Honour	8-12-0	F. Berry	50/1
Pulled Up – Royal Frolic	10-12-0	J. Burke	20/1
Pulled Up – Strombolus	8-12-0	J. Francome	10/1
Pulled Up – Otter Way	11-12-0	D. Goulding	50/1
Fell – Tied Cottage	11-12-0	T. Carberry	12/1

15 March 1979
Going – Heavy
Winner – £30,293.75
Time – 7mins 1sec
14 Ran

Alverton	Chestnut gelding by Midsummer Night II – Alvertona
Royal Mail	Chestnut gelding by Ballyroyal – Lency
Aldaniti	Chestnut gelding by Derek H – Renardeau

Winner bred by G.W. Pratt
Winner trained by M.H. Easterby

OTHER 1979 FESTIVAL RESULTS

Sun Alliance Novices' Hurdle	Venture To Cognac	Mr O. Sherwood	4/1
Two Mile Champion Chase	Hilly Way	Mr T.M. Walsh	7/1
Coral Golden Hurdle Final	Willie Wumpkins	Mr A.J. Wilson	25/1
Sun Alliance Chase	Master Smudge	R. Hoare	16/1
National Hunt Chase	Artic Ale	Mr J. Fowler	20/1
Grand Annual Chase	Casbah	G. Thorner	5/1
Waterford Crystal Nov Hurdle	Stranfield	T. Kinane	16/1
Arkle Ch Trophy Chase	Chinrullah	D.T. Hughes	10/11
Waterford Crystal C Hurdle	Monksfield	D.T. Hughes	9/4
Waterford Crystal Stayers' H	Lighter	P. Blacker	14/1
Kim Muir Mem Hcap Chase	Redundant Punter	Mr D. Jackson	14/1
Mildmay Of Flete Hcap Chase	Brawny Scot	R. Lamb	10/1
Daily Express Triumph Hurdle	Pollardstown	P. Blacker	12/1
Christies Foxhunter Chase	Spartan Missile	Mr M.J. Thorne	9/4
National Hunt Hcap Chase	Fair View	R. Lamb	12/1
County Handicap Hurdle	Monte Ceco	C. Tinkler	6/1
Cathcart Challenge Cup Chase	Roller-Coaster	J. Francome	6/4

Champion Hurdler, had taken to fences like a duck to water and was the second runner from Easterby's northern yard. The horse had won five races in succession before going down to Silver Buck in the Embassy Premier Final at Haydock. Gaffer, like Night Nurse a novice chaser, was a highly consistent, natural jumper from Fulke Walwyn's stable. With three wins during the season, Gaffer had proved he could mix with the highest competition by finishing close to Gay Spartan on his latest run in Wincanton's Jim Ford Challenge Cup.

With Gold Cup veterans Tied Cottage and Royal Frolic also among the fourteen-strong field, the race began amidst a concoction of rain and snow – conditions which ensured that the contest would prove a real war of attrition.

It was Tied Cottage that set a blazing pace, and before long the 1977 runner-up had built up a considerable lead, with only Alverton and Royal Mail anywhere near him. It was clear that the heavy ground and the blistering gallop set by Tied Cottage was taking its toll on the majority of the field and, incredibly, as the leader came down the hill for the final time only Alverton had a prayer of catching him.

Alverton was gaining rapidly, however, and between the final two fences he arrived with a menacing burst that sent him into a share of the lead at the last, clearly travelling the better of the pair.

The unlucky Tied Cottage, although probably facing an uphill battle anyway, clubbed the top of the fence and

As the snow comes down, Alverton (2) comes to take Tied Cottage at the last in the Gold Cup.

buckled over on the landing side, leaving Alverton and O'Neill to cruise home in emphatic style by twenty-five lengths. Royal Mail took second spot ahead of Aldaniti and Bob Champion (a partnership that will forever be remembered for their monumental win in the 1981 Grand National, Champion having overcome cancer and Aldaniti a string of devastating injuries).

The youngsters had disappointed this time, and although there would be another Gold Cup day for Night Nurse, Gaffer had pulled muscles in his neck on the final circuit and would not run in the Blue Riband again. The other joint favourite, the ageing Brown Lad, had never been able to get anywhere near the leaders given the furious pace, and eventually came home fifth of the seven that completed.

The hardy Alverton had been the one to cope best in the conditions and had jumped like a buck for the popular Irishman Jonjo O'Neill. It was the twelfth jumping success of Alverton's career, and it was hard not to warm to the big chestnut that clearly relished the battle of racing; the horse appeared set to go to war in at least a couple more Gold Cups.

Sadly, the ending to this Gold Cup tale would not stay happy for long. With a mouth-watering 10st 13lb on his back, Easterby realised that Alverton had to go for the Grand National a few weeks later, where the Gold Cup winner would never be so well treated again. It was mentioned by O'Neill after the Gold Cup win that Alverton would need to get higher at his fences in the National if he was to get round. At Becher's Brook second time round, absolutely hacking at the time, Alverton smacked into the fence and was killed. His death left O'Neill speechless. The rock-hard Alverton died a champion.

1980

MASTER SMUDGE

As with the year before, the King George VI Chase winner would miss the Gold Cup. This time the horse was the brilliant Tony Dickinson-trained Silver Buck. Unbeaten in all seven runs during the season, Silver Buck was naturally a leading fancy for the Gold Cup, but due to the continuous rain that fell on the course leading up to the race, Dickinson decided to pull the horse out at the last minute, knowing full well Silver Buck was far more effective on better ground.

Like Night Nurse before him, Monksfield had the chance to emulate the great three-time winners of the race in Tuesday's Champion Hurdle. The opposition included old adversaries Bird's Nest and Sea Pigeon, as well as an interesting newcomer in the form of the five-year-old Pollardstown. This day was to belong to the hugely popular Sea Pigeon, running for the fourth time in the race. Trained by Peter Easterby, the horse had been hampered by a poisoned foot in his preparation and was not thought to be at his best on the day. But expertly ridden by Jonjo O'Neill, Sea Pigeon produced a devastating finish to win the title from Monksfield and Bird's Nest. Having been so close on numerous occasions, Sea Pigeon's victory was understandably greeted with emotion and pride.

Earlier in the day, there had been an upset in the Arkle Trophy, as star novice Beacon Light – going for his eighth win from eight starts – came down two fences from home, with the race going to the Tommy Carberry-ridden Anaglog's Daughter.

On Wednesday, Mick O'Toole's highly talented Chinrullah confirmed the promise he had shown at the 1979 Festival by taking the Queen Mother Champion Chase – formerly the Two Mile Champion Chase – in blistering style, breaking Hilly Way's two-year grip on the race in the process. In beating Grand National candidate Another Dolly by twenty-five lengths, O'Toole was so impressed with the horse that he immediately stated that Chinrullah would run in the next day's Gold Cup.

A big field of seventeen lined up for the SunAlliance Chase later in the day, but mistakes plagued many in the field, including the well-fancied Little Owl, who fell at the tenth. In the end, only four got round, with victory going to

The classy Sea Pigeon won the first of his two Champion Hurdles under Jonjo O'Neill.

The Gold Cup favourite Diamond Edge takes the water jump.

Steve Knight aboard Lacson, beating Gold Cup withdrawal Flame Gun and the grey stayer Loving Words.

Despite the absence of Silver Buck, the Gold Cup of 1980 still preserved a good deal of class. The favourite was Diamond Edge, who was looking to provide his trainer Fulke Walwyn with a fifth Gold Cup. The horse had won all three of his races during the season – the John Bull Chase and the Jim Ford Challenge Cup at Wincanton sandwiching a defeat of Tied Cottage at Kempton – and he had the ground conditions he appreciated, which for the second year running happened to be heavy.

The big Irish hope, the Edward O'Grady-trained Jack Of Trumps, came into the race in puzzling form. Having made a winning start to the season, he had run very poorly at Leopardstown in February. In his favour, Jack Of Trumps

had the previous year's winning jockey, Jonjo O'Neill, in the saddle.

A pair of dark horses in the Gold Cup were Approaching and Border Incident, with both having missed considerable racing in recent seasons because of injury. John Francome's mount Border Incident had only run five times in three seasons, but was certainly a talented horse, having won his last two starts, while Approaching also had class on his side, as a win in the 1978 Hennessy Gold Cup proved. Since having a hobday operation, Approaching had slowly returned to his best, holding plenty of stamina in his locker.

The testing conditions were definitely in the favour of Tied Cottage, Chinrullah and the 1979 SunAlliance Chase winner Master Smudge, and this renewal of the Gold Cup was undoubtedly going to place an emphasis on staying power.

Jack of Trumps (8) was frustratingly brought down five out in the Gold Cup.

Before long, Tied Cottage had set about picking up where he had left off a year before, as he proceeded to deliver a bold display of jumping: after clearing the third fence, the horse had quickly opened up a lead of some ten lengths to Kas, Master Smudge and the fifteen-year-old Mac Vidi. Trying not to let the leader out of his sight, Bill Smith sent Diamond Edge forward to second position at the seventh fence, but already Tied Cottage had some of the field in trouble, such was his eagerness to run the legs off the opposition.

On the second circuit, the race pattern continued as Tied Cottage simply began to run his rivals into the ground as he kept up his march to glory. Could he really succeed where he so narrowly failed the year before? One contender that seemed sure to give the leader a run for his money was Border Incident, and Francome had crept the horse steadily into a threatening position before disaster struck six from home, the horse taking an untimely tumble. Francome later claimed that Border Incident had owned a real chance of winning, so well was he travelling until he fell.

The mishaps did not end there, however, as a fence later the 1979 runner-up Royal Mail came to grief, while Jack Of

Trumps was brought down, much to the frustration of O'Neill. Then, four fences from the finish, Diamond Edge began to tire and, making silly errors, lost his place and any chance of winning.

At the third last, Tied Cottage, who by now had Approaching as his nearest challenger, began to extend his lead and – just like that – the race was as good as over. Receiving tremendous cheers from the crowd, Tied Cottage marched to the finishing line an extremely popular winner, as those at Cheltenham realised the horse's gameness and fighting spirit, together with the fact he had come so close the year before. Eight lengths back came the staying on Master Smudge and then Mac Vidi, who had defied old age to hand a wonderful result to his owner/trainer Miss Pam Neal. Approaching and The Snipe were the only others to finish the gruelling contest.

The result should have been the crowning moment in the careers of trainer Dan Moore and jockey Tommy Carberry, both previous multi-winners of the race, as well as owner Tony Robinson – who had ridden the horse to an Irish Grand National victory in his time – and, for a while, they happily enjoyed Tied Cottage's marvellous, bold-jumping success. But some weeks later, it emerged that theobromine, a banned substance, had been discovered in a post-Gold Cup urine test carried out on Tied Cottage. It was revealed the substance originated from feed the horse had eaten and, heartbreakingly, Tied Cottage was disqualified and stripped of his title, with Master Smudge awarded the Gold Cup. The blame was not attributed to Moore or Mick O'Toole, who had used the same feed, meaning Chinrullah also lost his Queen Mother Champion Chase crown to Another Dolly. It was certainly a sad outcome though for Tied Cottage, who had run his heart out and had thoroughly deserved a place among the winners in Gold Cup history.

1980 PIPER CHAMPAGNE GOLD CUP RESULT

FATE – HORSE	AGE/WEIGHT	JOCKEY	ODDS
1st – MASTER SMUDGE	8-12-0	R. HOARE	14/1
2nd – MAC VIDI	15-12-0	P. LEACH	66/1
3rd – APPROACHING	9-12-0	B.R. DAVIES	11/1
4th – The Snipe	10-12-0	A. Webber	66/1
Fell – Border Incident	10-12-0	J. Francome	6/1
Brought Down – Jack Of Trumps	7-12-0	J. J. O'Neill	5/1
Fell – Royal Mail	10-12-0	P. Blacker	33/1
Fell – The Vintner	9-12-0	C. Grant	100/1
Pulled Up – Diamond Edge	9-12-0	W. Smith	5/2*
Pulled Up – Kas	8-12-0	J. Burke	100/1
Pulled Up – Kilcoleman	8-12-0	T. McGivern	50/1
Pulled Up – Narribinni	8-12-0	R. Linley	100/1
Pulled Up – Secret Progress	11-12-0	R. Barry	50/1
Disq. – Tied Cottage	12-12-0	T. Carberry	13/2
Disq. – Chinrullah	8-12-0	F. Berry	9/1

Tied Cottage originally finished first and Chinrullah fifth before disqualification.

13 March 1980
Going – Heavy
Winner – £35,997. 50
Time – 7mins 15secs (Tied Cottage)
15 Ran

Master Smudge — Chestnut gelding by Master Stephen – Lady Pond II
Mac Vidi — Bay gelding by Vidi Vici – Jockette
Approaching — Chestnut gelding by Golden Vision – Farm Hill

Winner bred by H. Radford (Master Smudge)
Winner trained and owned by Mr A. Barrow (Master Smudge).

OTHER 1980 FESTIVAL RESULTS

Waterford Crystal S N Hurdle	Slaney Idol	T. Carmody	9/1
Arkle Challenge Trophy Chase	Anaglog's Daughter	T. Carberry	9/4
Waterford Crystal C Hurdle	Sea Pigeon	J.J. O'Neill	13/2
Waterford Crystal S Hurdle	Mountrivers	T.J. Ryan	7/1
Kim Muir Mem Hcap Chase	Good Prospect	Mr A.J. Wilson	9/2
Grand Annual Chase	Stopped	B. DeHaan	7/2
Sun Alliance Novices' Hurdle	Drumlargan	T.J. Ryan	5/2
Queen Mother Cha Chase**	Another Dolly	S. Moreshead	33/1
Coral Golden Hurdle Final	Willie Wumpkins	Mr A.J. Wilson	10/1
Sun Alliance Chase	Lacson	S.C. Knight	16/1
National Hunt Chase	Waggoners Walk	Mr A. Fowler	10/1
Mildmay Of Flete Hcap Chase	Snowshill Sailor	A. Turnell	8/1
Daily Express Triumph Hurdle	Heighlin	S. Jobar	40/1
Christies Foxhunter Chase	Rolls Rambler	Mr O. Sherwood	9/4
National Hunt Hcap Chase	Again The Same	Mr A.J. Wilson	10/1
County Handicap Hurdle	Prince Of Bermuda	S.C. Knight	9/1
Cathcart Chase	King Weasel	J.J. O'Neill	5/2

** Chinrullah originally won the race but was subsequently disqualified.

But it was not meant to be for Tied Cottage and belated glory went to Master Smudge and his owner/trainer Arthur Barrow. The gutsy eight-year-old chestnut had proved his love of Cheltenham in the previous year's SunAlliance Chase, and had clearly shown a zest for the testing conditions by running a fine race in the big one itself under jockey Richard Hoare. Shortly after the announcement of Tied Cottage's disqualification, the Gold Cup was sent to Warwick racecourse and presented to a delighted Barrow. The trainer had bought Master Smudge from a local pig farmer as a two-year-old after seeing him running in a field. Six years later, the horse was the Gold Cup winner.

Master Smudge and jockey Richard Hoare were the eventual Gold Cup winners after Tied Cottage was disqualified.

1981

LITTLE OWL

Once again, a whole cluster of top names would be missing from the Gold Cup, including the defending champion Master Smudge. The 1980 winner was found to have pulled muscles in his hindquarters just days before the race, robbing trainer Arthur Barrow of a prime chance of winning another Gold Cup, with the ground again riding on the soft side. 1980 faller Border Incident, the Irish newcomer Daletta and the promising Artifice, were also all ruled out for one reason or another, but perhaps the biggest cause for disappointment among the 1981 absentees stemmed from the fact that Bright Highway would be missing. The brilliant youngster, trained in Ireland by Michael O'Brien, had won both the Mackeson and Hennessy Gold Cups and was consequently installed as the Gold Cup favourite. An injury in January sidelined Bright Highway from the 1981 Festival and the horse was again favourite for the Blue Riband in 1982 when injury struck again. In 1983, a persistent hock injury led to Bright Highway's retirement, and the horse goes down, along with Buona Notte and Flyingbolt, as among the best horses in recent times not to have competed in a Cheltenham Gold Cup.

The Tuesday of the 1981 Cheltenham Festival was all about John Francome, with an honourable mention going to Peter Easterby. The highlight for Francome was guiding Sea Pigeon to an effortless success from Pollardstown in the Champion Hurdle. In winning, the great Sea Pigeon became the ninth horse to win consecutive Champion Hurdles. Impressive for a different reason, the race was the sixth and final time Bird's Nest ran in a Champion Hurdle and he had equalled National Spirit's record for appearances in the event, departing the scene as arguably the best hurdler never to win the title. Francome's day was made even better with success aboard Derring Rose in the Stayers' Hurdle and then on Friendly Alliance in the Grand Annual Chase. As well as sending out Sea Pigeon, Easterby also saddled the prolific Clayside to win the Arkle Trophy under Alan Brown. This would prove to be a memorable Festival for Easterby, and the best was yet to come.

Grittar and Dick Saunders return having won the Foxhunters'.

Anaglog's Daughter displays exuberance during the
Queen Mother Champion Chase.

The hugely popular Willie Wumpkins on his way to a
third Coral Golden Hurdle triumph.

There were some interesting results on Wednesday, none more so than when 25/1 outsider Drumgora, ridden by Frank Berry, upset the applecart by overturning the Irish banker of the meeting, Anaglog's Daughter, in the Queen Mother Champion Chase.

After veteran Willie Wumpkins had brought the house down by winning his third Coral Golden Hurdle Final in his very last race, there was another sensation as the mare Lesley Ann – ridden by Colin Brown and trained by David Elsworth – upset the fancied Easter Eel, winner of five chases from six starts, and a future Grand National winner, Corbiere, in the SunAlliance Chase.

In what had developed into a truly exciting edition of the Cheltenham Festival, Thursday's Gold Cup arrived with no small amount of pomp and anticipation, as the fifteen-strong field prepared to bid for the richest prize yet in the race's illustrious history.

After a couple of years' speculation regarding the horse's participation in the Gold Cup, Silver Buck finally got the go-ahead to run in the race, even though the ground was probably softer than ideal for the horse (who ideally wanted good going). Silver Buck was now trained by Michael Dickinson, who had taken over from his father Tony at their Yorkshire-based Harewood stables. An extremely high-class brown gelding and a super athlete, Silver Buck had won all seven of his chases the previous season and his only defeat in six runs in the current campaign came when narrowly failing to give the useful Sunset Cristo 34lbs at Catterick. Silver Buck had comfortably won the season's King George and was to be ridden at Cheltenham by Irishman Tommy Carmody.

Having trained Alverton for his 1979 win, Peter Easterby was double handed on this occasion, with the powerful duo of Night Nurse and Little Owl representing him. The consistent Night Nurse, at ten, was three years older than his

1981 TOTE GOLD CUP RESULT

FATE – HORSE	AGE/WEIGHT	JOCKEY	ODDS
1st – LITTLE OWL	7-12-0	MR A.J. WILSON	6/1
2nd – NIGHT NURSE	10-12-0	A. BROWN	6/1
3rd – SILVER BUCK	9-12-0	T. CARMODY	7/2*
4th – Spartan Missile	9-12-0	Mr M.J. Thorne	33/1
5th – Diamond Edge	10-12-0	W. Smith	16/1
6th – Jack Of Trumps	8-12-0	N. Madden	7/1
7th – Royal Judgement	8-12-0	R. Rowe	100/1
8th – Approaching	10-12-0	R. Champion	33/1
9th – Midnight Court	10-12-0	J. Francome	14/1
Fell – Tied Cottage	13-12-0	L. O'Donnell	15/2
Pulled Up – Chinrullah	9-12-0	P. Scudamore	33/1
Pulled Up – Fair View	11-12-0	R. Barry	100/1
Pulled Up – Raffi Nelson	8-12-0	S. Smith-Eccles	100/1
Pulled Up – Royal Bond	8-12-0	T. McGivern	10/1
Pulled Up – So And So	12-12-0	Mr D. Gray	100/1

19 March 1981

Going – Soft

Winner – £44,258. 75

Time – 7mins 9. 9secs

15 Ran

Little Owl	Bay gelding by Cantab – Black Spangle
Night Nurse	Bay gelding by Falcon – Florence Nightingale
Silver Buck	Brown gelding by Silver Cloud – Choice Archlesse

Winner bred by Mrs J. Ferris

Winner trained by M. H. Easterby at Great Haston, Yorks.

OTHER 1981 FESTIVAL RESULTS

Waterford Crystal Sup Nov Hurdle	Hartstown	N. Madden	2/1
Arkle Challenge Trophy Chase	Clayside	A. Brown	5/2
Waterford Crystal C Hurdle	Sea Pigeon	J. Francome	7/4
Waterford Crystal Stayers' Hurdle	Derring Rose	J. Francome	3/1
Kim Muir Memorial Hcap Chase	Waggoners Walk	Mr C. Cundell	7/1
Cheltenham Grand Annual Chase	Friendly Alliance	J. Francome	11/2
Sun Alliance Novices' Hurdle	Gaye Chance	S. Moreshead	7/1
Queen Mother Champion Chase	Drumgora	F. Berry	25/1
Coral Golden Hurdle Final	Willie Wumpkins	Mr A.J. Wilson	13/2
Sun Alliance Chase	Lesley Ann	C. Brown	25/1
National Hunt Chase	Lucky Vane	Mr Stephen Bush	13/1
Mildmay Of Flete Hcap Chase	Political Pop	R. Earnshaw	15/8
Daily Express Triumph Hurdle	Baron Blakeney	P. Leach	66/1
Christies Foxhunter Chase Ch Cup	Grittar	Mr C. Saunders	12/1
Ritz Club Nat Hunt Hcap Chase	Current Gold	N. Doughty	10/1
County Handicap Hurdle	Staplestown	T.J. Ryan	11/2
Cathcart Challenge Cup Chase	Lord Greystoke	N. Doughty	7/2

stablemate and was partnered by Alan Brown. Little Owl had steadily risen through the chasing ranks as the season had progressed, winning all four of his races, and he came in to the race at the top of his game and sure to appreciate the soft ground. Little Owl was ridden by his owner, amateur Jim Wilson, who shared the horse with his brother Robert as a result of an inheritance from their late aunt. Night Nurse and Little Owl shared second place in the betting at 6/1.

The moral winner of the previous year, Tied Cottage, headed the Irish challenge. Sadly, trainer Dan Moore and owner Tony Robinson had both died since the 1980 Gold Cup and the horse, now a sprightly thirteen-year-old, was trained by Mrs Joan Moore and owned by Robinson's sister, Mrs Diane Price. The connections did not end there, as Mrs Moore's son, Arthur,

The impressive youngster Little Owl is almost home in the Gold Cup.

Winning jockey Jim Wilson and brother Robert, the owners of Little Owl, receive the Gold Cup from Lady Wyatt.

was responsible for the promising eight-year-old Royal Bond. Jack of Trumps completed the Irish contingent.

Just as he had done in numerous other runnings of the race, Tied Cottage set out at a frantic pace to try and win from the front. He was bowling along in his usual bold style, before making an untimely exit at the sixth. The luckless Tied Cottage was destined never to capture that elusive Gold Cup crown. Running in his second Gold Cup, Diamond Edge was left clear of Night Nurse and Spartan Missile, until the tough Night Nurse took hold of the race at the tenth fence.

There were no more fallers as Night Nurse continued to take them along, but it was noticeable that, even on ground that was far from ideal, Silver Buck was travelling nicely in the style of a very good horse just in behind the lead.

Coming down the hill for the final time, three horses began to draw clear of the trailing Royal Judgement, Approaching and Jack Of Trumps. The trio consisted of Night Nurse on the inside, the rangy Little Owl on the outside, and Silver Buck, seemingly going the best, in the middle.

Going into the second last, the youngster Little Owl put in a powerful burst of speed to draw away. Silver Buck tried in vain to go with him, but the ground was pegging him back. Finding a gigantic leap at the last, the white-faced Little Owl stormed up the finishing hill in the manner of a grand horse, and although Night Nurse battled on to the end, he simply could not overhaul his stablemate. Silver Buck had faded quickly after the last, clearly requiring better ground – although he had proved he could travel and jump with the best of them in the heat of a Gold Cup. Fourth was Spartan Missile, ridden by his owner/trainer/breeder Mr John Thorne. The same combination would go on to finish a brave second to Aldaniti in the Grand National. Trailing home as the last of the nine finishers was Midnight Court, the 1978 champion looking a shadow of former years having missed the last two Gold Cups.

Peter Easterby had won the Gold Cup for a second time. Little Owl had been a big, awkward, bumbling sort of horse when he was purchased as a three-year-old, but quickly developed into a tough warrior. Easterby became the first trainer to win both the Gold Cup and Champion Hurdle at the same Festival since Fulke Walwyn with Mandarin and Anzio in 1962. He also became the first person to train the first two home in the Gold Cup. In addition, the fine ride Jim Wilson gave Little Owl enabled the jockey to become the first amateur to win the race since Dick Black triumphed aboard Fortina back in 1947.

Little Owl was a very good winner of the Gold Cup; he had travelled well in the race, jumped with great zest and had thoroughly seen out the trip. With youth on his side, together with plenty of size and strength, the gallant Little Owl – in the same fashion as when Captain Christy and Midnight Court won – appeared set to be a key figure in Gold Cups of the future.

1982

SILVER BUCK

A week before the 1982 Cheltenham Festival, the reigning dual Champion Hurdler, Sea Pigeon, was retired. A son of the 1965 Derby winner Sea Bird II, Sea Pigeon won twenty-one races over hurdles and was undoubtedly one of the best Champion Hurdlers to grace the event. His retirement brought to a close a wonderful era for hurdling stars and, together with Night Nurse, Monksfield and Bird's Nest, Sea Pigeon had helped take the Champion Hurdle to new, glorious heights.

In the champion's absence, it was a fresh bunch of hopefuls that went to post for Tuesday's renewal, with the 1981 Triumph Hurdle failure Broadsword well fancied to give trainer David Nicholson his first Festival winner. Heavy rain was making its presence felt, and this was expected to be right up the street of the Irish hope Daring Run and jockey Ted Walsh. However, this new dawn of the great race was to provide a shock result, as both Broadsword and Daring Run were eclipsed by 40/1 shot For Auction. The winner was ridden by Mr Colin Magnier, who became the first amateur to win the Champion Hurdle since Alan Lillingston steered home Winning Fair in 1963. Another highlight of Magnier's riding career would come in the following season's Grand National, when he was narrowly beaten aboard Greasepaint by Jenny Pitman's chestnut Corbiere.

Wednesday's highlight was the victory by Rathgorman in the Queen Mother Champion Chase. The exciting two-mile specialist added to what was fast becoming a fine Festival for Michael Dickinson. As well as Rathgorman's win, the Yorkshire-based trainer also sent out Political Pop to win Tuesday's Kim Muir Chase, with the winner scoring by twenty lengths in ground he apparently detested!

Despite the hotly-fancied Drumlargan being beaten after a storming run up the hill by John Francome on Brown Chamberlin in the SunAlliance Chase, the Irish had won half of the races after the first two days, giving them every reason to be confident ahead of Thursday's Gold Cup.

After an underwhelming campaign cluttered with negative results, Peter Easterby's Little Owl continued the hugely disappointing trend in recent years of the previous year's Gold Cup winner failing to defend their crown. It is interesting to note that very few Gold Cup winners – with

For Auction storms away from Ekbalco to win the Champion Hurdle.

Rathgorman gets a kiss from owner Mr James Lilley after winning the Queen Mother Champion Chase.

The team behind Brown Chamberlin's Sun Alliance Chase win, John Francome, Fred Winter and owner Mrs Basil Samuel.

some obvious exceptions such as Arkle – ever seem able to rekindle the form that takes them to the top of the chasing tree. This may be because of the extra burden of weight the Gold Cup winner consequently shoulders in handicaps, or the fact that finely-tuned steeplechasers are obviously very difficult to maintain at their peak (due to factors like injury), or even that the sheer inner will a Gold Cup winner must project up that gruelling final hill to claim their crown is enough to ultimately send them over the top. Whatever the reason, many just cannot keep their place at the head of jumping's most prestigious table. Little Owl aside, Easterby still had the ever-popular Night Nurse to represent him, and a consistent season led to him stating as favourite. With a recent win at Doncaster to boost his claims, Night Nurse's connections retained strong aspirations that the horse could become the first to achieve that elusive Champion Hurdle/Gold Cup double.

Looking to increase Ireland's already bountiful haul at the 1982 Festival was the Arthur Moore-trained Royal Bond. The nine-year-old had been pulled-up in the previous year's Gold Cup, but had gone from strength to strength during the current season, culminating in a highly impressive, weight-carrying performance at Leopardstown in February where his previously suspect jumping was erased from memory with an immaculate display of fencing. With heavy ground present for the third time in four years, Royal Bond began as second favourite in a bid to give Tommy Carberry a fourth win in his final Gold Cup ride.

With the Dickinson horses in fine form, it was surprising that Silver Buck started as high as 8/1 in the betting. Punters were probably put off by the state of the ground and the fact that Silver Buck had seemingly been outbattled up the hill the previous year by Little Owl and Night Nurse. But the facts remained that the attractive brown horse was a two-

The top-class Silver Buck comes clear of stablemate Bregawn in the Gold Cup.

time King George winner, very rarely ran a bad race and, over the past three seasons, his defeats could be counted on one hand. Silver Buck had plenty of class about him and he was to be a first Gold Cup ride for young Robert Earnshaw.

Also having his first ride in the race was Graham Bradley, aboard Silver Buck's stablemate Bregawn. The chestnut gelding had soared dramatically through the handicap scene during the season, winning four times, including Haydock's Peter Marsh Chase and Doncaster's Great Yorkshire Chase. The horse's owner, Martin Kennelly, had insisted that Bregawn run in the Gold Cup, though the selection of Bradley – considering his lack of big-race experience – apparently worried Kennelly (whereas Dickinson reasoned it better to stick with a jockey that knew the horse). Wayward Lad, a horse that would go on to be a Gold Cup stalwart for years to come, would have been another Dickinson representative but for disappointing in his latest run at Haydock.

Grittar, ante-post favourite for the Grand National and a horse that had won both Cheltenham and Aintree Foxhunter Chases the season before, the 1980 hero Master Smudge, old favourites Diamond Edge and Border Incident, and the now fourteen-year-old Tied Cottage, were among a record field of twenty-two – beating by six the previous biggest field of 1945

– that lined up at the start, and the race got underway promising to be one of the most exciting and spectacular for years.

The now customary charge by Tied Cottage was again a feature of this Gold Cup, as the old warrior, jumping as well as ever, proceeded to take the other twenty-one 'spring chickens' along at a fair clip. Chasing the leader for most of the first circuit were the dual Whitbread Gold Cup winner Diamond Edge, Grittar and Earthstopper – although the lattermost horse was to suffer a fall later in the contest.

The pace that Tied Cottage set was severe for such testing ground and Royal Bond, expected to relish the stamina test, was soon in trouble, along with Master Smudge, the fancied Fred Winter-runner Venture To Cognac and the out-of-sorts Night Nurse.

Incredibly, for a horse of such years, Tied Cottage still headed a band of five that had broken free at the top of the hill second time around, and at the third last his familiar noseband touched down just ahead of northern raiders Sunset Cristo, Silver Buck and Bregawn, with Diamond Edge still in touch as well.

But rounding the turn for home, the long-time leader began to tread water and it was Earnshaw on Silver Buck that drove stylishly through the group to take command, with Diamond Edge and Bregawn travelling as his biggest dangers on either side of him.

By the second last, the almost black-looking Silver Buck quickened significantly, and only Bregawn was able to stay in touch as the leader put in a giant leap. Despite shaving the top of the last fence, Earnshaw kept Silver Buck up to his task and he held off his stablemate for a two-length victory. Sunset Cristo made it a northern cleansweep, coming home third for trainer Ray Hawkley, ahead of Diamond Edge. Tied Cottage had run another great race and signed off his Gold Cup participation with a highly creditable ninth of the thirteen

1982 TOTE GOLD CUP RESULT

FATE – HORSE	AGE/WEIGHT	JOCKEY	ODDS
1st – SILVER BUCK	10-12-0	R. EARNSHAW	8/1
2nd – BREGAWN	8-12-0	G. BRADLEY	18/1
3rd – SUNSET CRISTO	8-12-0	C. GRANT	100/1
4th – Diamond Edge	11-12-0	W. Smith	11/1
5th – Captain John	8-12-0	P. Scudamore	40/1
6th – Grittar	9-12-0	Mr C. Saunders	16/1
7th – Venture To Cognac	9-12-0	Mr O. Sherwood	6/1
8th – Royal Bond	9-12-0	T. Carberry	4/1
9th – Tied Cottage	14-12-0	G. Newman	25/1
10th – Two Swallows	9-12-0	A. Webber	100/1
11th – Lesley Ann	8-12-0	C. Brown	10/1
12th – Sugarally	9-12-0	C. Tinkler	100/1
13th – Peaty Sandy	8-12-0	T.G. Dun	40/1
Fell – Earthstopper	8-12-0	Mr G. Sloan	50/1
Pulled Up – Border Incident	12-12-0	J. Francome	33/1
Pulled Up – Drumroan	14-12-0	C. Dugast	150/1
Pulled Up – Henry Bishop	9-12-0	R. Rowe	25/1
Pulled Up – Master Smudge	10-12-0	S. Smith-Eccles	50/1
Pulled Up – Night Nurse	11-12-0	J.J. O'Neill	11/4*
Pulled Up – Snow Flyer	11-12-0	R. Champion	100/1
Pulled Up – Straight Jocelyn	10-12-0	H. Davies	100/1
Pulled Up – Wansford Boy	10-12-0	R. Dickin	300/1

18 March 1982
Going – Heavy
Winner – £48,386. 75
Time – 7mins 11. 3secs
22 Ran

Silver Buck — Brown gelding by Silver Cloud – Choice Archlesse
Bregawn — Chestnut gelding by Saint Denys – Miss Society
Sunset Cristo — Bay gelding by Derek H – Sunset Ramble

Winner bred by Mrs S. Booth
Winner trained by M. Dickinson at Dunkeswick, near Harewood, Yorks.

OTHER 1982 FESTIVAL RESULTS

Waterford Crystal Sup Nov' Hur	Miller Hill	T. Morgan	20/1
Arkle Challenge Trophy Chase	The Brockshee	T. Carberry	12/1
Waterford Crystal C Hurdle	For Auction	Mr C. Magnier	40/1
Waterford Crystal Stayers' Hurdle	Crimson Embers	S. Shilston	2/1
Kim Muir Memorial Hcap Chase	Political Pop	Mr D. Browne	15/2
Grand Annual Chase	Reldis	P. Barton	9/1
Sun Alliance Novices' Hurdle	Mister Donovan	T.J. Ryan	9/2
Sun Alliance Chase	Brown Chamberlin	J. Francome	7/1
Queen Mother C Chase	Rathgorman	K. Whyte	100/30
Coral Golden Hurdle Final	Tall Order	A. Stringer	15/1
National Hunt Chase	Hazy Dawn	Mr W. Mullins	8/1
Mildmay Of Flete Hcap Chase	Doubleuagain	F. Berry	11/1
Daily Express Triumph Hurdle	Shiny Copper	A. Webb	66/1
Christies Foxh Chase Ch Cup	The Drunken Duck	Mr B. Munro-Wilson	12/1
Ritz Club Nat Hunt Hcap Chase	Scot Lane	C. Smith	15/2
County Handicap Hurdle	Path Of Peace	J.J. O'Neill	4/1
Cathcart Challenge Cup Chase	Dramatist	W. Smith	15/8

finishers. Grittar, in sixth, went on to convincingly tame the big Aintree fences when winning the season's Grand National.

As a ten-year-old, Silver Buck had proved he had the strength and determination to turn his top-class form at easier three-mile tracks in to triumph on the most demanding of National Hunt courses – and on heavy ground too. There was no doubting that Silver Buck was one of the finest winners of recent times, given his record in elite chasing company.

Thirty-two-year-old Michael Dickinson had been a trainer for less than two years, but had garnered the Cheltenham Gold Cup and emulated Peter Easterby by saddling the first two home. Making Dickinson's training performance all the more impressive was the fact that Silver Buck, a notoriously nervous individual at home, had gone lame after Christmas and had been confined to his box for a month. As good as this achievement seemed for Dickinson, an even more glorious day lay in store for the young maestro, and in twelve months time, he would be the keyholder to surely the most astounding training result of them all.

1983

BREGAWN

Throughout the 1983 Cheltenham Festival, there was a feeling that the racing world was building up to something special. With the ground far less testing than in recent years, a plethora of splendid horses were on display, delivering some memorable performances.

As soon as Buck House – a chasing star of the future – got the meeting off to a flying start by beating future Gold Cup performer Golden Friend in the Supreme Novices' Hurdle, the Festival was competed at on the highest possible platform.

Soon after on Tuesday, the crowd were treated to a breathtaking show in the Champion Hurdle. The Michael Cunningham-trained For Auction – the defending champion – was well fancied to repeat his 1982 success, but the horse had no answer to the brilliant performance turned in by Gaye Brief, who simply destroyed the field in recording the fastest time since Another Flash in 1960. It was as romantic a win as it was emphatic, as Gaye Brief was the last horse bought by the late, great trainer Fred Rimell, and was now trained by Fred's wife Mercy. Gaye Brief's performance remains one of the highest rated of any running of the Champion Hurdle.

Later on the Tuesday, the Irish chestnut, the white-faced Greasepaint, won the Kim Muir Chase, booking his ticket to the Grand National in the process. Ridden at Aintree as at the Festival by amateur Colin Magnier, Greasepaint was a gallant runner-up to Corbiere. The popular Irish chaser would go on to become an Aintree specialist, finishing as runner-up again to Hallo Dandy in 1984 and then fourth and tenth in two other runnings of the National.

It is tough to imagine a Festival that provided more quality and history than that which would eventually emerge from the first three races on Wednesday. For instance, the first three home in the SunAlliance Novices' Hurdle stand out in bold lights. The winner was Sabin Du Loir, ridden by Graham Bradley, who would develop in to a fine, big-race chaser. The second horse was the mare Dawn Run – suffice to say she would make her own unique mark on future Cheltenham Festivals – while the third, West Tip, would go

Mercy Rimell and Champion Hurdle winner Gaye Brief, the last horse ever bought by Fred Rimell.

Badsworth Boy after the first of his
Queen Mother Champion Chase wins.

on to become a Grand National legend, running in the race six times, with a fine victory in 1986.

That classic SunAlliance Novices' Hurdle was quickly followed by the first of three wins in the Queen Mother Champion Chase for the lightning quick Badsworth Boy, ridden by Gold Cup-winning jockey Robert Earnshaw. It was a fifth win in an undefeated season for Badsworth Boy, and among his victims at Cheltenham was his stablemate and the defending champion, Rathgorman.

Another horse with a huge Cheltenham future was Forgive 'N' Forget, and jockey Mark Dwyer was able to beat off a highly competitive field to win the (always bustling) Coral Golden Hurdle Final.

The victories of Sabin Du Loir and Badsworth Boy on Wednesday had helped rectify what had been a disappointing start to the 1983 Festival for trainer Michael Dickinson, with four of his horses beaten favourites on Tuesday. Now it was Gold Cup day, and when discussing Michael Dickinson and the 1983 Blue Riband, the word to consider is domination. Of the eleven runners, five were trained at Dickinson's Harewood stables, and all held claims of winning, ranging from decent to outstanding.

The first of the bunch that would affectionately become known as 'the Famous Five' was the defending champion Silver Buck, who now, together with the total outsider Whiggie Geo, was the oldest horse in the race at eleven.

Nothing can stop Bregawn winning the Gold Cup.

Even entering the veteran stage of his career, Silver Buck was still an extremely hard horse to outpoint, and over the season had reaped another four victories, notably a fourth straight Edward Hamner Memorial Chase at Haydock where he beat a highly promising youngster named Burrough Hill Lad. Although he had been upstaged by stablemate Wayward Lad in the King George, Silver Buck had proved the year before that he had the stamina for the Gold Cup trip and, for once, the 1983 running presented him with near-perfect conditions, the going being good to soft.

The horse that started favourite was Silver Buck's stablemate, the ever-improving and battle-hardened Bregawn. The chestnut was a model of consistency, and while he had found Silver Buck too good the year before, Bregawn seemed to have progressed again and rarely ran a bad race. He had won the season's Hennessy Gold Cup and, with Bradley again on board, entered the battle at the top of his game.

Completing the Dickinson quintet were Captain John, Wayward Lad and Ashley House. Captain John had only joined the stable at the start of the season, having been labelled a suspect jumper. But that area of his game became a revelation under Dickinson and he had won three times from five runs, as well as finishing an interesting second to Bregawn in the Hennessy. Wayward Lad, who in upcoming years would repeatedly show his class, had won the King George (although doubts lingered over the stamina of Jonjo O'Neill's mount), while Ashley House had warmed up for the Gold Cup with a recent win at Doncaster.

The Dickinson quintet between them seemed to possess every quality required to win a Gold Cup. One horse that, on paper, had the potential to upset Yorkshire's raiding party was the David Elsworth-trained Combs Ditch. An exciting, front-running seven-year-old, Combs Ditch had improved in droves since falling earlier in the season, winning at Ascot, Cheltenham and Wincanton, latterly taking the scalp of Bregawn. If the chestnut had the stamina to match his bold jumping, he had the ability to thwart the Dickinson assault.

One thing was certain: this Gold Cup would be staying at home, as despite winning seven of the last sixteen Gold Cups since the Arkle years, there were no Irish runners present. This meant the race would be without its normal charge from Tied Cottage and, straight from the off, 500/1 shot Whiggie Geo burst into a crazy lead, seemingly gunning for a brief moment of fame. That moment lasted until the fifth fence when the rest of the field, headed by Bregawn, swallowed him up.

It was soon clear that Bradley was going to make this a battle of the fittest, and he sent Bregawn on at a thunderous gallop that caught a number of the runners cold. One of those that could not handle the pace was John Francome's mount Brown Chamberlin, who proceeded to make a number of blunders and, after a circuit, the previous year's SunAlliance Chase winner was pulled-up.

Michael Dickinson trained the first five home in a memorable Gold Cup.

Bregawn's lead was now four lengths from Ashley House, the improving Silver Buck, Wayward Lad, Captain John and the Fred Winter-trained Fifty Dollars More, but when the lattermost came down at the seventeenth – the last ditch – and with Combs Ditch struggling painfully, it was Bregawn that led his four stablemates onwards, although Ashley House began to drift out of contention from the fourth last.

Michael Dickinson must have been the proudest man on earth as four of his horses powered on towards the final three fences, all apparently in with a shout of winning. Captain John smacked the third last, a mistake that seriously affected his chances, although jockey David Goulding quickly had him back in contention. Silver Buck soon ran out of steam, and by the last fence, Bregawn, Captain John and Wayward Lad had it between them.

It seemed logical that, having led for so long and now being collared, Bregawn would be gobbled up by the other two. But Bregawn was a vigorously competitive warrior and, surging

One of the Dickinson 'Famous Five', Captain John.

1983 TOTE GOLD CUP RESULT

FATE – HORSE	AGE/WEIGHT	JOCKEY	ODDS
1st – BREGAWN	9-12-0	G. BRADLEY	100/30*
2nd – CAPTAIN JOHN	9-12-0	D. GOULDING	11/1
3rd – WAYWARD LAD	8-12-0	J.J. O'NEILL	6/1
4th – Silver Buck	11-12-0	R. Earnshaw	5/1
5th – Ashley House	9-12-0	Mr D. Browne	12/1
6th – Richdee	7-12-0	C. Hawkins	40/1
7th – Midnight Love	8-12-0	C. Grant	66/1
8th – Combs Ditch	7-12-0	C. Brown	9/2
Fell – Fifty Dollars More	8-12-0	R. Linley	8/1
Pulled Up – Brown Chamberlin	8-12-0	J. Francome	10/1
Pulled Up – Whiggie Geo	11-12-0	Mr N. Tutty	500/1

17 March 1983
Going – Good to Soft
Winner – £45,260
Time – 6mins 57. 6secs
11 Ran

Bregawn	Chestnut gelding by Saint Denys – Miss Society
Captain John	Chestnut gelding by Mon Capitaine – Aprolon Light
Wayward Lad	Bay or brown gelding by Royal Highway – Loughanmore

Winner bred by J. Fitzgerald
Winner trained by M. Dickinson at Harewood, Yorks.

OTHER 1983 FESTIVAL RESULTS

Waterford Crystal S Nov Hurdle	Buck House	T. Carmody	8/1
Arkle Challenge Trophy Chase	Ryeman	A. Brown	16/1
Waterford Crystal C Hurdle	Gaye Brief	R. Linley	7/1
Waterford Crystal Stayers' Hurdle	A Kinsman	T.G. Dun	50/1
Kim Muir Memorial Hcap Chase	Greasepaint	Mr C. Magnier	8/1
Grand Annual Chase	Churchfield Boy	J.P. Byrne	8/1
Sun Alliance Novices' Hurdle	Sabin Du Loir	G. Bradley	16/1
Queen Mother Champion Chase	Badsworth Boy	R. Earnshaw	2/1
Coral Golden Hurdle Final	Forgive 'N Forget	M. Dwyer	5/2
Sun Alliance Chase	Canny Danny	N. Madden	33/1
National Hunt Chase	Bit Of A Skite	Mr F. Codd	5/1
Mildmay Of Flete Hcap Chase	Mr Peacock	L. Bloomfield	20/1
Daily Express Triumph Hurdle	Saxon Farm	M. Perrett	12/1
Christies Foxhunter Chase Ch Cup	Eliogarty	Miss C. Beasley	3/1
Ritz Club Nat Hunt Hcap Chase	Scot Lane	C. Smith	20/1
County Handicap Hurdle	Robin Wonder	J.H. Davies	10/1
Cathcart Challenge Cup Chase	Observe	J. Francome	1/2

up the hill with keenness and courage, saw off his stablemates for a brave victory. Captain John came home five lengths behind in second, just edging Wayward Lad. Incredibly, Silver Buck claimed fourth place and then the gallant Ashley House, almost magnetised by the finishing line, took fifth. The Gold Cup had turned into a clean sweep for the Dickinson team.

It was a result that set the standards for every trainer in future Gold Cups, although it is unthinkable to suggest Dickinson's achievement will ever be matched. What makes it such a great training feat is that, of the five, only Ashley House had gone through the season problem-free, with the other four all suffering mishaps of some sort.

Almost lost in the remarkable nature of the result was the tenacious display the winner Bregawn had given. A real fighter, the nine-year-old reached his peak here under young Bradley, who in turn had ridden a dominant race from the head of affairs.

In winning the Gold Cup, Dickinson became the first trainer to scoop more than £300,000 in a season – which is staggering considering the little time he had officially been a trainer. However, like Bregawn, this blaze of glory would effectively signal the beginning of the end for Dickinson, at least in terms of the Cheltenham Festival, and he would soon be lost to National Hunt racing, turning his focus to Flat racing and eventually moving on to a highly successful career in America. His glory at Cheltenham will be remembered forever. 1983 and 'The Famous Five' – what a story!

1984

BURROUGH HILL LAD

The 1983 Cheltenham Festival had been the most spectacular of successes for Harewood trainer Michael Dickinson. The Yorkshire maestro had set an unmatchable standard in the Gold Cup, as well as scooping numerous other big prizes. 1984 was to prove groundbreaking in a very different manner. This would be a Festival for the ladies – in more ways than one.

Tuesday's Champion Hurdle was guaranteed a new winner, as the defending champion Gaye Brief was forced to miss the race after tearing ligaments in his back. In Gaye Brief's place was a worthy challenger in the shape of Very Promising, a horse that would have a big future over fences. So too would a pair of others in the contest: in fact, over time, they would develop into two of Cheltenham's all-time great chasers. The first was the imposing, bullishly-strong mare Dawn Run, trained by Paddy Mullins. The second was Desert Orchid, a horse that, come his finest hour in 1989, would be pure white in colour and almost unrecognisable from the speckled grey youngster that was sent out on this occasion. With former champion For Auction also in the field, it promised to be a hot contest. At the business end,

and with Desert Orchid and For Auction well beaten, Cheltenham got to witness the beast-like power of Dawn Run who, despite caning the last flight, steamed up the hill and held off the challenge from Cima and the late burst of Very Promising to win under Jonjo O'Neill. The cheers from the Irish contingent for their heroine were deafening and the scenes in the winner's enclosure were those of jubilation, as Dawn Run became the first mare to win the race since African Sister back in 1939.

The same day saw one of the most captivating runnings of the Arkle Trophy that there has ever been. Theoretically it was a match between the hugely promising Noddy's Ryde, trained by Gordon Richards, and the unbeaten Bobsline, and so it proved in the race. With both horses jumping like stags, Noddy's Ryde led most of the way until being overhauled by Bobsline and jockey Frank Berry as the line loomed. Neale Doughty, the Welsh jockey of Noddy's Ryde, was to gain compensation for this narrow defeat later in the season when he rode Hallo Dandy to victory in the Grand National.

Dawn Run (right) is challenged by Buck House in the Champion Hurdle, with the grey Desert Orchid further back.

One of the all time great Arkle Trophy's, Bobsline (nearside) eventually got the better of Noddy's Ryde.

In a year when John Francome became only the second jockey to reach the 1,000-winner mark aboard Gold Cup contender Observe, a new star made his first impact on the Festival. Northern Ireland's up-and-coming Richard Dunwoody, a man that would set the standards for horsemanship for the next fifteen years, guided Oyster Pond into second place behind Mossy Moore in the Grand Annual Chase.

On Wednesday, the Irish believed they had the horse to become the first from the Emerald Isle to win the SunAlliance Chase since Tied Cottage in 1976 in the shape of Harveystown, while the home favourite was Forgive 'N' Forget, a horse that had won at the previous year's Festival. However, both would have to yield glory to A Kinsman, the 1983 Stayers' Hurdle winner, trained by Cumbrian farmer John Brockbank.

Thursday began in horrible fashion for young trainer Nicky Henderson. In the Triumph Hurdle – a race that would become his speciality in future years – he saddled the hotly fancied See You Then. Sadly, not only was See You Then beaten into second place by Northern Game, but also Henderson's second runner, Childown, broke a leg.

Those trainers that had runners in the Gold Cup itself no doubt prayed for better luck in running than befell the unlucky Henderson as they prepared to send their horses out for battle for the fifty-eighth running of the great race.

As one of two members of the 'Famous Five' from 1983 to run on this occasion, Wayward Lad had enjoyed an extremely fruitful season which had seen him catapult to the head of the betting. He had won four of his five chases, the highlight being a second King George success, and even though doubts remained regarding his stamina, the Gold Cup ground was officially good for the first time in years – obviously helping the horse's chance.

In contrast to his stablemate, Bregawn had regressed since the memorable 1983 race and there were now signs in his game of stubbornness and lack of will. Indeed, Bregawn had fallen and refused on two of his recent starts and had failed to win a single race. Despite again having the highly capable Graham Bradley in the saddle, there was a distinct negative vibe surrounding the defending champion's chance this time around.

Although he had given a disappointing run in the 1983 Gold Cup, Brown Chamberlin had become something of a Cheltenham specialist, winning three times at the track. He had also progressed mightily throughout the season, his sole defeat coming in Wayward Lad's King George. Francome's mount had won the Hennessy at Newbury in good style and lined up as one of three runners for Fred Winter.

Even though Wayward Lad had stepped up his game and Brown Chamberlin had risen to new heights, the most improved chaser of the season hailed from Weathercock House, the Lambourn-based stable of Jenny Pitman. The

1984 TOTE GOLD CUP RESULT

FATE – HORSE	AGE/WEIGHT	JOCKEY	ODDS
1st – BURROUGH HILL LAD	8-12-0	P. TUCK	7/2
2nd – BROWN CHAMBERLIN	9-12-0	J. FRANCOME	5/1
3rd – DRUMLARGAN	10-12-0	MR F. CODD	16/1
4th – Scot Lane	11-12-0	C. Smith	100/1
5th – Fifty Dollars More	9-12-0	R. Linley	28/1
6th – Bregawn	10-12-0	G. Bradley	10/1
7th – Canny Danny	8-12-0	N. Madden	40/1
8th – Royal Bond	11-12-0	F. Berry	33/1
9th – Observe	9-12-0	B. De Haan	16/1
Pulled Up – Everett	9-12-0	S. Shilston	33/1
Pulled Up – Wayward Lad	9-12-0	R. Earnshaw	6/4*
Pulled Up – Foxbury	10-11-9	Mrs L. Sheedy	500/1

15 March 1984
Going – Good
Winner – £47,375
Time – 6mins 41.4secs
12 Ran

Burrough Hill Lad	Brown gelding by Richboy – Green Monkey
Brown Chamberlin	Brown gelding by Space King – Jocelin
Drumlargan	Bay gelding by Twilight Alley – Avro Jet

Winner bred by owner, R.S. Riley
Winner trained by Mrs J. Pitman at Upper Lambourn, Berks.

OTHER 1984 FESTIVAL RESULTS

Race	Horse	Jockey	Odds
Waterford Crystal Sup Nov Hurdle	Brownes Gazette	Mr D. Browne	11/2
Arkle Challenge Trophy Chase	Bobsline	F. Berry	5/4
Waterford Crystal Champion Hurdle	Dawn Run	J.J. O'Neill	4/5
Waterford Crystal Stayers' Hurdle	Gaye Chance	S. Morshead	5/1
Kim Muir Memorial Handicap Chase	Broomy Bank	Mr A.J. Wilson	16/1
Cheltenham Grand Annual Chase	Mossy Moore	J.J. O'Neill	11/2
Sun Alliance Novices' Hurdle	Fealty	S. O'Neill	33/1
Queen Mother Champion Chase	Badsworth Boy	R. Earnshaw	8/13
Coral Golden Hurdle Final	Canio	J. Francome	20/1
Sun Alliance Chase	A Kinsman	T.G. Dun	10/1
National Hunt Chase	Macks Friendly	Mr W.P. Mullins	11/4
Mildmay Of Flete Handicap Chase	Half Free	R. Linley	16/1
Daily Express Triumph Hurdle	Northern Game	T.J. Ryan	5/2
Christies Foxhunter Chase Ch Cup	Venture To Cognac	Mr O. Sherwood	7/1
Ritz Club National Hunt Hcap Chase	Tracys Special	Steve Knight	5/1
County Handicap Hurdle	Hill's Guard	A. Stringer	6/1
Cathcart Challenge Cup Chase	The Mighty Mac	Mr D. Browne	4/7

horse in question was a scope-rich, black-coloured, old-fashioned type of chaser named Burrough Hill Lad. Mrs Pitman had of course been the first woman to train a Grand National winner when Corbiere – as beautiful a jumper as one would wish to see – won in 1983. Burrough Hill Lad, big and powerful, had proved to be a slow learner, but it was clear he possessed buckets of class and during the season he had put together an unbeaten streak of four, including highly impressive displays to land the Welsh National and the Gainsborough Chase. Indeed Francome, who was a regular partner of the horse, believed Burrough Hill Lad to be the likely winner of the Gold Cup and had deserted him only through loyalty to the Winter stable. Phil Tuck, riding in his first Gold Cup, came in for the ride.

With the Irish represented by the 1983 Whitbread Gold Cup winner Drumlargan and the veteran Royal Bond, as well as the 500/1 outsider Foxbury (who was partnered by the first female jockey ever to ride in the race, Mrs Linda Sheedy), the twelve-strong field were sent on their way.

This was to be a true-run Gold Cup, with no hard luck stories – and definitely a Gold Cup where the best horse in the field came out on top. It was Francome and Brown Chamberlin that set a hot gallop and, for a short time at least, the partnership was closely followed by Mrs Sheedy on Foxbury.

Wayward Lad was struggling under Robert Earnshaw, somewhat surprisingly considering the going, and a mistake at the seventh was followed by further errors later in the

The splendid Burrough Hill Lad on his way to impressive Gold Cup glory.

The Queen Mother with the Burrough Hill Lad team, including trainer Jenny Pitman and jockey Phil Tuck.

race. Bregawn appeared to be sulking and it soon became obvious the Gold Cup would be going to a destination other than Yorkshire.

As the field ran to the third last fence, Brown Chamberlin still led and he, together with Burrough Hill Lad and Drumlargan, quickly drew clear of the chasing pack, headed by outsider Scot Lane and the former SunAlliance Chase winner Canny Danny, although Burrough Hill Lad did make a slight mistake at the downhill fence.

Brown Chamberlin appeared to be going marginally better coming down the hill, but Tuck was on board a horse at the top of his game and, surging up the inside, Burrough Hill Lad had Brown Chamberlin in real trouble at the second last. As the long-time leader jumped alarmingly to the right, Tuck was given all the incentive he needed.

Duly flying over the last, Burrough Hill Lad stormed up the hill in majestic style to win by three lengths from Brown Chamberlin, who had given his all. Drumlargan came next while, further back, Bregawn stayed on at the death,

eventually coming home sixth. The big disappointment was Wayward Lad, who was eventually pulled-up.

Jenny Pitman had scored another triumph for the ladies, becoming the first female to train the Gold Cup winner. Pitman had always had extreme confidence in her horse, which never wavered despite lingering rumours regarding the animal and broken blood vessels in the weeks leading up to the race. This would not be the last time Mrs Pitman would be at the peak of chasing's highest mountain.

For Burrough Hill Lad, an eight-year-old bred and owned by Mr Stan Riley, 1984 should really have been the beginning of a catalogue of Gold Cup challenges. He confirmed himself the best chaser in the land with a mesmerising win in the Hennessy Gold Cup later in the year and followed that up by winning the King George under Francome. But injuries had affected the horse before and in the future they would prevent him from running in any more Gold Cups. On this particular Thursday in March 1984 however, Burrough Hill Lad was King of Cheltenham.

1985

FORGIVE 'N' FORGET

The defending Gold Cup champion, Burrough Hill Lad, had been magnificent throughout the season and looked primed for a repeat win in 1985. Sadly, with under a week to go before the Gold Cup, he was found to have a cut behind his knee, an injury incurred when the horse had damaged himself with his own teeth, due to a low head carriage when running. With the horse not responding quickly enough to treatment, Jenny Pitman had no choice but to withdraw the race favourite, marking the thirteenth time since Mill House won in 1963 that the previous year's winner had failed to defend their crown. What Burrough Hill Lad's absence did provide was one of the most open Gold Cups in recent times, with no fewer than seven horses starting at 9/1 or shorter.

It looked an extremely strong field that lined-up for the Champion Hurdle on Tuesday, with horses such as Desert Orchid, Monica Dickinson's charge Brownes Gazette – a horse on a five-timer – and former champion Gaye Brief in the field. But the 1985 Champion Hurdle was to signal the start of a three-year dominance for See You Then, a horse beaten in the previous year's Triumph Hurdle. With the favourite Brownes Gazette swerving violently at the start and

losing twenty lengths of ground, See You Then was always handily placed and came through to win under Steve Smith-Eccles, who had been standing in for the injured John Francome. It was a first Cheltenham Festival success for trainer Nicky Henderson and, later in the meeting, he achieved his second as the versatile chaser The Tsarevich landed the Mildmay Of Flete Chase.

As one hat-trick of wins got underway courtesy of See You Then, another was coming to its conclusion, as the brilliant Badsworth Boy took his third Queen Mother Champion Chase on Wednesday. It had been billed as one of the races of the Festival, as the dual champion took on the 1984 Arkle winner Bobsline. Sadly, Bobsline's old foe Noddy's Ryde had been tragically killed following the 1984 Festival, leaving his immense promise unfulfilled. In the race itself, Badsworth Boy easily completed his glorious treble after Bobsline had capsized three fences from home. It was the first, and to date the only, time a horse has won the race three times, with all three wins coming under jockey Robert Earnshaw.

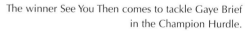

The winner See You Then comes to tackle Gaye Brief in the Champion Hurdle.

above: Nicky Henderson, trainer of See You Then.

right: West Tip – a cosy winner of the Ritz Club Chase, next to the trainer's wife, Mrs Michael Oliver.

While one big Irish hope was foiled in the Queen Mother Champion Chase, the Irish banker of the meeting duly obliged in the SunAlliance Chase. The horse in question was Antarctic Bay, with Frank Berry's mount winning the race after market rival Rhyme 'N' Reason – a horse that would ultimately win both an English and Irish Grand National – unshipped his jockey Graham Bradley at the seventh fence.

Some of Thursday's highlights included Richard Dunwoody's second Festival win aboard Grand National contender West Tip in the Ritz Club Chase – Dunwoody's first had been achieved on Von Trappe in the Coral Golden Hurdle Final earlier in the meeting – and the David Elsworth-trained Floyd maintaining an unbeaten season in the County Hurdle.

In a competitive betting market, the horse that eventually started favourite for the Gold Cup was Combs Ditch, who had flopped when Bregawn won in 1983. Combs Ditch was a classy animal, but never really found Cheltenham to his liking – at least not the red-hot battle the Gold Cup brought. His two most recent runs had ended in defeat, including when he finished second to Burrough Hill Lad in the King George.

As one of an interesting cluster of eight-year-olds in the race, the Jimmy Fitzgerald-trained Forgive 'N' Forget had landed a huge gamble when winning the Coral Golden Hurdle Final at the 1983 Festival and now he would become his trainer's first runner in the Gold Cup. There was no more consistent a horse in the field than the strongly-built chestnut

The novice Drumadowney (8) and Combs Ditch (6), both blinkered in the Gold Cup.

and Forgive 'N' Forget entered the race following a recent win in Haydock's Timeform Chase.

Other exciting newcomers to the race were Earl's Brig, Drumadowney, Righthand Man and Half Free. The progressive handicapper Earl's Brig, a big, dark-brown gelding, was the representative of Scottish permit holder Billy Hamilton, while the once inconsistent Drumadowney, a star novice, had been transformed by trainer Tim Forster, winning his last four races. With Monica Dickinson having taken over from Michael at Harewood stables, Righthand Man had developed into the trainer's most fancied prospect, having won the season's Welsh National. Old-hand Wayward Lad also lined-up for the Dickinson stable, while Cheltenham specialist Half Free, the Mackeson Gold Cup winner, was sent into battle by Fred Winter.

The Irish too had their hopes on this occasion, with Tuesday's Arkle winner Boreen Prince, the now Paddy Mullins-trained Bregawn, and the dark horse of the race, the injury plagued but talented Rainbow Warrior from Michael Cunningham's yard, all ready to run for their lives.

It was the novice Drumadowney, partnered by Welshman Hywel Davies, that set off at a fair pace and quickly built up a good lead.

In what turned out to be a fairly incident free but highly competitive race, the novice still had the edge at the fourth last, but behind him no fewer than seven horses were ready to swallow him up in their bid for glory, and these included Righthand Man, Half Free, Earl's Brig, Forgive 'N' Forget, Boreen Prince, Combs Ditch and Wayward Lad.

At the fourth last, Earl's Brig, who had been jumping majestically, made a blunder that could well have cost him a chance of triumph, knocking him to the back of the chasing pack. It was his only mistake of the race.

Jumping the third last, it was Half Free that now moved in to pole position, as Drumadowney's gallant bid began to falter. Even so, of the eight that had been in contention, only Wayward Lad was definitely out of it as they screamed towards the penultimate fence.

Going best of all, however, was Forgive 'N' Forget, and although Half Free held a fractional advantage two out, the sheepskin noseband-wearing chestnut surged through under Mark Dwyer and delivered a pair of tremendous leaps at the last two fences.

Earl's Brig came with one final effort and finishing like a train was Graham Bradley on Righthand Man, but Dwyer had timed his run perfectly and the courageous Forgive 'N' Forget marched on to the finishing line to win by a handy length-and-a-half. Not for the first time (and not for the last) Combs Ditch had proved disappointing, eventually finishing seventh. He was a smart performer at courses like Kempton Park, but on the severely undulating and stamina-sapping turf at Cheltenham, he simply never shone.

1985 TOTE GOLD CUP RESULT

FATE – HORSE	AGE/WEIGHT	JOCKEY	ODDS
1st – FORGIVE 'N FORGET	8-12-0	M. DWYER	7/1
2nd – RIGHTHAND MAN	8-12-0	G. BRADLEY	15/2
3rd – EARL'S BRIG	10-12-0	P. TUCK	13/2
4th – Drumadowney	7-12-0	H. Davies	9/1
5th – Half Free	9-12-0	R. Linley	9/1
6th – Boreen Prince	8-12-0	N. Madden	20/1
7th – Combs Ditch	9-12-0	C. Brown	4/1*
8th – Wayward Lad	10-12-0	R. Earnshaw	8/1
9th – Homeson	8-12-0	J.J. O'Neill	100/1
10th – Door Latch	7-12-0	J. Francome	25/1
11th – Ballinacurra Lad	10-12-0	P. Leach	33/1
12th – Sointulla Boy	10-12-0	Mr T. Houlbrooke	100/1
Refused – Bregawn	11-12-0	Mr W.P. Mullins	22/1
Pulled Up – Greenwood Lad	8-12-0	R. Rowe	40/1
Pulled Up – Rainbow Warrior	8-12-0	K. Morgan	22/1

14 March 1985
Going – Good
Winner –£52,560
Time – 6mins 48. 3secs
15 Ran

Forgive 'N Forget	Chestnut gelding by Precipice Wood – Tackienne
Righthand Man	Bay gelding by Proverb – Gleann Buidhe
Earl's Brig	Brown gelding by New Brig – Naughty Tara

Winner bred by Thomas F. Walsh
Winner trained by J. Fitzgerald at Malton, Yorks.

OTHER 1985 FESTIVAL RESULTS

Waterford Crystal Sup Nov Hurdle	Harry Hastings	C. Grant	14/1
Arkle Challenge Trophy Chase	Boreen Prince	N. Madden	15/2
Waterford Crystal Champion Hurdle	See You Then	S. Smith-Eccles	16/1
Waterford Crystal Stayers' Hurdle	Rose Ravine	R. Pusey	5/1
Kim Muir Memorial Handicap Chase	Glyde Court	Mr S. Sherwood	11/1
Cheltenham Grand Annual Chase	Kathies Lad	S. Smith-Eccles	7/1
Sun Alliance Novices' Hurdle	Asir	Mr R.J. Beggan	9/1
Queen Mother Champion Chase	Badsworth Boy	R. Earnshaw	11/8
Coral Golden Hurdle Final	Von Trappe	R. Dunwoody	12/1
Sun Alliance Chase	Antarctic Bay	F. Berry	6/4
National Hunt Chase	Northern Bay	Mr A. Fowler	12/1
Mildmay Of Flete Handicap Chase	The Tsarevich	J. White	5/1
Daily Express Triumph Hurdle	First Bout	S. Smith-Eccles	5/1
Christies Foxhunters' Chase Ch Cup	Elmboy	Mr A. Hill	10/1
Ritz Club National Hunt Hcap Chase	West Tip	R. Dunwoody	6/1
County Handicap Hurdle	Floyd	C. Brown	5/2
Cathcart Challenge Cup Chase	Straight Accord	S. Shilston	15/2

Shining like the brightest of stars though, had been Forgive 'N' Forget, registering his second win at the Festival in three years. He had clearly relished the battle, and the Yorkshire-based horse had jumped with great gusto to claim his prize.

Trainer Jimmy Fitzgerald, a former jockey, had ridden in two Gold Cups before a fractured skull had ended his riding career in the mid-1960s. He had bought Forgive 'N' Forget – a son of an Ascot Gold Cup winner, Precipice Wood – for Mr Tim Kilroe as a replacement for the owner's ill-fated duo Fairy King and Brave Fellow. Now trainer and owner alike could rejoice as Forgive 'N' Forget joined the Gold Cup's roll of honour.

Forgive 'N Forget would become a Gold Cup stalwart, starring under Mark Dwyer in 1985.

1986

DAWN RUN

Bitter weather had severely disrupted the National Hunt program in 1986. The nasty cold snap had led to virtually the whole of February, as well as the start of March, being lost, leaving many of the Cheltenham Festival-bound runners decidedly short of practice. Despite this inconvenience, the 1986 Festival provided the usual array of quality and quantity, which resulted in three days of magical racing.

See You Then, the reigning Champion Hurdler, had not really received the credit he deserved for winning in 1985, due to the favourite Brownes Gazette making a hash of the start. On this occasion though, there would be no doubt as to which horse was the best hurdler in the land as, ridden again by Steve Smith-Eccles, See You Then showed an electric turn of hoof to sprint clear of former champion Gaye Brief to win the title for a second time. See You Then was very difficult to keep right and was rarely seen on a racecourse. The performance was a credit to the blossoming training skills of Nicky Henderson, who got the horse to Cheltenham in grand shape, having had just one other run during the season. The hat-trick now beckoned for See You Then in 1987.

Having finished out of the frame in the previous two Champion Hurdles, the front-running, bold-jumping grey Desert Orchid, with a marked preference for right-handed tracks such as Kempton and Sandown, ran this time in the Arkle Chase. Even though he did not win, 'Dessie' – as he would become known – proved he could handle the course with a solid effort behind the Simon Christian-trained winner Oregon Trail.

On Wednesday, after the huge Ten Plus had illustrated to the racing world that he was a potential star of the future by winning the opening SunAlliance Novices' Hurdle, it was the turn of the top two-milers to enter combat in the Queen Mother Champion Chase. A surprise competitor was the three-time champion Badsworth Boy, who had been retired in mid-winter because of recurring arthritis. Badsworth Boy had apparently not taken to the idle life and had been reintroduced to training with Monica Dickinson, although he had yet to run during the season. The race figured to be a battle of the Irish horses, Buck House and Bobsline, and it was to be Buck House under Frank Berry who emerged to win in convincing manner. The victory for Buck House broke the Dickinson family's four-year grip on the event, with Badsworth Boy's three victories in the race being preceded by a win for Rathgorman. On this occasion, the gallant Badsworth Boy ran gamely before eventually coming home sixth.

Two Festival ducks were broken on Thursday after many years of toil. David Nicholson notched his first Festival win as a trainer when the 40/1 outsider Solar Cloud stormed home in the Triumph Hurdle. The horse was ridden by Peter Scudamore, who was having his first Festival win following a plethora of second-place finishes. You wait forever for a bus and then two come along at once – that saying certainly applied to the same partnership a short while later when

Jockey Kevin Mooney salutes Ten Plus' victory of promise in the Sun Alliance Novices' Hurdle.

Charter Party took the Ritz Club Chase. In the same race, those with one eye on the imminent Grand National would have done well to note West Tip finishing one place ahead of Young Driver. The same two horses would finish first and second at Aintree after a titanic duel.

It was time for the 1986 Cheltenham Gold Cup, and there was a big story brewing. The Irish-trained mare, the physically imposing Dawn Run, was attempting to complete the Champion Hurdle/Gold Cup double. What was more remarkable was the lack of experience Dawn Run had – a measly four outings over fences. With similar experience

and also a former Champion Hurdler, Lanzarote had run in the Gold Cup with tragic consequences back in 1977. Nevertheless, there was a romantic edge to Dawn Run's bid, together with a genuine feeling that the mare was something special; after all, she had won her first three chases in majestic style. Certainly, it appeared the whole of Ireland had backed her and those same individuals were adamant in their opinion of where the Gold Cup was heading. There was also controversy that came with Dawn Run's challenge. Her trainer, Paddy Mullins, had regularly given the leg up to his son Tony for the mare's races, but after her latest run, at

Cheltenham, had ended with a muddling fourth place finish, Tony was 'jocked-off' in favour of Jonjo O'Neill by the owner, Mrs Charmian Hill. Regardless of the jockey, a wave of money saw Dawn Run start the 15/8 favourite.

Trainer Jimmy Fitzgerald was extremely bullish about his defending champion Forgive 'N' Forget retaining his crown after the 1985 hero had destroyed fellow Gold Cup contenders Wayward Lad and Cybrandian in a recent workout. Although Forgive 'N' Forget had won only one of his four races during the season, he clearly adored Cheltenham and was primed for a strong showing.

The ground officially rode good, and this was expected to increase the respective chances of Wayward Lad and Combs Ditch – a pair that had experienced trouble in seeing out the Gold Cup distance in the past – while among the other contenders was Run And Skip, a fast-improving eight-year-old trailblazer that had won, among other races, the Welsh National and Sandown's Mildmay/Cazalet Memorial Chase during the season.

As the vast crowd settled down to watch a hungrily anticipated renewal of the Gold Cup, it was Forgive 'N' Forget that was the first to show at the opening fence, but it was not long before he was gobbled up by the menacing Dawn Run and the white-faced Run And Skip. Although the latter made a bad error at the third and almost came down, the pair set about delivering a fierce, cut-throat gallop.

The first casualty of the race was the Peter Easterby-trained Cybrandian, when jockey Alan Brown's leathers broke before the seventh fence. While Cybrandian was being pulled-up by Brown, Combs Ditch was struggling again and was unable to keep up with the volcanic pace set by the leaders.

The second circuit saw the battle heat up considerably and it was clear this was not going to be a race for the weak-

willed. At the second water jump, Dawn Run – who had not been jumping without error – dropped one of her legs in the water while six fences from home, Earl's Brig and jockey Phil Tuck actually came to grief, with Dawn Run making another mistake a fence later.

It appeared the advantage had shifted momentarily to the John Spearing-trained Run And Skip as they came down the hill, but in behind Wayward Lad was lurking and Dawn Run was still battling her heart out. Forgive 'N' Forget was also nicely poised under Mark Dwyer, having crept steadily into contention.

Two out, Dawn Run bravely responded to the urgings of O'Neill and briefly took control, but she, along with the three other principals, was getting painfully tired and it was the vastly experienced Wayward Lad that arrived at the last with what looked like a winning hold on the race.

Run And Skip had faded, Forgive 'N' Forget could give no more and it appeared that Dawn Run's brave bid would end in failure. Wayward Lad was running in his fourth Gold Cup. He had loved the ground and had never been so close to Gold Cup glory before. He seemed sure to finally triumph and give jockey Graham Bradley his second win in the race. What happened next was truly amazing. As Wayward Lad slowly began to falter in front, O'Neill switched Dawn Run to the stand side. Showing the utmost fighting spirit and digging to the very depths of her stamina, Dawn Run came with one pulsating final surge to snatch victory in the last twenty yards to win by a length. It was tough to tell whether the five pound mare's allowance Dawn Run was entitled to was the difference between victory and defeat, but no horse in Gold Cup history has ever looked so beaten only to get up and win. Wayward Lad was far from a mug, he had captured the King George for the third time during the season and had now delivered a

left: 'The Duke' David Nicholson trained his first Festival winner in 1986.

far left: Graham Bradley and Wayward Lad mean business before the 1986 Gold Cup.

performance good enough to win the majority of Gold Cups – he had simply been matched against a competitor with an iron will. Not surprisingly, the course record set by The Dikler in 1973 had been floored, and Cheltenham erupted as Dawn Run was led back in to the winner's enclosure. What followed were wild, Irish-dominated scenes of joy, that included seeing O'Neill chaired round the paddock in jubilant celebration. O'Neill was enjoying his second Gold Cup success following Alverton's win in 1979 and, being a true sportsman, he recognised the part Tony Mullins had played in the mare's rise to the top and promptly gave his unlucky colleague a piggy-back to collect the trophy from the Queen Mother.

So Dawn Run became the first, and to date the only horse to pull off the elusive Champion Hurdle/Gold Cup double and joined Ballinode, Kerstin and Glencaraig Lady as the only mares to win the Gold Cup. Sadly, the Dawn Run

Mrs Charmian Hill leads in her Gold Cup heroine Dawn Run.

1986 TOTE GOLD CUP RESULT

FATE – HORSE	AGE/WEIGHT	JOCKEY	ODDS
1st – DAWN RUN	8-11-9	J.J. O'NEILL	15/8*
2nd – WAYWARD LAD	11-12-0	G. BRADLEY	8/1
3rd – FORGIVE 'N FORGET	9-12-0	M. DWYER	7/2
4th – Run And Skip	8-12-0	S. Smith-Eccles	15/2
5th – Righthand Man	9-12-0	R. Earnshaw	25/1
6th – Observe	10-12-0	J. Duggan	50/1
Fell – Earl's Brig	11-12-0	P. Tuck	25/1
Fell – Von Trappe	9-12-0	R. Dunwoody	25/1
Pulled Up – Cybrandian	8-12-0	A. Brown	20/1
Pulled Up – Castle Andrea	8-12-0	G. Mernagh	500/1
Pulled Up – Combs Ditch	10-12-0	C. Brown	9/2

13 March 1986
Going – Good
Winner – £54,900
Time – 6mins 35. 3secs
11 Ran

Dawn Run	Bay mare by Deep Run – Twilight Slave
Wayward Lad	Brown gelding by Royal Highway – Loughanmore
Forgive 'N Forget	Chestnut gelding by Precipice Wood – Tackienne

Winner bred by owner, Mrs C.D. Hill
Winner trained by P. Mullins in Ireland.

OTHER 1986 FESTIVAL RESULTS

Waterford Crystal Supreme Novices' Hurdle	River Ceiriog	S. Smith-Eccles	40/1
Arkle Challenge Trophy Chase	Oregon Trail	R.J. Beggan	14/1
Waterford Crystal Champion Hurdle	See You Then	S. Smith-Eccles	5/6
Waterford Crystal Stayers' Hurdle	Crimson Embers	S.Shilston	12/1
Kim Muir Memorial Handicap Chase	Glyde Court	Mr J. Queally	13/2
Cheltenham Grand Annual Chase	Pearlyman	G. Bradley	14/1
Sun Alliance Novices' Hurdle	Ten Plus	K. Mooney	5/2
Queen Mother Champion Chase	Buck House	F. Berry	15/2
Coral Golden Hurdle Final	Motivator	G. McCourt	15/2
Sun Alliance Chase	Cross Master	R. Crank	16/1
National Hunt Chase	Omerta	Mr L. Wyer	9/4
Mildmay Of Flete Handicap Chase	The Tsarevich	J. White	8/1
Daily Express Triumph Hurdle	Solar Cloud	P. Scudamore	40/1
Christies Foxhunter Chase Challenge Cup	Attitude Adjuster	Mr T.M. Walsh	10/1
Ritz Club National Hunt Handicap Chase	Charter Party	P. Scudamore	12/1
County Handicap Hurdle	Jobroke	J.J. O'Neill	6/1
Cathcart Challenge Cup Chase	Half Free	S. Sherwood	11/8

fairytale ended there. Sent to France to attempt a second win in the French Champion Hurdle – despite her trainer's reservations – Dawn Run fell, breaking her neck, thus robbing racing of a genuine superstar whose like will not come around very often. She graced the world of racing for only a brief time but her legacy will live forever. She was something special.

The statue of Dawn Run and Jonjo O'Neill; eternal champions.

1987

THE THINKER

If ever the term 'quality over quantity' applied to a racehorse, then that horse would have to be the outstanding hurdler See You Then. During his years of dominance, the horse was seen on a racecourse about as often as the sighting of Halley's Comet (due to notoriously dodgy legs) and his build-up to the 1987 Champion Hurdle had mirrored the year before, with just one run beforehand. Without question, See You Then was, however, a class act and a cut above his contemporaries of the mid-1980s. Turned out again in peak condition by Nicky Henderson, there was rarely a moment's doubt in See You Then winning the race for the third time, as he cruised imperiously up to the leaders as they tuned for home, before Steve Smith-Eccles unleashed him up the run-in to win from the American horse Flatterer and the future star chaser Barnbrook Again. In winning, See You Then joined the illustrious trio of Hatton's Grace, Sir Ken and Persian War as three-time Champion Hurdlers, and his place among that group was richly deserved.

Later on Tuesday, there was a female victory in the Kim Muir Memorial Chase when Gee Armytage, an amateur,

guided The Ellier past the front-running chestnut Lean Ar Aghaidh to win. Miss Armytage followed that up on Wednesday by becoming the first female rider to topple the male professionals at the Festival when her mount Gee-A got the better of the Peter Scudamore-ridden Malya Mal in the Mildmay Of Flete Chase.

Wednesday's Queen Mother Chase featured a field of the highest quality, with two outstanding two-mile chasers, Very Promising and Pearlyman, competing against the King George winner Desert Orchid. The dashing grey put in his usual bold-jumping display, but in a thrilling finish it was Pearlyman that just held off the persistent Very Promising. Winning jockey Peter Scudamore was so impressed that he described Pearlyman as being as good as any horse he had ever ridden.

The SunAlliance Chase is traditionally one of the most reliable markers for all the big future staying chases. Over three tough miles, jumping at speed and with the famous Cheltenham hill to climb at the finish, the novices that come through this test have to demonstrate strength, stamina and quality in what is normally a brutal contest. The 1987 running threw forward a whole band of horses with extremely bright futures. The winner, Kildimo, went on to

Gee Armytage, twice a Festival winner in 1987.

The awesome Pearlyman heads for Queen Mother Champion Chase glory.

Clerk of the course, Major P.W.F. Arkwright, is passed by Combs Ditch
in the blizzard-like Gold Cup parade ring.

run in all the top chases for the next six seasons, the runner-up Playschool would win a Hennessy Gold Cup, the third, Brittany Boy, would win an Irish National, Mr Frisk a Grand National, while Cavvies Clown, Dixton House and Lastofthebrownies would all develop in to fine chasers.

The 1987 Gold Cup was perhaps not the finest renewal of the race, with Burrough Hill Lad again absent and Mrs Pitman's Welsh National victor Stearsby also missing, but it was one of the most interesting to watch, not only for the red-hot action, but also for the extraordinary scenery that accompanied the great race. During the Foxhunter Chase – the race before the Gold Cup – snow started falling, and it was not long before the turf was carpeted in white flakes, giving the stewards no choice but to delay racing and the runners for the Gold Cup were temporarily sent back to their waiting boxes. After a break of some eighty-one minutes, the snow had faded sufficiently for racing to continue, although

the ground conditions – while officially good – were going to make it a real test of stamina with the snow turning the turf loose.

Probably counting their lucky stars were the team responsible for The Thinker, a horse that adored a thorough examination of stamina. Trained in County Durham by the legendary Arthur Stephenson, The Thinker had impressed when winning his last two races, Haydock's Peter Marsh Chase and the Rowland Meyrick at Wetherby. A rugged, sturdy chestnut with a flash-white streak on his face, The Thinker was ridden by Stephenson's stable jockey Riddley Lamb.

Apart from Combs Ditch and the twelve-year-olds Wayward Lad and Earl's Brig, only Forgive 'N' Forget had any previous experience of the race. The 1985 champion was out to become the first horse to regain his crown and was strongly fancied to do so, starting the 5/4 favourite. With

The Thinker still has work to do as Cybrandian leads over the last in the Gold Cup.

four wins from five outings during the season and with a field consisting mainly of decent handicappers, it was easy to see why Forgive 'N' Forget was so short in the betting.

Among those decent handicappers were West Tip and Door Latch. Both had run in the 1986 Grand National – with totally contrasting outcomes. West Tip had won the race in convincing style while Door Latch had fallen at the first! However, Door Latch had run very well for trainer Josh Gifford when finishing second in the season's King George, although he had been hampered by injury problems since.

The Gold Cup resembled a scene from the Winter Olympics as the twelve runners were finally sent on their way. It was the Peter Easterby-trained Cybrandian that set the pace early on from Door Latch, Charter Party, Mr Moonraker, Earl's Brig and Nick Gaselee's charge, Bolands Cross. In the opening stages, The Thinker, appreciating the easier ground, was kept towards the back of the pack by Lamb.

At the fifth fence, the first ditch, Charter Party took a fall, sending Richard Dunwoody diving in to the snow, while at the twelfth, Forgive 'N' Forget shocked those in the stands by

making a serious blunder that seemed to shake him for the remainder of the race.

Cybrandian was travelling smartly deep in to the second circuit, with Door Latch his nearest pursuer, but Bolands Cross – who had been jumping well – was so untidy at the ditch eight from home that Peter Scudamore was unseated.

By the time the field had reached the top of the snow-capped hill, the leading group had assembled into single-file, with Cybrandian leading Door Latch, The Thinker, Forgive 'N' Forget and the fast-improving veteran Wayward Lad. At the third last, The Thinker made a monumental blunder that looked to have dented his chances severely.

Flying two out, there were still six in with a shout and Cybrandian was still going strongly under Chris Grant. However, running in his fifth Gold Cup, Wayward Lad had suddenly swept into a menacing position with Graham Bradley on board, and the classy twelve-year-old finally appeared set to end his Gold Cup heartache as he took the last, surging up the inside.

It was not to be. The famous Gold Cup trophy was destined never to be graced with the name of Wayward Lad and, just as the year before, he folded badly as he tried to climb the finishing hill and it was The Thinker – only third at the last fence – who showed the guts of a streetfighter to storm up the hill and break the veteran's heart once more. Cybrandian, Door Latch and West Tip also managed to pip Wayward Lad, who finished exhausted in fifth place. Grant had ridden a particularly admirable race aboard Cybrandian, but second place was a position that would continue to plague the jockey in the big races. As well as here, he had finished second on Young Driver in the 1986 Grand National, and would fill the same berth on Stephenson's Durham Edition in the same race in 1988 and 1990.

1987 TOTE GOLD CUP RESULT

FATE – HORSE	AGE/WEIGHT	JOCKEY	ODDS
1st – THE THINKER	9-12-0	R. LAMB	13/2
2nd – CYBRANDIAN	9-12-0	C. GRANT	25/1
3rd – DOOR LATCH	9-12-0	R. ROWE	9/1
4th – West Tip	10-12-0	Peter Hobbs	11/1
5th – Wayward Lad	12-12-0	G. Bradley	11/1
6th – Golden Friend	9-12-0	D. Browne	16/1
7th – Forgive 'N Forget	10-12-0	M. Dwyer	5/4*
8th – Mr Moonraker	10-12-0	B. Powell	50/1
Fell – Charter Party	9-12-0	R. Dunwoody	25/1
Unseated Rider – Bolands Cross	8-12-0	P. Scudamore	8/1
Pulled Up – Combs Ditch	11-12-0	C. Brown	9/1
Pulled Up – Earl's Brig	12-12-0	P. Tuck	25/1

19 March 1987
Going – Good
Winner – £55,500
Time – 6mins 56. 5secs
12 Ran

The Thinker	Chestnut gelding by Cantab – Maine Pet
Cybrandian	Bay gelding by Prince Regent – Lavenham Rose
Door Latch	Chestnut gelding by Cantab – Kelly's Door

Winner bred by Victor Semple
Winner trained by W.A. Stephenson at Bishop Auckland, Co. Durham.

OTHER 1987 FESTIVAL RESULTS

Waterford Crystal Sup Nov Hurdle	Tartan Tailor	P. Tuck	14/1
Arkle Challenge Trophy Chase	Gala's Image	R. Linley	25/1
Waterford Crystal Champion Hurdle	See You Then	S. Smith-Eccles	11/10
Waterford Crystal Stayers' Hurdle	Galmoy	T. Carmody	9/2
Kim Muir Memorial Hcap Chase	The Ellier	Miss G. Armytage	16/1
Cheltenham Grand Annual Chase	French Union	R. Dunwoody	13/2
Sun Alliance Novices' Hurdle	The West Awake	S. Sherwood	16/1
Queen Mother Champion Chase	Pearlyman	P. Scudamore	13/8
Coral Golden Hurdle Final	Taberna Lord	L. Harvey	10/1
Sun Alliance Chase	Kildimo	G. Bradley	13/2
National Hunt Chase	Mighty Mark	Mr J. Walton	8/1
Mildmay Of Flete Hcap Chase	Gee-A	Miss G. Armytage	33/1
Daily Express Triumph Hurdle	Alone Success	S. Smith-Eccles	11/1
Christies Foxhunter Chase Ch Cup	Observe	Mr C. Brooks	14/1
Ritz Club National Hunt Hcap Chase	Gainsay	B. De Haan	10/1
County Handicap Hurdle	Neblin	R. Guest	14/1
Cathcart Challenge Cup Chase	Half Free	P. Scudamore	5/4

The Thinker braved the snow to land the Gold Cup.

The Thinker had given his sixty-six-year-old trainer the biggest success of his forty-one-year career, but remarkably the trainer had elected to oversee a bunch of his other horses at Hexham the same day and was not there to see his hardy warrior win the Blue Riband, or to pick up the Cup itself. In his absence, Stephenson's nephew Peter Cheesborough did the honours. It was also a particularly emotive win for Riddley Lamb, who had suffered a badly dislocated hip three years previously, and had been warned he may never race again. Thankfully, the jockey recovered and could now join in the post-race fun – together with all those present on the day Cheltenham resembled the North Pole – in celebrating The Thinker becoming the Gold Cup hero of 1987.

1988

Having won the SunAlliance Novices' Hurdle the year before, the Oliver Sherwood-trained The West Awake became the first horse to follow up and take the SunAlliance Chase after beating Bob Tisdall. So impressed by The West Awake's jumping performance was Sherwood, that the trainer suggested the horse could develop in to a Gold Cup contender in time.

The famous maroon and yellow halved colours of the Courage family, synonymous with Royal Relief and Spanish Steps in the 1970s, were carried to further glory in the Mildmay Of Flete Chase when Smart Tar gave the leading conditional jockey, Carl Llewellyn, his first Festival success. Llewellyn would go on to have a hugely successful career that included victories in the Grand National aboard Party Politics in 1992 and Earth Summit in 1998.

CHARTER PARTY

The great trainer Fred Winter had been on the easy-list since unfortunately suffering a fractured skull in a fall at home in September. However, the opening day of the 1988 Cheltenham Festival was about to give him a much-needed lift to his current plight. Winter had sent out the winner of the Champion Hurdle three times, twice with Bula in 1971 and 1972, and in 1974 with Lanzarote, and Winter was represented on this occasion by Celtic Shot – a horse that had suffered his only defeat during the season to the race favourite Celtic Chief, who was trained by Mercy Rimell. This time it was Celtic Shot that came out on top with Celtic Chief only third.

Another trainer with plenty to smile about on the opening day was Josh Gifford. Having gone seventeen years without a winner, Gifford broke his Festival duck when Golden Minstrel won the Kim Muir Chase. Having waited an age to record his first Festival success, the Findon-based trainer then recorded a one-two courtesy of Vodkatini and Clay Hill in the Grand Annual Chase and an incredible hat-trick was then completed on the Wednesday as Pragada stormed home in front in the Coral Hurdle Final.

Celtic Shot gets a pat from Peter Scudamore after winning the Champion Hurdle.

above: Josh Gifford (right) celebrates his first Festival win as a trainer.

left: Golden Minstrel (red & white colours) leads the field in the Kim Muir Chase.

The Gold Cup had been the original Festival target of the lightning-bolt grey Desert Orchid, but as the Festival had worn on, the poor weather had caused the ground to become increasingly soft and tacky. Bearing in mind his charge may have not seen out the trip in such conditions, David Elsworth switched Dessie to the Queen Mother Champion Chase. Despite putting up a customary brave performance and improving a place on his 1987 third, Desert Orchid met his match in the classy Pearlyman, who became the seventh multiple winner of the race. Trained again by John Edwards, Pearlyman was ridden on this occasion by Tom Morgan.

Despite the fact that Desert Orchid would be missing from the Gold Cup, there were still plenty of horses in the fifteen-strong field that stood a good chance of winning this open renewal of the race and at the head of the betting market stood perhaps the most improved horse in training, Playschool. A runner-up in the 1987 SunAlliance Chase, the David Barons-trained and New Zealand-bred horse had developed from a decent stayer into a true Gold Cup contender after brilliant wins in the Hennessy, the Welsh National and Leopardstown's Vincent O'Brien Irish Gold Cup. With courage and stamina his forte, the track and the prevailing soft ground were expected to be right up Playschool's street.

The winner of that 1987 SunAlliance Chase was the Toby Balding-trained Kildimo. The horse was a talented performer and had won twice during the season, but he really needed

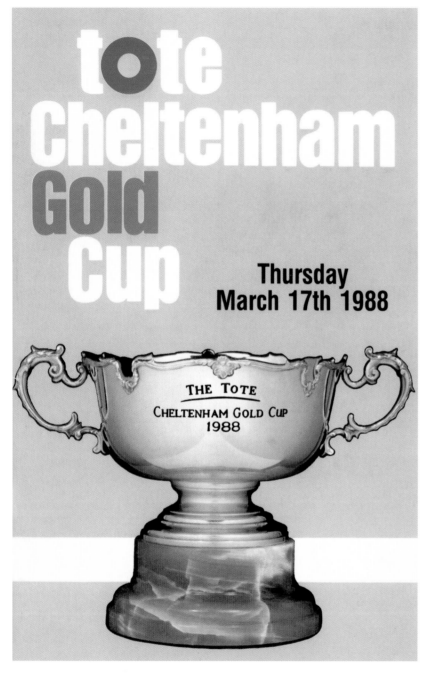

THE TOTE
CHELTENHAM GOLD CUP
1988

1988 Racecard.

good ground to be at his optimum. The same could be said of the French raider, Nupsala, the surprise King George winner trained by Francois Doumen.

Other notable challengers were Cavvies Clown, Charter Party, Yahoo and Forgive 'N' Forget. The mud-loving Cavvies Clown had won his last four races, although following three of the victories – at Newbury, Wincanton and Cheltenham – it was revealed the horse had failed dope tests, so there was a degree of uncertainty surrounding his true ability. Charter Party, despite winning his latest start, had fallen in the previous Gold Cup and still held the tag of an unreliable jumper, while running in his fourth Gold Cup, Forgive 'N' Forget had experienced an up-and-down season. One dark horse was Yahoo, a highly capable seven-year-old trained by John Edwards, and a horse that was looking to emulate Royal Frolic and Alverton by winning the Greenall Whitley Chase at Haydock before striking Gold at Cheltenham.

Even though the ground at Cheltenham was undeniably sticky, the field set off at a fast pace, headed by the Martin Pipe-trained Beau Ranger and pressed by the likes of fellow trailblazers Run And Skip and Cybrandian. The leaders remained the same until the outsider Golden Friend strode up to take control at the seventh fence.

The big move on the second circuit came from jockey Simon Sherwood on Cavvies Clown. Sherwood had only come in for the ride after fellow jockey Ross Arnott had broken his collar-bone in a fall at Wincanton just a week before the race and now his grateful replacement sent Cavvies Clown into a commanding lead eight fences from home, with the horse clearly enjoying the soft conditions.

At the fourth last, the race really kicked off in earnest as Rhyme 'N' Reason – much to the frustration of jockey Brendan Powell – met the final ditch wrong and crashed out of contention. A much bleaker episode lay in wait a fence

Charter Party clears the last fence in the Gold Cup.

later, and must be considered one of the saddest moments in Gold Cup history. Jumping the fence, the 1985 hero Forgive 'N' Forget – when travelling imperiously – shattered an off-hind pastern and tragically had to be put down. The horse had been simply cruising at the time, and his death left trainer Jimmy Fitzgerald understandably distraught. Forgive 'N' Forget ran in four Gold Cups and at six Festivals in all and, fittingly, his ashes are buried at Cheltenham near the Royal Box.

The challengers to Cavvies Clown were starting to drop away dramatically. Playschool's bid filtered out rather timidly while Kildimo had never been in the mix on unfavourable ground. Yahoo and Nupsala too were struggling to stay in contention, so it was left to Charter Party to throw down the gauntlet to the leader.

At the second last, Cavvies Clown made his one jumping error, but it was enough to cost him the race as Charter Party had caught him running and, after jumping the last, the David Nicholson-trained gelding promptly battled up the hill to great effect to gain a six-length victory under Richard Dunwoody. Beau Ranger had stayed on gamely at the end to take third place. The huge disappointment of the race had been Playschool, who had run so indifferently that jockey Paul Nicholls was forced to pull him up and, although David

Richard Dunwoody returns victorious to joint owner Mrs Jenny Mould aboard Gold Cup hero Charter Party.

Barons was adamant the horse must have been tampered with in some way, routine tests proved nothing – but it was an extremely puzzling run from the favourite. Playschool would not be the last favourite to go down in controversial circumstances: a crystal ball would have revealed possible 'stalking' tactics on the 1992 hot-pot.

Obviously, the tragedy that befell poor Forgive 'N' Forget took a good deal of gloss off Charter Party's somewhat surprising Gold Cup win, although the 'Duke' David Nicholson was very courteous and thoughtful on acceptance of his prize, recognising the sadness of the situation. Nicholson had only broken his Festival duck two

years previously and he deserved no small amount of credit for the training performance, bearing in mind that Charter Party had been suffering from a blood disorder the previous season. Nicholson's father, Frenchie, had won the race in 1942 on Medoc II, while David had been third aboard Snaigow in 1966. Winning jockey Richard Dunwoody had joined Nicholson's stable at the start of the year, and had begun Gold Cup day with a victory aboard the blazing grey Kribensis in the Triumph Hurdle.

Charter Party had looked a very good horse when winning the Ritz Club Chase at the 1986 Festival, only for injury and jumping problems to hamper his progress. Now though,

1988 TOTE GOLD CUP RESULT

FATE – HORSE	AGE/WEIGHT	JOCKEY	ODDS
1st – CHARTER PARTY	10-12-0	R. DUNWOODY	10/1
2nd – CAVVIES CLOWN	8-12-0	S. SHERWOOD	6/1
3rd – BEAU RANGER	10-12-0	P. SCUDAMORE	33/1
4th – Nupsala	9-12-0	A. Pommier	8/1
5th – Yahoo	7-12-0	T. Morgan	12/1
6th – West Tip	11-12-0	M. Hammond	80/1
7th – Kildimo	8-12-0	G. Bradley	6/1
8th – Golden Friend	10-12-0	D. Browne	40/1
9th – Run And Skip	10-12-0	Peter Hobbs	50/1
Fell – Rhyme 'N Reason	9-12-0	B. Powell	11/1
Fell – Stearsby	9-12-0	G. McCourt	100/1
Pulled Up – Cybrandian	10-12-0	C. Grant	40/1
Pulled Up – Forgive 'N Forget	11-12-0	M. Dwyer	8/1
Pulled Up – Foyle Fisherman	9-12-0	R. Rowe	50/1
Pulled Up – Playschool	10-12-0	P. Nicholls	100/30*

17 March 1988
Going – Soft
Winner – £61,960
Time – 6mins 58. 9secs
15 Ran

Charter Party	Bay gelding by Document – Ahoy There
Cavvies Clown	Bay gelding by Idiot's Delight – Cavallina
Beau Ranger	Chestnut gelding by Beau Chapeau – Sand Martin

Winner bred by A.W. Ridell Martin
Winner trained by D. Nicholson at Condicote, Glos.

OTHER 1988 FESTIVAL RESULTS

Waterford Crystal Sup Nov Hurdle	Vagador	M. Perrett	4/1
Arkle Challenge Trophy Chase	Danish Flight	M. Dwyer	11/2
Waterford Crystal Champion Hurdle	Celtic Shot	P. Scudamore	7/1
Waterford Crystal Stayers' Hurdle	Galmoy	T. Carmody	2/1
Kim Muir Memorial Handicap Chase	Golden Minstrel	Mr T. Grantham	7/1
Cheltenham Grand Annual Chase	Vodkatini	R. Rowe	4/1
Sun Alliance Novices' Hurdle	Rebel Song	S. Sherwood	14/1
Queen Mother Champion Chase	Pearlyman	T. Morgan	15/8
Coral Golden Hurdle Final	Pragada	R. Rowe	16/1
Sun Alliance Chase	The West Awake	S. Sherwood	11/4
National Hunt Chase	Over The Road	Mr T. Costello	10/1
Mildmay Of Flete Handicap Chase	Smart Tar	C. Llewellyn	11/1
Daily Express Triumph Hurdle	Kribensis	R. Dunwoody	6/1
Christies Foxhunter Chase Ch Cup	Certain Light	Mr P. Hacking	9/1
Ritz Club Nat Hunt Hcap Chase	Aquilifer	P. Croucher	9/2
Cathcart Challenge Cup Chase	Private Views	B. Powell	7/1
County Handicap Hurdle	Cashew King	T. Wall	9/1

Nicholson, Dunwoody and owners Mrs Claire Smith and Mrs Jenny Mould could enjoy Charter Party's rise to Gold Cup stardom.

1989

DESERT ORCHID

If a general survey was taken to discover the most popular chaser of modern times, then the likes of Mill House, Arkle and Dawn Run would probably be the names most commonly unearthed. However, it is tough to say whether there has been, or ever will be, a more popular, flamboyant and endearing character than the wonderful grey horse that the racing public took to their hearts. Desert Orchid was a big, strapping, hugely athletic specimen that jumped every fence with a zest rarely encountered in the sport. Now, with five well-fought but ultimately fruitless Festivals behind him, Dessie was going for the Gold Cup. It would be a tough nut to crack for the seemingly invincible grey, for he had a distinct favour for right-handed tracks and had never won at Cheltenham (and indeed had only once won on a left-handed course – Aintree). The record books too were against Dessie, with no horse of his colour having ever won the Gold Cup, and only Shaef (second in 1952) and Stalbridge Colonist (second in 1967 and third in 1968) ever placed. Despite all this, the racing world held its collective breath to see if one of jump racing's finest could scale the highest mountain.

The big shock of the opening day – and one of the biggest shocks in the history of the Cheltenham Festival – came in the Champion Hurdle. Beech Road, a 50/1 shot trained by Toby Balding, stunned a strong field, including the Celtics – Shot and Chief – and the previously unbeaten Kribensis, a horse that was trying to become the first to complete the Triumph/Champion Hurdle double since the great Persian War twenty-one years before. The victorious chestnut Beech Road, ridden by the stylish Richard Guest, became the joint longest-priced winner of the Champion Hurdle, mirroring Kirriemuir's winning odds in 1965.

An interesting young horse won the Kim Muir Chase in the shape of Cool Ground. Ridden by six-foot amateur Anthony Tory, the mud-loving chestnut would be back at Cheltenham in future years attempting to win far bigger prizes.

Barnbrook Again jumps clear of his rivals en route to Queen Mother Champion Chase glory.

A saturated Tom Morgan with the Ritz Club Chase winner Dixton House.

The absence of the dual champion Pearlyman took away some of the spice from Wednesday's Queen Mother Champion Chase. Even so, there was a fine replacement lying in wait in the form of Barnbrook Again, and the horse gave trainer David Elsworth the perfect boost ahead of Desert Orchid's Gold Cup bid by winning the race from the outsider Royal Stag. Barnbrook Again was a horse that loved Cheltenham and had been placed in a Champion Hurdle and an Arkle Chase. He would now become the dominant force in the two-mile chasing division for a number of years.

As usual, the SunAlliance Chase was a monster of a race to win, even with a horse on a sizzling-hot streak. The 9/2 favourite Nick The Brief had won his last five races, but on this occasion found Josh Gifford's runner Envopak Token just too good. Nick The Brief certainly would not remain the last horse to enter the race in tremendous form only to come unstuck. The same fate awaited the lofty reputations of Harcon, Mr Mulligan and Nick Dundee in future years.

Without wishing to dampen the achievements of the winners of all the other races at the 1989 Festival, this particular year really was centred on the Gold Cup itself, with everyone wanting to know the fate of their favourite grey. The day finally arrived and there was an almost irresistible feeling that, with Dessie at the absolute peak of his powers, the fairytale ending that most people desired could actually be realised. Then the weather arrived. The

The waterlogged Cheltenham turf on Gold Cup morning.

ground had ridden soft for the opening two days, but an early morning mixture of snow and rain changed the going to heavy, a factor considered a severe detriment to Dessie's chances. The horse was already sure to lose ground by jumping naturally right at his fences and now the conditions would sap even more of his valuable reserves. Simon Sherwood, who entered the race unbeaten on the grey, admitted to fearing the worst when discovering the state of the ground on the big day and for a while it looked doubtful whether the horse would run at all, until David Elsworth decided once and for all to let the horse take his chance. Nevertheless, Desert Orchid had been in stupendous form during the season, winning at a variety of distances, including a second King George VI Chase where he thrashed the one-two from the 1988 Gold Cup, Charter Party and Cavvies Clown. Perhaps his most impressive performance though had come in Sandown's Gainsborough Chase where he gave a hefty 18lbs and a beating to a rising star and fellow

Gold Cup aspirant Pegwell Bay. With a record crowd of over 51,000 present at Cheltenham to cheer him on, Dessie started as the 5/2 favourite.

There was plenty of dangerous opposition for the grey to be concerned about. Both the two previous champions, The Thinker and Charter Party, were back together with Cavvies Clown and Yahoo, but perhaps the biggest threats were likely to come from two imposing, well-built challengers, both Gold Cup newcomers, Ten Plus and Carvill's Hill.

Carvill's Hill, a seven-year-old, was the top novice in Ireland, and was a classic, old-fashioned chaser trained by Jim Dreaper. The horse bypassed a bid for the SunAlliance Chase in favour of the Gold Cup and, astonishingly, became Ireland's first Gold Cup runner since Dawn Run. Ten Plus, a big bay horse with a strong neck, was potentially the best horse in the field. Having won the SunAlliance Novices' Hurdle in 1986, the horse had always looked a real chaser, but had surprisingly struggled the season before and had also suffered injury problems. But during the current season, Ten Plus had really blossomed, improving dramatically every time he ran, and he had taken four races in a row as he attempted to give trainer Fulke Walwyn a fifth Gold Cup win. Interestingly, Ten Plus lived in the same box at Saxon House that Mill House and The Dikler had occupied before their triumphs.

It was Desert Orchid that bounded out into an early lead, pressed closely by Ten Plus, Charter Party, the mud-loving Bonanza Boy, Slalom and Yahoo. Early on, Carvill's Hill was towards the rear together with the strangely reluctant Cavvies Clown.

Unusually, there were a number of fallers on the first circuit. The doubtful stayer Golden Freeze fell at the sixth fence while groans could be heard from the Irish contingent as their raider Carvill's Hill hit the turf at the next, dislocating

Desert Orchid leads, from left to right, Ten Plus, Yahoo, Slalom and Charter Party at half way in the Gold Cup.

jockey Ken Morgan's shoulder in the process. The Carvill's Hill incident summed up Ireland's luck at the meeting, as none of their runners managed to win a race. Quite out of character, the normally safe-jumping 1987 hero The Thinker crashed out at the tenth. Dessie was still out in front, with Charter Party for company.

By the fourteenth fence, Ten Plus had ranged up to take the lead and, as the race progressed, the nine-year-old was looking increasingly dangerous; such was the elegance of his jumping and the determination of his jockey Kevin Mooney.

At the third last, tragedy struck. Still bounding clear in front and having shaken off most of his rivals, Ten Plus brushed through the top of the fence and slammed down to the turf, landing in an ugly heap. The horse got up and carried on running, but the damage had been done. Ten Plus had broken his near-hind fetlock and had to be destroyed. It was a terribly sad episode in the race's history and it will never be known if Ten Plus' brave bid for glory would have ultimately been successful. One only had to witness the tearful Mooney after the race to understand the severity of the loss. In the same incident, Ballyhane, one of only five left in contention, had been brought down.

Rounding the turn for home and with Charter Party beaten, the crowd rose in sheer excitement as Desert Orchid and

The Queen Mother and 'Dessie' after the grey's Gold Cup win.

Yahoo settled down for a grandstand finish. It was the smaller Yahoo though that was going better (and he was a horse that loved the mud) and he took a slight lead over the last two fences.

Desert Orchid was now totally exhausted and slowed right down to jump the last, though Yahoo did the same on his inside. With the whole crowd roaring him home, the incredible happened as Dessie slowly began to peg back the weakening Yahoo halfway up the run-in and, as the two came together in the last hundred yards, the noise was deafening. Through sheer guts and unflinching courage, it was Desert Orchid that miraculously edged ahead and held

on to win by a length-and-a-half. The gallant Yahoo could not have done more in defeat, and had been beaten by a truly special horse. Back in third came Charter Party, with Bonanza Boy and West Tip the only others to finish.

Needless to say, the reception awaiting Desert Orchid in the winner's enclosure was rapturous, with a burst of three cheers thrown in for good measure. The horse was fully deserving of such praise, having demonstrated the heart of a lion to deliver the most popular of wins.

Somewhat masked in the grey's glory was the role played by Elsworth. The horse's owner, Richard Burridge, had never been ultra-keen for the horse to take his chance and was

1989 TOTE GOLD CUP RESULT

FATE – HORSE	AGE/WEIGHT	JOCKEY	ODDS
1st – DESERT ORCHID	10-12-0	S. SHERWOOD	5/2*
2nd – YAHOO	8-12-0	T. MORGAN	25/1
3rd – CHARTER PARTY	11-12-0	R. DUNWOODY	14/1
4th – Bonanza Boy	8-12-0	P. Scudamore	15/2
5th – West Tip	12-12-0	Peter Hobbs	66/1
Fell – Ten Plus	9-12-0	K. Mooney	11/2
Fell – Slalom	8-12-0	J. White	33/1
Fell – The Thinker	11-12-0	C. Grant	15/2
Fell – Golden Freeze	7-12-0	B. Sheridan	16/1
Fell – Carvill's Hill	7-12-0	K. Morgan	5/1
Brought Down – Ballyhane	8-12-0	R. Rowe	50/1
Refused – Cavvies Clown	9-12-0	R. Arnott	8/1
Pulled Up – Pegwell Bay	8-12-0	C. Llewellyn	25/1

16 March 1989
Going – Heavy
Winner – £66,635
Time – 7mins 17. 60secs
13 Ran

Desert Orchid	Grey gelding by Grey Mirage – Flower Child
Yahoo	Bay gelding by Trombone – Coolroe Aga
Charter Party	Bay gelding by Document – Ahoy There

Winner bred by J.D. Burridge
Winner trained by D.R.C. Elsworth at Whitsbury, Hants.

OTHER 1989 FESTIVAL RESULTS

Waterford Crystal Sup Nov Hurdle	Sondrio	J. Lower	25/1
Arkle Challenge Trophy Chase	Waterloo Boy	R. Dunwoody	5/4
Waterford Crystal Champion Hurdle	Beech Road	R. Guest	50/1
Waterford Crystal Stayers' Hurdle	Rustle	M. Bowlby	4/1
Kim Muir Memorial Handicap Chase	Cool Ground	Mr A. Tory	7/2
Cheltenham Grand Annual Chase	Pukka Major	P. Scudamore	4/1
Sun Alliance Novices' Hurdle	Sayfar's Lad	M. Perrett	12/1
Queen Mother Champion Chase	Barnbrook Again	S. Sherwood	7/4
Coral Golden Hurdle Final	Rogers Princess	S. Keightley	8/1
Sun Alliance Chase	Envopak Token	Peter Hobbs	16/1
National Hunt Chase	Boraceva	Mr S. Mullins	4/1
Mildmay Of Flete Handicap Chase	Paddyboro	R. Rowe	9/2
Daily Express Triumph Hurdle	Ikdam	N. Coleman	66/1
Christies Foxhunter Chase Ch Cup	Three Counties	Miss K. Rimell	6/1
Ritz Club National Hunt Hcap Chase	Dixton House	T. Morgan	13/2
Cathcart Challenge Cup Chase	Observer Corps	T. Morgan	66/1
Racegoers Club County Hcap Hurdle	Willsford	M. Bowlby	11/1

understandably concerned over the ground conditions. Elsworth's total belief in the horse had been gloriously rewarded and was a major tonic for a trainer that had lost a star novice and a potential future Gold Cup contender in Sir Blake on the gallops earlier in the season.

This was, of course, Desert Orchid's finest hour: even though he recorded a record four King George victories, a Whitbread Gold Cup and an Irish National over the course of his career, that mud-soaked March Thursday in 1989 will forever be remembered as his day, the day the people's star achieved the dream. The ultimate grey day.

1990

trained by another great Flat trainer, Barry Hills, and carried the blue and green colours of Robert Sangster.

In the Arkle Chase earlier in the day, the drying ground was expected to be in the favour of one of the season's leading novices, the Oliver Sherwood-trained six-year-old Young Snugfit. However, in the aftermath of the race, Josh Gifford hoped he had a potential Gold Cup candidate on his hands as Comandante won the race from the Irish hope Kiichi, with Young Snugfit third. Sadly, the dream never materialised for Gifford, as Comandante was tragically killed before he had a chance to line-up in the Gold Cup.

On Wednesday, there was a steward's enquiry following a dramatic tussle up the hill to conclude the Queen Mother Champion Chase. After an anxious wait for connections, it

NORTON'S COIN

There are occasions when sporting stars greatly overachieve to gain success. There are occasions when there are surprise outcomes. Then there are the downright shocks. It is fair to say throughout the entire history of the Cheltenham Gold Cup, no result caused as big a shock as the outcome of the 1990 edition.

The Festival began on Tuesday with ground on the fast side, and this was of great benefit to a number of runners in the Champion Hurdle. Rather ungracefully, the triple-champion of the mid-1980s, See You Then, was asked to bid for glory again after a two-year absence, while the defending champion Beech Road, an unsteady favourite in the light of the quicker ground, was back to defend his crown. The race was, however, dominated by horses with Flat racing links, and it was the grey Kribensis – a horse that had suffered his only ever National Hunt defeat in the 1989 race – that took the spoils from Nomadic Way. On the fastest ground since 1976, Beech Road finished fourth and See You Then last (and was thankfully then retired). The Flat racing personalities involved were Kribensis' legendary trainer, Sir Michael Stoute, and the horse carried the famous red silks with white sleeves of Sheikh Mohammed, while Nomadic Way was

The grey Kribensis unleashes his bid for victory in the Champion Hurdle. Nomadic Way, the runner-up, is on the far side.

far left: One of Flat racing's finest trainers, Sir Michael Stoute, tasted Champion Hurdle glory with Kribensis.

left: The reigning champion Desert Orchid canters to the post for the Gold Cup under Richard Dunwoody.

emerged Barnbrook Again had won his second title, following a thrilling duel with the gutsy 1989 Arkle winner Waterloo Boy. The two-time winner of the race, Pearlyman, had been pulled-up during the contest.

After the hot favourite, the chestnut Royal Athlete, had fallen in the SunAlliance Chase, Jenny Pitman's second-string, Garrison Savannah, was able to pick up the pieces and win the race under Ben De Haan. Both Garrison Savannah and Royal Athlete would develop in to two of Mrs Pitman's all-time great horses.

At eleven, Desert Orchid was now the elder statesman of the Gold Cup field, yet the season had seen the grey reach new levels of brilliance. After suffering a rare fall at Aintree to finish the previous season in a race where Yahoo gained compensation for the Gold Cup defeat, Dessie had come out in scintillating form this time around. Among his season's highlights were a third victory in the King George, in which he easily disposed of many of the Gold Cup field, and perhaps his best performance yet back at Kempton as he beat the useful chaser Delius by eight lengths in the Racing

Post Chase – despite giving that rival a huge 28lbs. Having proved his Gold Cup worth in testing conditions the previous year, it seemed plausible that he would become the first horse since L'Escargot in 1971 to retain his crown, especially since the ground on this occasion was in his favour. The enormous faith put in the horse, partnered by Richard Dunwoody after Simon Sherwood had retired, saw Dessie start odds-on at 10/11.

With many of the field, including the two-time Welsh National winner Bonanza Boy, the 1989 runner-up Yahoo and the increasingly stubborn Cavvies Clown, in need of the mud to win such a race, it appeared Dessie's main challengers would be a bunch of newcomers. One of those was John Upson's charge Nick The Brief, runner-up in the 1989 SunAlliance Chase. Although he too would have preferred softer ground, Nick The Brief had progressed in to a lively contender during the season, narrowly losing to Cool Ground at Haydock before returning to that course to win the Peter Marsh Chase before downing Ireland's great hope Carvill's Hill in the Vincent O'Brien Gold Cup at

1990 TOTE GOLD CUP RESULT

FATE – HORSE	AGE/WEIGHT	JOCKEY	ODDS
1st – NORTON'S COIN	9-12-0	G. McCOURT	100/1
2nd – TOBY TOBIAS	8-12-0	M. PITMAN	8/1
3rd – DESERT ORCHID	11-12-0	R. DUNWOODY	10/11*
4th – Cavvies Clown	10-12-0	G. Bradley	10/1
5th – Pegwell Bay	9-12-0	B. Powell	20/1
6th – Maid Of Money	8-11-9	A. Powell	25/1
7th – Yahoo	9-12-0	T. Morgan	40/1
8th – Bonanza Boy	9-12-0	P. Scudamore	15/2
Fell – Ten Of Spades	10-12-0	K. Mooney	20/1
Fell – Kildimo	10-12-0	J. Frost	50/1
Pulled Up – Nick The Brief	8-12-0	M. Lynch	10/1
Pulled Up – The Bakewell Boy	8-12-0	S. Smith-Eccles	200/1

15 March 1990
Going – Good to Firm
Winner – £67,003. 40
Time – 6mins 30. 90secs
12 Ran

Norton's Coin	Chestnut gelding by Mount Cassino – Grove Chance
Toby Tobias	Bay gelding by Furry Glen – Aurora Lady
Desert Orchid	Grey gelding by Grey Mirage – Flower Child

Winner bred by G.P. Thomas
Winner trained by S.G. Griffiths at Natgaredig, Dyfed.

OTHER 1990 FESTIVAL RESULTS

Waterford Crystal Sup Nov Hurdle	Forest Sun	J. Frost	7/4
Arkle Challenge Trophy Chase	Comandante	Peter Hobbs	9/2
Waterford Crystal Champion Hurdle	Kribensis	R. Dunwoody	95/40
Waterford Crystal Stayers' Hurdle	Trapper John	C. Swan	15/2
Kim Muir Memorial Handicap Chase	Master Bob	Mr J. Berry	20/1
Cheltenham Grand Annual Chase	Katabatic	H. Davies	11/4
Sun Alliance Novices' Hurdle	Regal Ambition	P. Scudamore	3/1
Queen Mother Champion Chase	Barnbrook Again	H. Davies	11/10
Coral Golden Hurdle Final	Henry Mann	A. Mulholland	20/1
Sun Alliance Chase	Garrison Savannah	B. De Haan	12/1
National Hunt Chase	Topsham Bay	Mr P. Hacking	40/1
Mildmay Of Flete Handicap Chase	New Halen	E. Tierney	66/1
Daily Express Triumph Hurdle	Rare Holiday	B. Sheridan	25/1
Christies Foxhunter Chase Ch Cup	Call Collect	Mr R. Martin	7/4
Ritz Club National Hunt Hcap Chase	Bigsun	R. Dunwoody	15/2
Cathcart Challenge Cup Chase	Brown Windsor	J. White	13/8
County Handicap Hurdle	Moody Man	Peter Hobbs	9/1

Leopardstown. It was after the latter contest that Upson was advised, by none other than Vincent O'Brien, to tackle the Gold Cup this time around.

With Ladbrokes bracing themselves for a £2million pay-out if Desert Orchid should win, the grey set off in the lead and hurtled directly in to a blistering gallop. His stablemate Cavvies Clown, who now had a reputation as a troublesome individual, lost ten lengths at the start through reluctance, despite the urgings of his trainer David Elsworth.

Early on, it was Kildimo that sparred with Dessie for the lead, but soon it was Fulke Walwyn's injury-plagued runner Ten Of Spades that went up to almost fight the grey for supremacy.

As the field passed the stands having completed a circuit, jockey Martin Lynch pulled-up Nick The Brief, who had bitterly disliked the ground and the electric pace.

As Desert Orchid and Ten Of Spades continued to throw more coal on an already scorching fire, Kildimo became a casualty at the fifteenth as he began to feel the strain, but two horses that were biding their time cosily behind the leaders were Jenny Pitman's progressive youngster Toby Tobias and the 100/1 outsider Norton's Coin.

Ten Of Spades had held a two-length lead at one point on the second circuit, but coming down the hill for the final time, and with Bonanza Boy, Yahoo and the Mackeson Gold Cup winner Pegwell Bay already beaten off, he too began to tire; in fact, he made such a hash of the second last that he fell to the turf, although his jockey Kevin Mooney reported that the horse had broken down.

Now there were only three horses left in contention. Desert Orchid, Norton's Coin and Toby Tobias had been

Norton's Coin and Toby Tobias (11) battle out the finish of the Gold
Cup. Desert Orchid is back in third.

Sirrell Griffiths meets the Queen Mother after his 100/1 outsider
Norton's Coin had shocked the Gold Cup field.

inseparable at the penultimate fence, but as the vast crowd
looked on, it was the grey hero Dessie that was the first to
weaken as they approached the last.

Norton's Coin under Graham McCourt and Toby Tobias
under Jenny's son Mark then settled down to battle to the
line. It was a gripping fight, but ultimately, the huge outsider
unbelievably got his head in front in the last fifty yards to
win in front of a stunned audience. Ironically, Toby Tobias
had kicked Norton's Coin before the start of the race, and the
winner was found to be lame afterwards, a true indication of
a brave horse with unbelievable courage. Desert Orchid had
run his heart out again, but came home four lengths adrift of
the principals, while the infuriating Cavvies Clown stormed
home to take fourth, despite the considerable advantage he
had handed the field at the start.

Norton's Coin became the longest priced winner in Gold
Cup history, with Gay Donald in 1955 and L'Escargot in

1970 the nearest rivals at 33/1. But the result was no fluke:
the horse had been runner-up in the Cathcart Chase at the
1989 Festival and his victory here had taken 4.4 seconds off
Dawn Run's 1986 record time.

The proud man responsible for Norton's Coin was cattle
farmer and permit holder Sirrell Griffiths. He ran a tiny yard
with just three horses at his Herefordshire farm near
Carmarthen and, remarkably, had milked seventy cows at
4 a.m. on the morning of his horse's glory day. Originally,
Norton's Coin was to be aimed at another bid for the
Cathcart, but on discovering his horse's ineligibility, then
finding out the Mildmay Of Flete deadline had been missed,
Griffiths decided to let Norton's Coin go for gold. In
hindsight, the entry mishaps were the best mistakes Griffiths
would ever make, for he could now say he had trained the
winner of the Cheltenham Gold Cup. Shock? Certainly.
Deserving? Totally.

1991

GARRISON SAVANNAH

All Cheltenham Festivals have quality horses in abundance – after all, it is the most important and prestigious National Hunt Festival of the year. But the 1991 Festival seemed to go one step further. There were simply countless horses with star quality at every turn, including dozens that would win big races over the next few years. One need not look any further than the Gold Cup runners for proof of this. The fourteen-strong field included no less than five past, present or future winners of chasing's Blue Riband, plus a former Champion Hurdler and a future Grand National winner, as well as winners of numerous important handicap races.

In Tuesday's Champion Hurdle, the absence of the defending champion Kribensis presented the Irish with a decent chance of landing the race for the first time since Dawn Run in 1984. The progressive, Willie Fennin-trained Athy Spirit and the hugely backed The Illiad were both strongly fancied, but the Irish drought in this race was to continue – indeed it would not be until the start of an amazing trilogy in seven years time that they would finally be able to celebrate – and it was Morley Street that gave his trainer Toby Balding a second win in three years in the race, following Beech Road

in 1989. Morley Street was ridden by Jimmy Frost, who had won the Grand National for Balding aboard Little Polveir two years earlier. The 1991 Champion Hurdle was a race that, in time, would produce some very good chasers through the likes of Deep Sensation, Bradbury Star and Black Humour.

The Arkle Chase featured three unbeaten novices that had won five chases each during the season: Remittance Man, Uncle Ernie and Last O' The Bunch. In the end, it was Remittance Man that demonstrated sheer class under Richard Dunwoody to win. Trainer Nicky Henderson went on to describe Remittance Man as the most exciting horse he had ever trained.

Jockey Simon McNeill was a proud man after Wednesday's Queen Mother Champion Chase, following a fine win aboard Katabatic. McNeill, at thirty-five years of age, was having his first success at the Festival and it arrived in fine

A Grand National in their near future, Nigel Hawke and Seagram first claimed the Ritz Club Chase.

above: The superb Remittance Man (12)
bides his time in the Arkle Chase.

below: Katabatic (far side) leads Waterloo
Boy in a gripping Queen Mother
Champion Chase.

style as Katabatic jumped the last level with Waterloo Boy
and Young Snugfit, before scorching up the hill to win by
seven lengths.

Despite winning an incredible and record-breaking
fourth King George VI Chase at Kempton, the now almost
pure white Desert Orchid was twelve years old, and there
had been signs during the season that the horse may have
lost a shade of ability. In view of this, it was the 1988
Champion Hurdle winner Celtic Shot that began the Gold
Cup as favourite. Trained by Charlie Brooks, Celtic Shot had
been matched against high-class chasers from an early age
and had nearly run in the Gold Cup the year before. His
only defeat from five runs in the current season had come in

125

The beautiful and blinkered Garrison Savannah before his finest hour.

the King George, but impressive wins at Wetherby and Haydock had seen the horse escalate to the top of the betting market.

The Cheltenham ground had turned good for Gold Cup day, conditions that seemed likely to be against the soft ground horses such as Nick The Brief, the gambled-on Welsh National winner Cool Ground and the intriguing Gordon Richards-trained pair, Twin Oaks and Carrick Hill Lad. The duo had been in sparkling form during the season. Twin Oaks had missed most of the previous two seasons with leg trouble, but had put together a string of fine wins at Haydock – five on the trot – this time around, while his stablemate Carrick Hill Lad, a superb jumper, had only been defeated once in the campaign, when giving weight away to Cool Ground in the Welsh National.

Among those that figured to appreciate the better ground were a future Grand National winner, the giant Party Politics, the front-running Hennessy Gold Cup winner Arctic Call, the young French hope The Fellow, and the 1990 SunAlliance Chase winner Garrison Savannah. The latter had only run once all season for trainer Jenny Pitman due to a shoulder injury and was ridden in the race by the trainer's son Mark, who had been second on Toby Tobias in 1990.

As the horses jumped off for what promised to be an extremely competitive renewal of the race, it was Desert Orchid that quickly went in to a lead. Celtic Shot tried to go with him, but clearly he did not enjoy being taken on for supremacy, so his jockey, Peter Scudamore, decided to drop him back and it was Arctic Call that then raced up at the second fence to take command.

By the sixth fence, the veteran Kildimo and the other French raider Martin D'Or had become detached from the main group, while Garrison Savannah and the sizeable Twin Oaks took much closer order. Celtic Shot was still not enjoying himself and dropped further back.

Arctic Call was always a horse that was inclined to make an error. At the eleventh, he made a monumental one, crashing through the fence, and, with his frame of mind rattled, he too began to fade away.

On the second circuit, it was Desert Orchid that again took over, while at last Celtic Shot began a positive move, being encouraged via the inside rail by Scudamore, tracked closely by the sure-staying Cool Ground.

Nick The Brief and the impressive Carrick Hill Lad began to make ominous moves going up the hill, while The Fellow, despite an awkward jump at the fifteenth, was travelling dangerously for Polish-born jockey Adam Kondrat. Defending champion Norton's Coin was an unlucky faller, having been unseated at the seventeenth.

The picture of the race began to change dramatically at the third last, as a number of the leading contenders began to drop away. With Desert Orchid struggling, Celtic Shot, who had temporarily held the lead moments before, faded alarmingly, while the bitterly unlucky Carrick Hill Lad went lame having jumped the fence and jockey Mark Dwyer was forced to pull up the horse when he looked sure to play a big part in the finish.

It was now Garrison Savannah that led and Pitman sent him surging on over the final two fences, getting a huge jump out of the horse at the last to gain a four-length advantage over the chasing Kondrat on The Fellow.

Going up the finishing hill, Garrison Savannah suddenly began to tire as The Fellow chased him furiously. Images of his father Richard being caught close to home on Pendil by The Dikler in the 1973 Gold Cup must have been patrolling through Mark's mind (along with his own narrow defeat aboard Toby Tobias twelve months previously) and as the

1991 TOTE GOLD CUP RESULT

FATE – HORSE	AGE/WEIGHT	JOCKEY	ODDS
1st – GARRISON SAVANNAH	8-12-0	M. PITMAN	16/1
2nd – THE FELLOW	6-12-0	A. KONDRAT	28/1
3rd – DESERT ORCHID	12-12-0	R. DUNWOODY	4/1
4th – Cool Ground	9-12-0	L. Harvey	7/1
5th – Kildimo	11-12-0	R. Stronge	66/1
6th – Nick The Brief	9-12-0	R. Supple	12/1
7th – Celtic Shot	9-12-0	P. Scudamore	5/2*
8th – Yahoo	10-12-0	N. Williamson	100/1
Fell – Norton's Coin	10-12-0	G. McCourt	16/1
Pulled Up – Carrick Hill Lad	8-12-0	M. Dwyer	11/1
Pulled Up – Twin Oaks	11-12-0	N. Doughty	11/1
Pulled Up – Arctic Call	8-12-0	J. Osborne	10/1
Pulled Up – Party Politics	7-12-0	A. Adams	33/1
Pulled Up – Martin D'Or	7-12-0	J-M. Joly	250/1

14 March 1991
Going – Good
Winner – £98,578
Time – 6mins 50secs
14 Ran

Garrison Savannah	Bay gelding by Random Shot – Merry Coin
The Fellow	Bay gelding by Italic – L'oranaise
Desert Orchid	Grey gelding by Grey Mirage – Flower Child

Winner bred by John McDowell
Winner trained by Mrs J. Pitman at Upper Lambourn, Berks.

OTHER 1991 FESTIVAL RESULTS

Race	Horse	Jockey	Odds
Trafalgar House Sup Nov Hurdle	Destriero	P. McWilliams	6/1
Waterford Castle Arkle Chase	Remittance Man	R. Dunwoody	85/40
Smurfit Champion Hurdle	Morley Street	J. Frost	4/1
Bonusprint Stayers' Hurdle	King's Curate	M. Perrett	5/2
Fulke Walwyn – Kim Muir Chase	Omerta	Mr A. Maguire	11/1
Cheltenham Grand Annual Chase	Aldino	J. Osborne	15/2
Sun Alliance Novices' Hurdle	Crystal Spirit	J. Frost	2/1
Queen Mother Champion Chase	Katabatic	S. McNeill	9/1
Coral Golden Hurdle Final	Danny Connors	M. Dwyer	9/1
Sun Alliance Chase	Rolling Ball	P. Scudamore	7/2
National Hunt Chase	Smooth Escort	Mr A.J. Martin	7/1
Mildmay Of Flete Hcap Chase	Foyle Fisherman	E. Murphy	33/1
Daily Express Triumph Hurdle	Oh So Risky	P. Holley	14/1
Christies Foxhunter Chase Ch Cup	Lovely Citizen	Mr W. O'Sullevan	14/1
Ritz Club Nat Hunt Hcap Chase	Seagram	N. Hawke	6/1
Cathcart Challenge Cup Chase	Chatam	P. Scudamore	3/1
County Handicap Hurdle	Winnie The Witch	D. Bridgwater	33/1

two horses plunged for the line, there was nothing to separate them. It had been a fantastic battle, but as they walked back to the winner's enclosure, unaware of the outcome of the race, it was revealed over the loudspeaker system that Garrison Savannah had prevailed by a short-head. Both trainers, Jenny Pitman and the Frenchman, Francois Doumen, were very proud of their brave horses and it was a particularly sweet result for Mark Pitman, having been so close to glory the year before.

The win once again proved the training qualities of Mrs Pitman. Garrison Savannah had been bothered by injury and had been kept wrapped in cotton wool in the run-up to the race, only to display heart, strength and desire to see off the Gallic challenge of The Fellow. Garrison Savannah demonstrated the rich range of depth at Mrs Pitman's Weathercock House stables as, originally, the sidelined trio of Royal Athlete, Toby Tobias and Golden Freeze had been the intended Gold Cup runners.

With a now featherweight-looking 10st 11lbs to carry at Aintree, Garrison Savannah – who Mrs Pitman likened in ability to Corbiere – headed for the Grand National. Despite morning rain turning the Aintree going to a rather

discouraging good-to-soft, Garrison Savannah looked like achieving the near impossible double, jumping brilliantly and leading over the last, only for the Festival's Ritz Club Chase winner Seagram to steal victory in the dying strides. It was, nevertheless, a brave show from the newest Gold Cup winner and his equally brave jockey, Mark Pitman, who hours after Garrison Savannah's finest hour in the Gold Cup had broken his pelvis in a fall in the closing County Hurdle. To be able to recover so soon after such an injury illustrated what a tough, determined jockey he was and Garrison Savannah's efforts at Aintree underlined the wonderful abilities of the 1991 Gold Cup winner.

The Pitman Gold Cup. Trainer/mother Jenny and jockey/son Mark.

1992

COOL GROUND

The 1992 running of the Champion Hurdle promised to be one of the most competitive for years. Morley Street, the defending champion, had been beaten in only one of his four races since his 1991 success and certainly appeared capable of repeating his finest hour, despite a recent training setback that cast a shadow over his general condition. Even without that worry, there was plenty of tough competition for Morley Street and his connections to be concerned about, with the unbeaten Granville Again, the top-class, ex-Flat horse Royal Gait, the 1991 Triumph Hurdle winner Oh So Risky and the 1990 Champion Hurdle winner Kribensis all in the field. In a bruising encounter, it was Royal Gait that survived a steward's enquiry to provide his owner Sheikh Mohamed with his second winner in the race in three years. Royal Gait, who had been disqualified after winning the 1988 Ascot Gold Cup – one of Flat racing's most prestigious events – was trained by James Fanshawe, and the novice got the better of Oh So Risky in a bumpy passage to the winning line.

Nomadic Way, a horse that had been second in the previous two Champion Hurdles, finally had his day in the Stayers' Hurdle when he beat the French-trained Ubu III.

The winning jockey was Jamie Osborne, who had a sensational opening day of the Festival, winning the first two races before taking the Stayers'.

It was to get even better for Osborne on Wednesday in a vintage renewal of the Queen Mother Champion Chase. With two-mile demons Katabatic and Waterloo Boy contributing to an electric pace over the final fences, it was the Osborne-ridden Remittance Man that proved his class by coming home best of all for a thrilling win. Remittance Man goes down as one of the very best two-milers of recent times and one of trainer Nicky Henderson's best ever horses. Remittance Man had won the Arkle Chase the previous year and had been given a terrific ride by Osborne, who completed a stupendous Festival with a win aboard Dusty Miller in Thursday's County Hurdle.

The 1992 SunAlliance Chase was a race that turned out to be an excellent provider of future big race winners. A pulsating finish saw Miinnehoma, owned by comedian

Royal Gait (right), won a roughhouse Champion Hurdle. Oh So Risky (left) was second and Fidway (centre) fourth.

Miinnehoma is led in after winning the Sun Alliance Chase.
In the leather jacket is trainer Martin Pipe.

Freddie Starr, hold off the Josh Gifford-trained Bradbury Star. Despite some injury problems, Miinnehoma would ultimately capture the Grand National in extremely testing conditions in 1994, while Rough Quest, among the beaten horses on this occasion, would win the National in 1996. As for Bradbury Star, he would go on to become a dual winner of the Mackeson Gold Cup as well as a key contributor to races such as the King George.

Although the field for the 1992 Gold Cup was on the small side with just eight runners taking part, the race turned out to be one of the most exciting – and controversial – of all time. Adding to the interest was the presence in the field of a new equine hero, a horse that had developed into one potentially good enough to compare with Mill House, Arkle and Dawn Run. The horse in question was officially rated the best since the 1990 version of the great Desert Orchid and that horse was Carvill's Hill. He had been a revelation since joining Martin Pipe's stable from that of Jim Dreaper, and his

The Gold Cup favourite Carvill's Hill.

previous jumping problems – which had come to light during his Gold Cup debut in 1989 – seemed to have been vanquished. A strongly-built horse in the mould of a classic steeplechaser, Carvill's Hill had destroyed the opposition on his three runs during the season, with the highlights being a thrashing of the imminent Grand National winner Party Politics in the Welsh National and an imperious victory in the Irish Hennessy at Leopardstown. The style of Carvill's Hill's wins had seen him lead from the front, where he was able to get in to a smooth and fluent jumping rhythm. What remained to be seen was if such tactics could be employed to equally good effect in the simmering cauldron of the Gold Cup.

Expected to give the even money favourite Carvill's Hill most to think about were the good ground-loving pair of The Fellow and Toby Tobias. The Fellow had enjoyed a fine season having won a cluster of races, including a King George win that broke the time record for the race, while Toby Tobias had won his last two races for Jenny Pitman, who also saddled the trailblazing outsider Golden Freeze.

Right from the start, it was clear that Carvill's Hill was not going to have the race handed to him and, as the field dashed frantically to the first fence, Golden Freeze was right up with the favourite, almost fighting Pipe's runner for supremacy. It is quite possible that Carvill's Hill was unsettled by these events and he promptly crashed through the first, Peter Scudamore doing well to stay aboard.

Carvill's Hill was having his feathers well and truly ruffled by Golden Freeze and, although the favourite briefly composed himself well enough to take control, the first fence confidence-shaker, together with the incurrence of what later was to be revealed as chest and tendon injuries, meant he made further blunders along the way, allowing Golden Freeze to constantly challenge him for the lead.

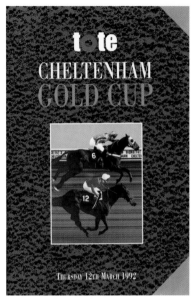

above: 1992 Racecard

left: The Fellow (centre) leads at the last from Docklands Express, but it was to be Cool Ground (far side) that came out on top.

As the second circuit developed, it became clear that Carvill's Hill would not be winning the Gold Cup, as the eventual principals began their challenge for glory. Unluckily, the huge nine-year-old King's Fountain, who had been running a fine race, came down at the fifteenth and as Carvill's Hill gave out his distress signals coming down the hill for the final time, it was The Fellow that appeared to be travelling best of all, with Docklands Express and the Adrian Maguire-ridden Cool Ground just behind.

The Fellow was just in front at the last, but jockey Mark Perrett swiftly sent Docklands Express into the lead on the run in. In hindsight, Docklands Express probably hit the front too soon, as he then proceeded to wander alarmingly to the right, giving The Fellow the edge again on the inside. However, in what was his first ride in the race, Maguire conjured up a spectacular late run from the robust chestnut Cool Ground – who had only been third at the last – to win by a short-head from The Fellow (a gallant runner-up when one considers that his owner, the Marquesa de Moratalla, did not condone the use of a whip on any of her horses, preventing jockey Adam Kondrat from using every weapon in his arsenal). In an ultra-tight finish, Docklands Express was only a length back in third. Carvill's Hill's run had petered out so badly that he staggered home last of five finishers, even eclipsed on the run-in by the lame Toby Tobias.

1992 TOTE GOLD CUP RESULT

FATE – HORSE	AGE/WEIGHT	JOCKEY	ODDS
1st – COOL GROUND	10-12-0	A. MAGUIRE	25/1
2nd – THE FELLOW	7-12-0	A. KONDRAT	7/2
3rd – DOCKLANDS EXPRESS	10-12-0	M. PERRETT	16/1
4th – Toby Tobias	10-12-0	M. Pitman	15/2
5th – Carvill's Hill	10-12-0	P. Scudamore	Evens*
Unseated Rider – King's Fountain	9-12-0	A. Tory	8/1
Pulled Up – Norton's Coin	11-12-0	G. McCourt	33/1
Pulled Up – Golden Freeze	10-12-0	M. Bowlby	150/1

12 March 1992
Going – Good
Winner – £97,028. 75
Time – 6mins 47. 60secs
8 Ran

Cool Ground	Chestnut gelding by Over The River – Merry Spring
The Fellow	Bay gelding by Italic – L'oranaise
Docklands Express	Bay gelding by Roscoe Blake – Southern Moss

Winner bred by N.J. Conmore
Winner trained by G.B. Balding at Whitcombe, Dorset.

OTHER 1992 FESTIVAL RESULTS

Trafalgar House Sup Nov Hurdle	Flown	J. Osborne	13/2
Waterford Castle Arkle Chase	Young Pokey	J. Osborne	4/1
Smurfit Champion Hurdle	Royal Gait	G. McCourt	6/1
Bonusprint Stayers' Hurdle	Nomadic Way	J. Osborne	15/2
Fulke Walwyn – Kim Muir Chase	Tug Of Gold	Mr M. Armytage	11/1
Cheltenham Grand Annual Chase	My Young Man	G. Bradley	7/1
Sun Alliance Novices' Hurdle	Thetford Forest	R. Dunwoody	7/1
Queen Mother Champion Chase	Remittance Man	J. Osborne	Evens
Coral Golden Hurdle Final	My View	J. Titley	33/1
Sun Alliance Chase	Miinnehoma	P. Scudamore	7/2
National Hunt Chase	Keep Talking	Mr M. Armytage	5/2
Mildmay Of Flete Handicap Chase	Elfast	M. Lynch	10/1
Daily Express Triumph Hurdle	Duke Of Monmoth	M. Richards	33/1
Ritz Club National Hunt Hcap Chase	Tipping Tim	C. Llewellyn	20/1
Christies Foxhunter Chase Ch Cup	Rushing Wild	Mr J. Farthing	9/1
County Handicap Hurdle	Dusty Miller	J. Osborne	9/1
Cathcart Challenge Cup Chase	Repeat The Dose	M. Richards	14/1
Tote Festival Bumper Nat Hunt Flat	Montelado	R. Dunwoody	8/1

Understandably, much of the post race attention focused on the dismal performance of Carvill's Hill, an effort that visibly upset his trainer Martin Pipe. There were suggestions that Jenny Pitman had run Golden Freeze simply to rattle the favourite's cage for the benefit of her other runner, Toby Tobias. An enquiry was held and although Mrs Pitman and jockey Michael Bowlby were cleared of all allegations, the whole controversy of the 1992 Gold Cup remains a clouded issue to this day. Poor Carvill's Hill had suffered more than most and, unfortunately, the injuries he had gathered in the race were ultimately enough to end his career. It was a sad outcome for a horse that was undeniably a brilliant, if flawed, machine of a chaser. Certainly that was the opinion held by Scudamore, who placed Carvill's Hill at the top of the tree of chasers he had partnered when his excellent riding career came to an end.

It was happy times though for the Cool Ground team and trainer Toby Balding became the first trainer since Fred Winter to register wins in the Gold Cup, Champion Hurdle and Grand National. Indeed, it was the Grand National that was the original principal target for the mudlark Cool Ground and he eventually went on to finish a far from disgraced tenth in the big race at Aintree a few weeks later. But it was this Gold Cup day in 1992 that Cool Ground will forever be remembered. It was the day he proved strongest in an epic battle up the hill, guided home by a young gem by the name of Adrian Maguire.

Adrian Maguire receives some much-appreciated
congratulations after winning the Gold Cup on Cool Ground.

1993

JODAMI

Incredibly, L'Escargot still remained the last horse, way back in 1971, to successfully have defended his Gold Cup crown. Since then, ten horses had tried to retain their titles and all had failed. Could Cool Ground be the horse to break the trend? It seemed particularly unlikely given the state of the ground. On the Monday prior to the Festival, Cheltenham officials were forced to water the course to prevent it from becoming too hard. Even so, the going for this Festival would ride on the fast side, allowing for some scintillating performances and a breathtaking three days.

The meeting got off to a pulsating start as the 1992 Champion Bumper winner Montelado gave the Irish an electric opening by breaking the course record under Charlie Swan in the Supreme Novices' Hurdle. The win signalled the beginning of a fine Festival for Swan – a hugely popular figure who would enjoy countless Festival victories in the future, particularly over hurdles – as he would later capture the Handicap Hurdle Final aboard Fissure Seal, as well as taking two races on Thursday, the Triumph Hurdle aboard Shawiya and the Stayers' Hurdle on Shuil Ar Aghaidh. The four victories were good enough to secure Swan the Festival's top jockey award.

With rising Irish star Soft Day, trained by Arthur Moore, forced to miss the Arkle Chase because of the fast ground, the focus turned on Sybillin, rated by Jimmy Fitzgerald as his best horse since Forgive 'N' Forget. However, the odd-on chance – many people's banker for the meeting – ran disappointingly and finished third behind Travado. Fitzgerald would later claim he was unhappy with a blood test carried out on Sybillin.

The favourite for the Champion Hurdle on this occasion was Flown, a horse that was looking to give his trainer Nicky Henderson a fourth win in the race. Although Flown was a fast ground-lover, the day belonged to the duo of Martin Pipe and Peter Scudamore, as Granville Again made up for an ultimately fruitless bold-show in the 1992 edition, by battling home to beat the outsider Royal Derbi by a length. Pipe – who would later scoop a £50,000 bonus when his Olympian won Wednesday's Coral Cup, having won the Sunderlands Imperial Cup at Sandown the previous Saturday – praised Cheltenham legend Michael Dickinson for his help

The Festival's leading jockey, Charlie Swan.

Peter Scudamore is all smiles after landing the Champion Hurdle aboard Granville Again.

in assisting to correct a problem Granville Again had been hampered by earlier in the season. The disappointing Flown could only finish eighth.

Another disappointing favourite on Tuesday was Esha Ness – fifth behind Strong Beau in the Fulke Walwyn-Kim Muir Chase – and Esha Ness would suffer more cruel luck later in the season, controversially winning the Grand National, only for that particular fiasco to be declared void. However, there was joy for Declan Murphy in Wednesday's Queen Mother Champion Chase, as the rider gained his first Cheltenham win aboard the Josh Gifford-trained Deep Sensation.

Despite the late withdrawals of Bradbury Star, King's Fountain and Another Coral, an extremely competitive field of sixteen took their places in the line-up for Thursday's Gold Cup, with the official going good to firm.

The heavily-backed favourite was The Fellow, a gallant runner-up in each of the last two renewals of the Gold Cup. The French raider's season had again been a fruitful one, just failing to give fellow Gold Cup aspirants Sibton Abbey and Jodami two-stone in the Hennessy at Newbury, before thrashing the useful Pat's Jester to win his second consecutive King George. With Kondrat again in the saddle, the fast ground seemed ideal to make The Fellow's third bid for glory a lucky one.

The Fellow was just one member of an interesting bunch of eight-year-old challengers, a group that also included Jodami, Rushing Wild, Sibton Abbey and Cherrykino. Between 1979 and 1987, the north had dominated the Gold Cup scene, with the likes of Silver Buck and Bregawn, but they had been relatively quiet since. Now the region had a grand representative in Peter Beaumont's bay Jodami, an old-fashioned type of chaser, typical of the sort his likeable trainer admired, and the horse had improved throughout the season – his biggest success coming in the Irish Hennessy at

far left: Beneath the stunning backdrop, Deep Sensation (left) is about to collar Cyphrate and win the Queen Mother Champion Chase.

left: Jodami (nearside) was a fine winner of the Gold Cup, beating Rushing Wild.

Leopardstown. Rushing Wild, a promising ex-hunter, had the benefit of Richard Dunwoody in the saddle after the jockey had switched from the withdrawn Another Coral, while Sibton Abbey – trained by Ferdy Murphy – had provided the shock of the season when winning the Hennessy Gold Cup at odds of 40/1. Then there was Cherrykino, a relative of Arkle and a horse that carried the same yellow and black colours. Trained by Tim Forster, the horse was having only his eighth run over fences, but had won all four of his races during the season. Cherrykino was held in such high regard by his trainer that he was described as being potentially the best horse he had trained.

With the likes of former Gold Cup winners Garrison Savannah and Cool Ground, the season's Welsh National winner Run For Free, and the fast ground-loving Docklands Express all in the field, the winner of this Gold Cup would truly be a worthy champion. It was Rushing Wild that took them along at a steady pace from Run For Free, Sibton Abbey, Docklands Express, Tipping Tim and Jodami.

Adam Kondrat had The Fellow settled towards the rear of the field early on, but the first signs that this was not going to be his day came at the sixth fence, which the horse brushed through the top of. The Fellow promptly made a mess of the seventh, but here a far worse fate befell poor Cherrykino, as the youngster fell fatally, tragically breaking a shoulder.

As the field went out for their second circuit, Jodami was travelling well and was nicely placed in fifth under Mark Dwyer, as Dunwoody and Rushing Wild attempted to up the tempo of the race, with Garrison Savannah too going strongly until he made a costly error at the last ditch.

As Rushing Wild continued to accelerate coming down the hill from the improving Jodami and the now struggling Sibton Abbey, it was clear The Fellow had been caught out and the race now lay between Rushing Wild and Jodami.

The latter had been going very easily indeed and Dwyer could afford to take a pull on his mount going to the last fence. Although Rushing Wild narrowly led over the last, it was only a matter of time before Dwyer unleashed Jodami and when he did, the big-striding bay coasted to a comfortable two-length win from the game Rushing Wild.

1993 TOTE GOLD CUP RESULT

FATE – HORSE	AGE/WEIGHT	JOCKEY	ODDS
1st – JODAMI	8-12-0	M. DWYER	8/1
2nd – RUSHING WILD	8-12-0	R. DUNWOODY	11/1
3rd – ROYAL ATHLETE	10-12-0	B. DE HAAN	66/1
4th – The Fellow	8-12-0	A. Kondrat	5/4*
5th – Sibton Abbey	8-12-0	S. Smith-Eccles	22/1
6th – Docklands Express	11-12-0	J. Osborne	8/1
7th – Garrison Savannah	10-12-0	M. Pitman	25/1
8th – Run For Free	9-12-0	M. Perrett	11/1
9th – Cool Ground	11-12-0	A. Maguire	50/1
10th – Tipping Tim	8-12-0	D. Bridgwater	25/1
11th – Chatam	9-12-0	P. Scudamore	10/1
12th – Topsham Bay	10-12-0	J. Frost	200/1
13th – Cahervillahow	9-12-0	C. Swan	14/1
Fell – Black Humour	9-12-0	G. Bradley	66/1
Fell – Cherrykino	8-12-0	H. Davies	16/1
Pulled Up – Very Very Ordinary	7-12-0	R. Supple	66/1

18 March 11993

Going – Good to Firm

Winner – £99,448

Time – 6mins 34. 60secs

16 Ran

Jodami	Bay gelding by Crash Course – Masterstown Lucy	
Rushing Wild	Bay gelding by Rushmere – Lady Em II	
Royal Athlete	Chestnut gelding by Roselier – Darjoy	

Winner bred by Eamon Phelan
Winner trained by P. Beaumont at Brandsby, Yorks.

OTHER 1993 FESTIVAL RESULTS

Trafalgar House Sup Nov Hurdle	Montelado	C. Swan	5/1
Waterford Castle Arkle Chase	Travado	J. Osborne	5/1
Smurfit Champion Hurdle	Granville Again	P. Scudamore	13/2
Ritz Club National Hunt Hcap Chase	Givus A Buck	P. Holley	11/2
Fulke Walwyn – Kim Muir Chase	Strong Beau	Mr T. Jenks	6/1
Am. Exp. Gold Card Hcap Hurdle F	Fissure Seal	C. Swan	14/1
Sun Alliance Novices' Hurdle	Gaelstrom	C. Llewellyn	16/1
Sun Alliance Chase	Young Hustler	P. Scudamore	9/4
Coral Cup Handicap Hurdle	Olympian	P. Scudamore	4/1
Queen Mother Champion Chase	Deep Sensation	D. Murphy	11/1
National Hunt Chase	Ushers Island	Mr N. Wilson	15/2
Mildmay Of Flete Handicap Chase	Sacre D'Or	G. McCourt	7/1
Guinness Festival Bumper N. H. Flat	Rhythm Section	P. Carberry	16/1
Daily Express Triumph Hurdle	Shawiya	C. Swan	12/1
Bonusprint Stayers' Hurdle	Shuil Ar Aghaidh	C. Swan	20/1
Christies Foxhunter Chase Ch Cup	Double Silk	Mr R. Treloggen	12/1
Cheltenham Grand Annual Chase	Space Fair	A. Maguire	5/1
Cathcart Challenge Cup Chase	Second Schedual	A. Maguire	6/1
Tote County Handicap Hurdle	Thumbs Up	R. Dunwoody	16/1

Royal Athlete, totally unconsidered at 66/1, illustrated what a good horse he was on his day by finishing third for the Jenny Pitman team and earning himself a place at the head of the market for the Grand National at Aintree. The favourite The Fellow eventually filled fourth spot.

It was an extremely impressive performance from Jodami, who had jumped imperiously all the way round and had beaten a strong Gold Cup field. Virtually every horse in the race had won or would win a major chase in their career: Gold Cups, Grand Nationals, Hennessy's, Welsh and Scottish Nationals, Whitbread's and Mackeson's – a fine collection, yet Jodami's performance suggested that here,

finally, was a horse that seemed sure to register multiple wins in the great race, barring injury. He was certainly young enough, with excellent temperament, size and jumping ability, plus the expert touch of a caring trainer.

Peter Beaumont had farmed for twenty-five years and came into training from the point-to-point arena, while proud owner John Yeadon had turned away numerous bids for his star, including one reputed offer of £150,000.

Immediately, the first two home were installed as the top two in the betting for the 1994 race. Sadly, the highly promising Rushing Wild was killed when fracturing a pelvis in the Irish National later that season.

1994

THE FELLOW

In a sense, there was a strange sort of confusion surrounding the likely outcome of the 1994 Cheltenham Gold Cup, so muddling had been the form of most of the leading contenders. Jodami, on paper, still appeared to have the best credentials, but had suffered a topsy-turvy season, while the highly impressive King George winner, Barton Bank, trained by David Nicholson, was not taking part. For those hoping that The Fellow could provide the first French success in the Blue Riband, it was worth noting that although a plethora of horses had won the race at their second attempt, only two – Red Rower in 1945 and Mandarin in 1962 – had suffered defeat in the Gold Cup twice before winning on their third go and only The Dikler had achieved the near impossible by taking the race at the fourth time of asking.

In a relatively weak renewal of the Champion Hurdle on Tuesday, the final outcome proved to be a heart-warming one. The race provided the peak of Herefordshire farmer Richard Price's training career as his charge, the game mare Flakey Dove, came home best of all to beat Oh So Risky and the promising novice Large Action. The victory gave winning jockey Mark Dwyer a real chance of becoming the first

jockey to win both the Champion Hurdle and the Gold Cup in the same year since Fred Winter in 1961, with Jodami still to come in the big one.

An absolutely rapturous reception was reserved for the new star of Ireland, Danoli, after the horse won the SunAlliance Novices' Hurdle on Wednesday. Danoli, the favourite, was coolly ridden by Charlie Swan and the horse would go on to share a romantic relationship with the Irish public for many years to come.

Without a doubt, the most exciting finish at the 1994 Festival (in what was possibly the best ever edition of this particular race) came in the Queen Mother Champion Chase. With three previous winners of the race, Katabatic, Deep Sensation and the unbeaten Remittance Man – who had made a most pleasing comeback from injury – plus the 1993 Arkle hero Travado and young-gun Viking Flagship all in the field, it was always going to be an ultra-hot renewal.

Flakey Dove (nearside) gets the better of the novice Large Action in the Champion Hurdle.

Danoli and Charlie Swan return triumphant from the Sun
Alliance Novices' Hurdle.

The cap-less Adrian Maguire on Viking Flagship would narrowly edge out Travado (left) and Deep Sensation in a thrilling Queen Mother Champion Chase.

The big shock of the race happened when Remittance Man ruined his fantastic record with a surprising fall and it was left to Deep Sensation, Travado and Viking Flagship to endure a three-way fight up the finishing hill, with the capless Adrian Maguire winning the day on the supremely tough Viking Flagship. With Richard Dunwoody absent from the Festival because of a ban picked up for causing intentional interference to Maguire – his big rival for the season's leading jockey title – this Festival was Maguire's big chance to prove to the racing world he deserved to be recognised as the number one rider. There is probably no race that better demonstrates what a strong jockey Maguire was and although he was helped by a magnificent horse in Viking Flagship, Maguire's strength and determination were there for all to see, just as they had been when Cool Ground triumphed in the 1992 Gold Cup. Unfortunately, Maguire would ultimately finish a narrow second in the season's jockey title race, while future Festivals were ruined for the humble Irishman through cruel injuries and personal circumstances.

The most exciting grey horse since Desert Orchid put his blossoming reputation on the line later on Wednesday, as the Gordon Richards-trained One Man took on a highly talented SunAlliance Chase field that included a horse that trainer Paul Nicholls regarded as a future Gold Cup winner in See More Indians and a future winner of the Scottish, Welsh and Aintree Nationals in Earth Summit. Sadly for the hoards that followed the athletic One Man, this race was to prove an insight into Gold Cups of the future, as he folded badly at the business end of the race and had virtually stopped at the second last, while the victory went to the honest and game Monsieur Le Cure, giving jockey Peter Niven his first Festival success.

While victories for Christmas Gorse – a giant half-brother to the 1992 Grand National winner Party Politics – in the four-mile National Hunt Chase and the talented hunter-chaser Double Silk in the Foxhunters' provided reasons to think about future Grand Nationals, naturally it was the Gold Cup that once again was the major talking point of the Festival.

Jodami was favourite – and rightly so on his 1993 showing – but the horse had thrown in a couple of howlers during the season, although another win in the Irish Hennessy had given his supporters plenty of encouragement and the horse certainly looked a picture in the pre-race paddock. After one of his poor runs at Chepstow earlier in the season, Peter Beaumont had shut down his operation and did not re-open until two months later. Also against Jodami was the fact that no English-trained horse had won consecutive Gold Cups since the legendary Golden Miller in 1933.

The horse that Barton Bank had narrowly defeated in the season's King George, Bradbury Star, took his place in the line-up for trainer Josh Gifford. Although there was a worry about his stamina, no horse loved Cheltenham more than Bradbury Star, with Declan Murphy's mount having won seven times at the track.

Interesting newcomers to the race included the previous two winners of the SunAlliance Chase, the injury-plagued Miinnehoma and the bonny, front-running chestnut Young Hustler. As well as those two, Ireland was represented by the talented giant Flashing Steel, while trainer Peter Cheesborough saddled the race's dark horse in Blazing Walker, a horse that had looked a serious proposition until injury had restricted him to just three runs in two years.

As for The Fellow, trainer Francois Doumen had equipped him with blinkers after the horse had finished only third in both the King George and the Racing Post Chase at Kempton. Although still only a nine-year-old, there was a slight feeling that The Fellow may have missed out on his chance of Cheltenham glory.

It was Young Hustler and Topsham Bay that disputed the lead over the first fence until Run For Free took control a fence later. The first circuit as a whole played out in a cagey manner, with Jodami and The Fellow both travelling nicely just behind the leaders.

When Young Hustler jumped into the lead at the sixteenth, only the struggling pair of Garrison Savannah and Blazing Walker were out of contention, as a whole host of horses, including The Fellow, Run For Free, Jodami, Deep Bramble and Bradbury Star began to make bids for glory. In total, twelve horses still had something of a chance at the fourth last fence.

The chestnut Deep Bramble proceeded to make a couple of untimely errors, while Miinnehoma and the veteran Docklands Express both began to feel the noose tightening around their necks, and once Run For Free began to go backwards at the second last, those in contention were reduced to four – the main players being Young Hustler, The Fellow, Jodami and Bradbury Star.

1994 TOTE GOLD CUP RESULT

FATE – HORSE	AGE/WEIGHT	JOCKEY	ODDS
1st – THE FELLOW	9-12-0	A. KONDRAT	7/1
2nd – JODAMI	9-12-0	M. DWYER	6/4*
3rd – YOUNG HUSTLER	7-12-0	C. LLEWELLYN	20/1
4th – Flashing Steel	9-12-0	J. Osborne	10/1
5th – Bradbury Star	9-12-0	D. Murphy	5/1
6th – Docklands Express	12-12-0	D. Gallagher	14/1
7th – Miinnehoma	11-12-0	A. Maguire	11/1
8th – Deep Bramble	7-12-0	P. Niven	20/1
9th – Run For Free	10-12-0	M. Perrett	11/1
10th – Topsham Bay	11-12-0	J. Frost	100/1
11th – Chatam	10-12-0	G. McCourt	33/1
Unseated Rider – Ebony Jane	9-11-9	C. Swan	100/1
Pulled Up – Garrison Savannah	11-12-0	G. Bradley	50/1
Pulled Up – Blazing Walker	10-12-0	C. Grant	20/1
Pulled Up – Capability Brown	7-12-0	M.A. Fitzgerald	200/1

17 March 1994
Going – Good (Good to Soft in places)
Winner – £118,770
Time – 6mins 40. 70secs
15 Ran

The Fellow	Bay gelding by Italic – L'Oranaise
Jodami	Bay gelding by Crash Course – Masterstown Lucy
Young Hustler	Chestnut gelding by Import – Davett

Winner bred by Mlle A.M. Gaulin
Winner trained by F. Doumen in France.

OTHER 1994 FESTIVAL RESULTS

Citroen Supreme Novices' Hurdle	Arctic Kinsman	C. Llewellyn	50/1
Guinness Arkle Ch Trophy Chase	Nakir	J. Osborne	9/1
Smurfit Champion Hurdle	Flakey Dove	M. Dwyer	9/1
Ritz Club National Hunt Hcap Chase	Antonin	J. Burke	4/1
Fulke Walwyn – Kim Muir Chase	Fighting Words	Mr T. McCarthy	9/2
Hamlet Cig. G Card Hcap Hur Final	Tindari	P. Williams	20/1
Sun Alliance Novices' Hurdle	Danoli	C. Swan	7/4
Queen Mother Champion Chase	Viking Flagship	A. Maguire	4/1
Coral Cup Handicap Hurdle	Time For A Run	C. Swan	11/1
Sun Alliance Chase	Monsieur Le Cure	P. Niven	15/2
National Hunt Chase	Christmas Gorse	Mr M. Armytage	14/1
Mildmay Of Flete Handicap Chase	Elfast	G. McCourt	8/1
Bromsgrove Ind Festival Bumper	Mucklemeg	C. Swan	7/2
Daily Express Triumph Hurdle	Mysilv	A. Maguire	2/1
Bonusprint Stayers' Hurdle	Balasani	M. Perrett	9/2
Christies Foxhunter Chase Ch Cup	Double Silk	Mr R. Treloggen	2/5
Cheltenham Grand Annual Chase	Snitton Lane	D. Bridgwater	33/1
Cathcart Challenge Cup Chase	Raymylette	M.A. Fitzgerald	7/4
County Handicap Hurdle	Dizzy	A. Dobbin	12/1

As the quartet bounded down to the final flight, it was obvious that the stamina doubts that had tarred Bradbury Star were starting to come to fruition, and as he weakened, the crowd began to roar as the three remaining challengers met the fence in a line.

Though Young Hustler was merely hanging on for dear life, Jodami had looked to be going in fine style, but when he brushed the fence, the advantage fell to the French raider, and The Fellow was quickly away up the hill. With memories of two short-head defeats no doubt in his mind, Adam Kondrat kept The Fellow going, and although Jodami battled back bravely, this was to be, at last, The Fellow's day. To a mighty cheer, he passed the post as the winner by a length-and-a-half from Jodami, with Young Hustler third.

There was a real feeling of potential fulfilled following The Fellow's superb effort. He had been so close to winning before and his jockey had come in for, at times, unfair criticism. Trainer Doumen had never lost faith in his horse's ability to win a Gold Cup, and now The Fellow had become the first Gallic winner of the great race. Doumen also singled out praise for Kondrat following the jockey's impressive display on this occasion.

The Fellow went on to run in the Grand National later in the season, but the prevailing heavy ground put pay to any

chance he may have had of winning. In fact, it was a major surprise he raced at all. In the event, The Fellow capsized at the second Canal Turn, and Doumen could only watch as Miinnehoma slogged home victorious.

The Fellow would run in one more King George before being retired by his owner, the Marquesa de Moratalla. He left the game having finally captured the Blue Riband he had threatened to win for so many years. Perhaps it was the sprig of shamrock he wore on that St Patrick's Day in 1994 that ultimately tipped the balance in his favour!

1995

MASTER OATS

The elusive double of the Champion Hurdle and the Gold Cup had not been achieved in the same year by the same trainer/jockey combination since 1950. It is fair to say that the combination that finally ended the drought had a couple of extremely talented racehorses to remedy the cause.

Tuesday's Champion Hurdle had been robbed of the presence of the imposing grey Relkeel on the eve of the Festival because of tendon trouble. It was a further blow to Relkeel's trainer, David Nicholson, who had already been denied the services of stable jockey Adrian Maguire, following the sad death of the Irishman's mother. However, carrying the hopes of Ireland was the 'People's Horse', Danoli, who took his place in the line-up together with another heralded Irish raider, Dermot Weld's smart Fortune And Fame. Hotly fancied was the 1994 third, the ever-improving Large Action, but all these challengers were to be eclipsed by the emergence of a new star in the form of the Kim Bailey-trained, ex-Flat horse Alderbrook. Locked in battle at the last flight with Large Action, Alderbrook delivered a turn of foot that had not been seen in the race for a number of years, as he shot clear on the run-in under

Norman Williamson to win from Large Action and Danoli. It was a first Festival winner for Bailey, and general opinion was that Alderbrook – having just his third race over hurdles – was one of the best winners of the Champion Hurdle in recent years, and could possibly go on to run up a sequence in the race, so devastatingly had he burst onto the scene.

In the race before Alderbrook proclaimed himself the new hurdling star, Klairon Davis got the better of Sound Man in a titanic duel for the Arkle Chase. Showing great speed and grit under Francis Woods, the winner showed he had what it took to be seriously considered for the following season's Queen Mother Champion Chase. The two Irish stars had come well clear of the remaining pack by the last fence, with high profile runners, the flamboyant grey Morceli and the talented-but-erratic Dancing Paddy, failing to shine. Indeed, Morceli had led the field at a hectic pace before crashing out of contention in the back straight.

Klairon Davis (left) and Sound Man fought out a titanic, all-Irish duel for the Arkle Trophy.

Brief Gale (right) sinks the 'new Arkle', Harcon, in the Sun Alliance Chase.

After Viking Flagship had easily won his second consecutive Queen Mother Champion Chase on Wednesday, the focus switched to one of the most hyped horses to emerge from Ireland for a long time. The horse in question was the giant chestnut, Harcon, hailing from the very same box as Arkle in Jim Dreaper's yard. Harcon had certainly been impressive up to this point, but as always, the SunAlliance Chase would prove a huge test for future Gold Cup aspirants. Martin Pipe too believed he had the week's banker in the trailblazing Banjo, and in what turned out to be a blistering, brutally-run race, both Banjo and Harcon held the lead for long periods. However, biding her time behind the big two was the Josh Gifford-trained mare, Brief Gale, and as Banjo faded tamely, Philip Hide aboard Brief Gale was able to pick off the lumbering Harcon to cause an upset. As is so often the case, the hype surrounding Harcon never materialised, and the horse was never the same again after this race, with injuries crippling the rest of his short career.

After future Gold Cup prospect Dorans Pride had scored a memorable victory for the Irish in Thursday's Stayers' Hurdle, the anticipation and excitement grew to eruptive levels as the crowds awaited the running of the 1995 Cheltenham Gold Cup.

Without any shadow of a doubt, Kim Bailey's Master Oats had been the most improved chaser of the season and fully deserved his place at the head of the betting market. In truth, the improvement had begun the season before with a sequence of victories including the Greenalls Gold Cup at Kempton (thrashing the capable Grand National favourite Moorcroft Boy in the process). Master Oats had then himself run in the National and was absolutely cruising when tipping up, along with numerous others, at the thirteenth fence. The current season had seen the nine-year-old go from strength to strength, winning the Rehearsal Chase at Chepstow before making a mockery of the Welsh National field when the race was transferred to Newbury. Master Oats had been available at 40/1 for the Gold Cup prior to his Welsh National win, and these odds were to come tumbling down considerably after the horse's Gold Cup warm up in the Pillar Property Investments Chase at Cheltenham, when he sauntered home from fellow Gold Cup hopefuls Dubacilla and Barton Bank to shoot to the top of the market. The key to Master Oats was the ground, as he was a truly relentless galloper on his favoured soft or heavy surfaces, and although the course had dried up a little come Gold Cup day, the soft going seemed ideal for Master Oats to confirm his position as the season's top chaser.

The opposition to Master Oats was strong, with Jodami, fresh from winning his third Irish Hennessy, most fancied to give the favourite a battle. Even though The Fellow had now retired, Francois Doumen still had two useful challengers to represent him, and although Algan was a very fortunate

Brilliantly guided round by Norman Williamson, Master Oats
eventually slaughtered the Gold Cup field.

sixth and of Nuaffe a fence later, but it was the jumping of the favourite that was the most noticeable aspect of the race. Master Oats had been making niggling mistakes and, at the eleventh, he made one that probably changed the direction of the race.

Merry Gale had been bowling along in front from Monsieur Le Cure, Barton Bank, Miinnehoma and Master Oats, with Dubacilla, Deep Bramble and Algan somewhat detached with a circuit to go. Then came the incident at the eleventh; Master Oats clattered into it, and for a moment it looked as though Williamson may be unseated. But the pair remained together and after jumping the water for a second time, Williamson cleverly realised a change of tactic was needed if Master Oats was going to win. Visibly switching the horse to the wide outside so as to gain a better view of the fences, the change in Master Oats was instant, as he proceeded to jump far more fluently and with increased zest, quickly coming back on the bridle.

Five from home, the inevitable happened for Barton Bank as he crashed out of contention, hampering Monsieur Le Cure, and leaving Merry Gale and Master Oats clear of the struggling Jodami.

At the second last, Master Oats jumped into the lead, and with two fences omitted because of the ground, Williamson saw the chance to kick Master Oats for home on the long run to the last and devastatingly left Merry Gale for dead rounding the final turn, with only Dubacilla plugging on from the back.

Just as he had done in his previous victories, Master Oats continued to gallop on relentlessly, churning his way through his favoured ground and sealing victory with a fine jump at the last, much to the appreciation of the crowd. He passed the post fifteen lengths clear of Dubacilla, with Miinnehoma third and the plucky Merry Gale fourth.

winner of the King George – Barton Bank had the race at his mercy only to fall at the last – the unexposed Val D'Alene was many people's idea of the dark horse of the race, having won the season's Racing Post Chase impressively at Kempton.

Of the remainder, Barton Bank had developed into an unreliable jumper, but Grand National hopeful Deep Bramble, running in his second Gold Cup, had won a pair of useful handicaps including the Mildmay/Cazalet Chase at Sandown, while Pipe's Miinnehoma looked as good as ever following his Grand National win of the year before. Ireland too had a worthy challenger in the form of the front-running Merry Gale, a seven-year-old that trainer Jim Dreaper hoped would atone for the failure of Harcon the day before.

The first circuit of the race was a puzzling affair, and certainly an uncomfortable one for the followers of Master Oats. Blunders caused the departures of Val D'Alene at the

1995 TOTE GOLD CUP RESULT

FATE – HORSE	AGE/WEIGHT	JOCKEY	ODDS
1st – MASTER OATS	9-12-0	N. WILLIAMSON	100/30*
2nd – DUBACILLA	9-11-9	D. GALLAGHER	20/1
3rd – MIINNEHOMA	12-12-0	R. DUNWOODY	9/1
4th – Merry Gale	7-12-0	G. Bradley	10/1
5th – Young Hustler	8-12-0	C. Llewellyn	33/1
6th – Monsieur Le Cure	9-12-0	P. Niven	10/1
7th – Beech Road	13-12-0	A. P. McCoy	100/1
8th – Jodami	10-12-0	M. Dwyer	7/2
9th – Commercial Artist	9-12-0	C.N. Bowens	100/1
Fell – Flashing Steel	10-12-0	J. Osborne	25/1
Fell – Barton Bank	9-12-0	D. Bridgwater	8/1
Unseated Rider – Nuaffe	10-12-0	S.H. O'Donovan	50/1
Unseated Rider – Algan	7-12-0	Philippe Chevalier	16/1
Unseated Rider – Val D'Alene	8-12-0	A. Kondrat	10/1
Pulled Up – Deep Bramble	8-12-0	C. Maude	14/1

16 March 1995
Going – Soft
Winner –£122,540
Time – 6mins 56. 20secs
15 Ran

Master Oats	Chestnut gelding by Oats – Miss Poker Face
Dubacilla	Bay mare by Dubassoff – Just Camilla
Miinnehoma	Bay or brown gelding by Kambalda – Mrs Cairns

Winner bred by R.F. and Mrs Knipe
Winner trained by K.C. Bailey at Upper Lambourn, Berks.

OTHER 1995 FESTIVAL RESULTS

Citroen Supreme Novices' Hurdle	Tourist Attraction	M. Dwyer	25/1
Guinness Arkle Ch Trophy Chase	Klairon Davis	F. Woods	7/2
Smurfit Champion Hurdle	Alderbrook	N. Williamson	11/2
Ritz Club National Hunt Hcap Chase	Rough Quest	M. A. Fitzgerald	16/1
Fulke Walwyn – Kim Muir Chase	Flyer's Nap	Mr P. Henley	11/1
Astec Vodafone G Card Hcap Hur Final	Miracle Man	Peter Hobbs	9/2
Sun Alliance Novices' Hurdle	Putty Road	N. Williamson	7/1
Queen Mother Champion Chase	Viking Flagship	C. Swan	5/2
Coral Cup Handicap Hurdle	Chance Coffey	G.M. O'Neill	11/1
Sun Alliance Chase	Brief Gale	P. Hide	13/2
National Hunt Chase	Front Line	Mr J. Berry	7/1
Mildmay Of Flete Handicap Chase	Kadi	N. Williamson	11/2
Prestige Medical Festival Bumper	Dato Star	M. Dwyer	7/2
Daily Express Triumph Hurdle	Kissair	J. Lower	16/1
Bonusprint Stayers' Hurdle	Dorans Pride	J.P. Broderick	11/4
Christies Foxhunter Chase Ch Cup	Fantus	Miss P. Curling	8/1
Cheltenham Grand Annual Chase	Sound Reveille	G. Bradley	7/1
Cathcart Challenge Cup Chase	Coulton	J. Osborne	11/2
Vincent O'Brien County Hurdle	Home Counties	D.J. Moffatt	14/1

Despite the problems he had encountered on the first circuit, the race was all about the winner, and he had gloriously confirmed himself the top chaser in the land. It was a fine testament to Bailey, as the horse had suffered from broken blood vessels and injury problems early in his career. The Lambourn trainer had successfully pulled off the Champion Hurdle/Gold Cup double, with Norman Williamson the winning jockey both times.

After much debate, Master Oats eventually lined up for the Grand National three weeks later with the burden of top weight. The ground though had gone against him on this occasion, and despite travelling beautifully – again on the wide outside – all the way to the last fence, never making a trace of a jumping error, the horse was eventually overhauled on the run-in and finished a gallant seventh, as former Gold Cup third Royal Athlete enjoyed his moment in the sun. Even in defeat, Master Oats came away with credit in a season when he ruled as the number one chaser.

1996

IMPERIAL CALL

Just ten days before he was due to defend his Cheltenham Gold Cup crown, the brilliant 1995 winner Master Oats was forced out of the upcoming renewal after aggravating a troublesome leg injury during a workout. In truth, Master Oats had always been a particularly fragile individual and was trained with the optimum caution at Kim Bailey's Lambourn yard. Even if he had made the Gold Cup line-up on this occasion, Master Oats' form during the season suggested he would have struggled to recapture his title, with a disappointing reappearance at Chepstow preceding placed efforts in both the King George and Irish Hennessy. It was time for a new batch of chasers to make their mark on the Gold Cup picture.

The jockey who partnered Master Oats to his success in 1995, Norman Williamson, would also be missing from action this time around. The previous Festival's leading rider had suffered a broken leg and a dislocated shoulder during the season, and had then dislocated his shoulder again during a schooling session, ruling him out of Cheltenham. As well as Williamson's woes, Adrian Maguire would be missing having broken a collarbone in a recent incident at Newbury.

One jockey that seemed spoiled for choice heading in to Tuesday's Champion Hurdle was Jamie Osborne. With sunshine enriching the Cheltenham turf on Monday, Osborne elected to ride the good ground-loving, former Triumph Hurdle winner Mysilv, in favour of Collier Bay, who definitely required soft ground to be at his best. However, by the time Tuesday's race rolled around, the heavens had opened, leaving the ground much in the favour of Collier Bay and the defending champion Alderbrook, the latter starting a hot odds-on favourite. Also in the field, miraculously, was Danoli – a horse that had, if anything, increased his popularity with the Irish after recovering from a near fatal injury to a fetlock at Aintree the previous year. But on this day, neither he nor any of the others could overcome the brilliant ride Graham Bradley gave Collier Bay. Bradley, knowing his horse loved the conditions and

Collier Bay found conditions ideal in the Champion Hurdle.

The Arkle winner Ventana Canyon.

that Alderbrook would be held up under Richard Dunwoody, shot clear from the second last, and the deficit proved too great for Alderbrook to pull back. Dunwoody's ride on the favourite came in for much scrutiny, but Bradley had been at his tactical best and rewarded trainer Jim Old with one of the finest moments of his career. One trainer out of luck in the race though was Martin Pipe, whose runner Mack The Knife, owned by Darren Mercer, broke down fatally towards the end of the race. It had developed into a particularly sad day for Pipe and Mercer, as earlier they had lost their star mare Draborgie to a freak injury on the flat in the early stages of the Arkle Chase.

The Arkle Chase – for totally contrasting reasons – was typical of the pattern at the 1996 Festival. Firstly, the race was won by an Irish raider in the shape of Ventana Canyon, commencing a bumper crop of winners for the Emerald Isle that would total a grand haul of seven by the time the dust had settled on Thursday. The second trend though was more disturbing, as Draborgie's death was just one of a sickening ten that would occur over the three days, with five coming in bewildering fashion on the flat.

There was no doubt that the star two-mile chaser of the season had been the brilliant, Edward O'Grady-trained Sound Man, and despite rumours surrounding his wellbeing, the horse was strongly fancied to capture Wednesday's Queen Mother Champion Chase. However, just as in the previous year's Arkle Chase, Sound Man would have to give way to the electrifying finishing drive of Klairon Davis and jockey Francis Woods, who timed their run to perfection. The dual winner Viking Flagship once again ran a brave race to be second.

The highly impressive and unbeaten novice chaser, the flashy, bold chestnut Mr Mulligan, was the hot favourite for the SunAlliance Chase. The horse possessed magnificent power, but after a terrible mistake at the first fence the huge gelding simply could not dominate as he had in his previous races, and consequently went down to the Jenny Pitman-trained Nathen Lad. Despite only finishing second, Mr Mulligan displayed a vast amount of potential and his trainer Noel Chance indicated that races such as the King George and Gold Cup would be on the menu for his charge the following season.

When Desert Orchid dominated the jumping scene in the late 1980s and early '90s, it was tough to imagine a more popular or magnetic grey flyer to ever take his place. However, come 1996, the Gordon Richards-trained One Man was certainly at the forefront of the race to be the next grey wonder. Although not as big or headstrong as Dessie, One Man was every bit as athletic, and certainly harboured the potential to join the greats of the chasing game. One Man had dominated the chasing season, winning all three of his races – including the King George, which had been rerouted to Sandown. In fact, the handsome grey had won ten of his eleven completed chases, with the only jumping failure arriving through a spectacular crashing fall in the previous season's Racing Post Chase at Kempton. The pre-race hype had One Man virtually home and dry as the winner, such had become his lofty status, but the shrewd judges among the bubbling Festival crowd had not forgotten One Man's dismal failure on his last visit to Cheltenham, when he had folded badly in the closing stages of the 1994 SunAlliance Chase and his stamina remained a worry for his vast army of supporters.

With the likes of the Hennessy winner Couldn't Be Better, the swift Mackeson Gold Cup winner Dublin Flyer and the Racing Post Chase winner Rough Quest in the field, the opposition to One Man was strong, but many believed this would be the year Ireland recaptured the Blue Riband. It had

Soon to be Kings – Imperial Call and
Conor O'Dwyer before the Gold Cup.

A great Festival for the Irish; Imperial Call is swamped after his Gold Cup win.

been ten years since Dawn Run had brought the house down with her emotional triumph, yet no Irish runner had even made the frame since. Here though, they finally had a candidate in the shape of the rapidly improving seven-year-old, Imperial Call, that they could believe in. Imperial Call had been steadily brought along by trainer Fergie Sutherland before demonstrating in emphatic style what a horse he may become by winning the Irish Hennessy at Leopardstown in blistering fashion from Master Oats and Monsieur Le Cure. Partnering the youngster was Conor O'Dwyer, who had got the ride at Leopardstown after Charlie Swan and Richard Dunwoody had opted for other horses.

It was Dublin Flyer that set the early gallop, as expected, followed by Young Hustler, Couldn't Be Better, Barton Bank and Monsieur Le Cure, with One Man settled patiently at the rear by Dunwoody.

Tragedy struck at the sixth fence when Monsieur Le Cure crashed straight into the fence and was dead before he touched the ground. It was a bitter end for a fine horse whose greatest moment had come on the course in 1994, when he won the SunAlliance Chase.

As the race progressed under a dark cloud, mistakes cost Dublin Flyer his place in the lead and at the top of the hill for the final time, Couldn't Be Better, Imperial Call and One Man had broken clear of Rough Quest.

Although Couldn't Be Better was soon to crack, One Man appeared full of running as he and Imperial Call came to the second last, but almost as if his power had been switched off, One Man began to curl up like a shocked hedgehog as the Irish runner powered on.

With only Rough Quest now trying in vain to catch him, Imperial Call flew the last and surged up the hill a very impressive four-length winner. Rough Quest, who would go on to win the Grand National a few weeks later, had run a fine race in second with Couldn't Be Better third. Obviously, the major disappointment of the race had been One Man, and although Gordon Richards was bemused by the horse's performance, time would show that the grey simply did not stay the Gold Cup trip against top opposition – although he would have his day in the sun eventually.

The reception that awaited Imperial Call in the winner's enclosure was nothing short of riotous, with hoards of Irish rejoicing the coming of a new hero, and rightly so – the horse had won in eyecatching fashion, giving O'Dwyer his first Festival winner.

The victory proved to be the career highlight of Fergie Sutherland, a man that had suffered having part of his leg blown off while serving in the Korean War. Sutherland, from Peebles, Scotland, was always confident that Imperial Call was the horse to end the Irish drought in the race. As a

1996 TOTE GOLD CUP RESULT

FATE – HORSE	AGE/WEIGHT	JOCKEY	ODDS
1st – IMPERIAL CALL	7-12-0	C. O'DWYER	9/2
2nd – ROUGH QUEST	10-12-0	M.A. FITZGERALD	12/1
3rd – COULDN'T BE BETTER	9-12-0	G. BRADLEY	11/1
4th – Barton Bank	10-12-0	A. P. McCoy	16/1
5th – Young Hustler	9-12-0	C. Maude	25/1
6th – One Man	8-12-0	R. Dunwoody	11/8*
7th – King Of The Gales	9-12-0	C. Swan	50/1
Fell – Monsieur Le Cure	10-12-0	J.F. Titley	14/1
Pulled Up – Dublin Flyer	10-12-0	B. Powell	5/1
Pulled Up – Lord Relic	10-12-0	D. Bridgwater	100/1

14 March 1996
Going – Good
Winner – £131,156
Time – 6mins 42. 40secs
10 Ran

Imperial Call	Brown gelding by Callernish – Princess Menelek
Rough Quest	Bay gelding by Crash Course – Our Quest
Couldn't Be Better	Brown gelding by Oats – Belle Bavard

Winner bred by T.A. O'Donnell
Winner trained by F. Sutherland at Killnardish, Co. Cork.

OTHER 1996 FESTIVAL RESULTS

Race	Horse	Jockey	Odds
Citroen Supreme Novices' Hurdle	Indefence	W. Marston	25/1
Guinness Arkle Ch Trophy Chase	Ventana Canyon	R. Dunwoody	7/1
Smurfit Champion Hurdle	Collier Bay	G. Bradley	9/1
Ritz Club National Hunt Hcap Chase	Maamur	A. Thornton	13/2
Fulke Walwyn – Kim Muir Chase	Stop The Waller	Mr K. Whelan	16/1
Hamlet Cig Gold Card Hcap Hur Final	Great Easeby	R. McGrath	7/1
Sun Alliance Novices' Hurdle	Urubande	C. Swan	8/1
Queen Mother Champion Chase	Klairon Davis	F. Woods	9/1
Coral Cup Handicap Hurdle	Trainglot	M. Dwyer	11/2
Sun Alliance Chase	Nathen Lad	W. Marston	7/1
National Hunt Chase	Loving Around	Mr P. Fenton	10/1
Mildmay Of Flete Handicap Chase	Old Bridge	G. Crone	14/1
B. I. Group Festival Bumper	Wither Or Which	Mr W. Mullins	11/4
Daily Express Triumph Hurdle	Paddy's Return	R. Dunwoody	10/1
Bonusprint Stayers' Hurdle	Cyborgo	D. Bridgwater	8/1
Christies Foxhunter Chase Ch Cup	Elegant Lord	Mr E. Bolger	3/1
Cheltenham Grand Annual Chase	Kibreet	A. P. McCoy	7/1
Cathcart Challenge Cup Chase	Challenger Du Luc	D. Bridgwater	10/1
Vincent O'Brien County Hurdle	Star Rage	D. Gallagher	14/1

seven-year-old, Imperial Call looked to have the chasing world at his mercy and appeared set for at least one more Gold Cup victory. Indeed, he was promptly given odds of 7/2 for a repeat win in 1997. However, similar to previous impressive winners of his age – such as Captain Christy, Midnight Court and Little Owl – things would never quite go his way again. On this occasion though, Imperial Call was not only the toast of Cheltenham, but of a whole nation.

Fergie Sutherland (right) discusses Imperial Call's Gold Cup win with the Queen Mother.

1997

MR MULLIGAN

There have been some magnificent National Hunt jockeys in recent times. The stylish John Francome, the passionate Peter Scudamore and the wonderfully natural Richard Dunwoody are three, among a countless list of gifted horseman that come to mind. However, in the second half of the 1990s emerged a talent that, to this day, continues to build upon his peerless reputation at an unfathomable rate. He is none other than Anthony 'AP' McCoy. An unrivalled will to win combined with masterful strength in the saddle, not to mention a rich bounty of top-class horses from the yard of Martin Pipe, are the traits that currently set McCoy apart from his contemporaries, yet at the time of the 1997 Cheltenham Festival, McCoy had recorded just one previous Festival winner, guiding home Kibreet to win the 1996 Grand Annual Chase. 1997, however, would be 'McCoy's Festival'.

Unbeaten in five novice chases, the bouncy little chestnut Mulligan was, by general consensus, the Festival banker in Tuesday's Arkle Chase. Mulligan was viewed as an eventual successor to his trainer David Nicholson's top two-mile chaser Viking Flagship, but the Festival was to prove the first step backwards in Mulligan's promising career. The horse crashed out of contention four fences from home and it was left to a pair of quirky individuals in Or Royal and Squire Silk to battle out the finish. Giving the grey horse all the encouragement he needed, McCoy got Or Royal home in a pulsating climax for his first win of the meeting.

In the very next race, McCoy took advantage of the drying ground – conditions very much against the defending champion Collier Bay – to charge Martin Pipe's Make A Stand to an easy victory in the Champion Hurdle. Make A Stand had roared up the handicap ladder during the season, and his victory here could not have been more impressive, blazing a trail for much of the way and consequently shattering the course record in the process.

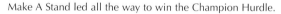

Make A Stand led all the way to win the Champion Hurdle.

Tony McCoy lifts the Champion Hurdle trophy.

The first race on Wednesday, the Royal & SunAlliance Novices' Hurdle included a very interesting contender as regards to future Champion Hurdles, as Istabraq and jockey Charlie Swan danced up the hill to land the Irish Festival banker. Trainer Aiden O'Brien, owner J.P. McManus and Swan, each paid tribute to John Durkan – the man who had discovered Istabraq, and who was courageously battling for his life against leukaemia in a New York hospital. Sadly, it was a battle he would lose.

With just one fence jumped in public in sixteen months, there seemed little cause for optimism as regards to Martha's Son bid for the Queen Mother Champion Chase. On this occasion though, and again later at Aintree, the horse proved how devastating he could be on his day. Jumping frightfully low and flat, albeit at tremendous speed, Martha's Son split Viking Flagship and Ask Tom at the final fence before tearing up the run-in to win. It was a much-needed tonic for trainer Tim Forster, who sadly had lost his star grey chaser Maamur – the 1996 Festival's William Hill National Hunt Handicap Chase winner – to a broken hock the day before.

Adding to his success with Wither Or Which in the same race the year before, Willie Mullins sent out Florida Pearl to storm up the hill in the Champion Bumper beating, among others, French Holly. Florida Pearl, a big strong bay horse with a striking white face, would go on to become a star chaser in Ireland, and would figure prominently at future Festivals.

Buoyed by Imperial Call's success the previous year, the Irish challenge for the 1997 Gold Cup was strong, with their three representatives among the top six in the betting. Although Imperial Call's preparation had been hampered by training problems, the manner of his 1996 win saw him go off the 4/1 favourite, although his two compatriots were also

Martha's Son shoots through to split Ask Tom (left) and Viking Flagship
in the Queen Mother Champion Chase.

The Hennessy winner Coome Hill exercises on the morning of the Tote Gold Cup.

attracting a lot of interest. Dorans Pride had, for many, been the novice of the season, winning his seven previous starts before uncharacteristically falling in his latest race at Thurles. Trained by Michael Hourigan and ridden by Shane Broderick, the horse always seemed to run a true race, although the worry for his first Gold Cup bid lay with the state of the ground as Dorans Pride appreciated far softer conditions than the good-to-firm going he was about to encounter. Danoli too was a novice chaser full of promise, and one that, if winning, would surely create an eclipsing of the celebrations reserved for Imperial Call the previous year. Unlike Dorans Pride though, Danoli was an unreliable jumper, with a clutter of falls clouding his otherwise impressive record over fences.

The Hennessy winner Coome Hill, trained by Walter Dennis near Bude in Cornwall, was among the leading home fancies, although One Man again garnered the majority of focus. Having won another King George with great ease, One Man had removed the Cheltenham monkey from his back with a tight win over Barton Bank earlier in the season, but the doubts over the flamboyant grey's ability to see out the Gold Cup trip lingered on. Trainer Gordon Richards also saddled the tough Unguided Missile and could have been represented further by fast ground-loving Addington Boy and the rangy Hennessy runner-up The Grey Monk. The former was forced to pull out with injury, while the unlucky grey had a sheer dislike for faster surfaces that, together with an unfortunate series of injuries, would see him miss out on

1997 TOTE GOLD CUP RESULT

FATE – HORSE	AGE/WEIGHT	JOCKEY	ODDS
1st – MR MULLIGAN	9-12-0	A.P. McCOY	20/1
2nd – BARTON BANK	11-12-0	D. WALSH	33/1
3rd – DORANS PRIDE	8-12-0	J.P. BRODERICK	10/1
4th – Go Ballistic	8-12-0	A. Dobbin	50/1
5th – Challenger Du Luc	7-12-0	C. Maude	16/1
6th – One Man	9-12-0	R. Dunwoody	7/1
7th – Coome Hill	8-12-0	J. Osborne	15/2
8th – Cyborgo	7-12-0	C. Swan	12/1
Fell – Danoli	9-12-0	T. P. Treacy	7/1
Fell – Unguided Missile	9-12-0	N. Williamson	16/1
Pulled Up – Dublin Flyer	11-12-0	B. Powell	8/1
Pulled Up – Imperial Call	8-12-0	C. O'Dwyer	4/1*
Pulled Up – Nathen Lad	8-12-0	R. Farrant	20/1
Pulled Up – Banjo	7-12-0	D. Bridgwater	33/1

13 March 1997
Going – Good (Good to Firm in places)
Winner – £134,810
Time – 6mins 35. 50secs
14 Ran

Mr Mulligan	Chestnut gelding by Torus – Miss Manhatten
Barton Bank	Brown gelding by Kambalda – Lucifer's Daughter
Dorans Pride	Chestnut gelding by Orchestra – Marians Pride

Winner bred by J. Rowley
Winner trained by N.T. Chance at Lambourn, Berks.

OTHER 1997 FESTIVAL RESULTS

Race	Horse	Jockey	Odds
Citroen Supreme Novices' Hurdle	Shadow Leader	J. Osborne	5/1
Guinness Arkle Ch Trophy Chase	Or Royal	A.P. McCoy	11/2
Smurfit Champion Hurdle	Make A Stand	A. P. McCoy	7/1
Astec Buzz Shop Nat H Hcap Chase	Flyer's Nap	D. Bridgwater	20/1
Fulke Walwyn – Kim Muir Chase	King Lucifer	Mr R. Thornton	7/2
Hamlet Cig Gold Card Hcap Hur F	Pharanear	Mr R. Thornton	14/1
Royal & SunAlliance Novices' Hurdle	Istabraq	C. Swan	6/5
Queen Mother Champion Chase	Martha's Son	R. Farrant	9/1
Coral Cup Handicap Hurdle	Big Strand	Jamie Evans	16/1
Royal & SunAlliance Chase	Hanakham	R. Dunwoody	13/2
National Hunt Chase	Flimsy Truth	Mr M. Harris	33/1
Mildmay Of Flete Handicap Chase	Terao	T.J. Murphy	20/1
Weatherbys Champion Bumper	Florida Pearl	R. Dunwoody	6/1
Elite Racing Club Triumph Hurdle	Commanche Court	N. Williamson	9/1
Bonusprint Stayers' Hurdle	Karshi	J. Osborne	20/1
Christies Foxhunter Chase Ch Cup	Fantus	Mr T. Mitchell	10/1
Cheltenham Grand Annual Chase	Uncle Ernie	G. Bradley	20/1
Cathcart Challenge Cup Chase	Sparky Gayle	B. Storey	3/1
Vincent O'Brien County Hurdle	Barna Boy	R. Dunwoody	14/1

Gold Cups and Grand Nationals throughout his career (a great shame, given the horse's natural talent).

Fourteen runners did eventually face the starter, and it was Dublin Flyer that set a steady pace on the first circuit from Mr Mulligan, – who had been running a fine race in the season's King George only to fall at the last – Barton Bank, Coome Hill and Danoli.

Throughout the first circuit, the champion Imperial Call raced on the wide outside and never looked happy, and as McCoy sent the giant chestnut Mr Mulligan in to the lead at the start of the second lap, the hot pace seemed to have Imperial Call cooked.

Mr Mulligan was clearly loving the occasion, being allowed to bowl along in front and bouncing off the ground. He put in a pair of mighty leaps at the fifteenth and sixteenth, and it was here that it started to become apparant that the leader was not stopping. In behind, Barton Bank was still there, and One Man and Dorans Pride were creeping closer, but the likes of Danoli and Coome Hill could not maintain the throat-cutting pace, while Imperial Call pulled-up altogether.

Surviving a mistake four out, McCoy sent Mr Mulligan on rounding the turn for home and the leader was quick to respond to the champion jockey's urgings, as he went clear from Barton Bank, One Man and Dorans Pride. One Man had looked a real threat jumping the second last, but history was to repeat itself, and while Mr Mulligan jumped the final fence with power, One Man had virtually come to a standstill; it was a sad sight to see him clambering over the last, with barely enough energy left to get him over the line. The questions surrounding One Man's stamina had been emphatically answered once and for all. Mr Mulligan powered home, beneath glorious sunshine, under McCoy to record something of a surprise victory. Next came Barton Bank with the game Dorans Pride third.

Despite his starting price of 20/1, Mr Mulligan's win was no fluke. The horse had been a top novice the season before, one that trainer Noel Chance had always maintained would be good enough to contest a Gold Cup. In the current season, Mr Mulligan had been bothered by injury, including damaged ligaments following his King George tumble. A workout at Newbury prior to the Gold Cup had been a complete shambles and left both Chance and McCoy wondering if the horse would be ready in time for Cheltenham. But after a schooling session a week before the big race where Mr Mulligan showed signs of coming back to his best, it was all systems go, and in the race itself the horse was able to show the full extent of his ability. It would have been tough to find a stronger-looking horse than Mr Mulligan; built like an ox, it was the horse's relentless galloping and awesome power that set him apart from the rest.

It was Chance's first Festival winner. Mr Mulligan, like half of the horses he trained in Lambourn, was owned by ice-cream cone manufacturer Michael Worcester. As for McCoy, the Gold Cup had capped a marvellous personal Festival, one where he had become only the fifth jockey to win both the Champion Hurdle and Gold Cup in the same year. At the conclusion of the 1997 Festival, McCoy had recorded three winners, three seconds and two thirds.

The blazing chestnut Mr Mulligan ran his rivals ragged to win the Gold Cup.

1998

was receiving weight because of his age, but this victory was definitely the result of McCoy's expert persuasion.

The Champion Hurdle was deemed to be a battle between the new star of Ireland, Istabraq, and Malcolm Jefferson's northern-trained challenger, Dato Star. Those that had been unconvinced by Istabraq's win in the Royal & SunAlliance Novices' Hurdle the previous year or that had been put off by another failed Irish hot-pot, His Song – who disappointed behind the exciting French Ballerina in the opening Supreme Novices' Hurdle – were left to eat humble pie, as Istabraq delivered a devastating display under Charlie Swan to win by twelve lengths. In fact, this was just the beginning of Istabraq's domination of the hurdling division. Dato Star had run miserably in defeat. The race was not without tragedy, as Shadow Leader, the brilliant Supreme Novices' Hurdle winner of the 1997 Festival, plunged to his death when behind at the final flight.

COOL DAWN

The 1997 Gold Cup winner Mr Mulligan had run twice during the current campaign, winning the Sean Graham Chase at Ayr on his second start. The champion was then struck down by an injury to his near-fore tendon. Realising the severity of the damage and the sheer amount of time the horse would be sidelined, the decision was taken by Michael Worcester and his wife Gerry to retire the big chestnut. Unfortunately, and with a spell of hunter-chasing beckoning for the still sprightly star, an accident at the Worcester's farm in the summer of 1999 led to Mr Mulligan being put down, the horse having sustained a fracture to a leg.

It was a shame that Mr Mulligan was not present to defend his crown, as he would have undoubtedly appreciated the rapidly drying ground at Cheltenham during Festival week. Mr Mulligan's pilot for the horse's finest hour, Tony McCoy, had of course enjoyed a fine Festival in 1997 and on this occasion he seemed to merely carry on where he had left off twelve months before. McCoy was involved in the finish of the day in Tuesday's Arkle Chase, where he gave the five-year-old grey Champleve a masterful ride to pip the Irish-raider Hill Society by a nose at the death. True, Champleve

Istabraq and Charlie Swan about to capture the first of three Champion Hurdle titles.

The wonderfully athletic One Man flies the last to finally bury his Festival hoodoo.

Richard Dunwoody with the connections of the striking bay Florida Pearl.

There was no moment more heart-warming at the 1998 Festival than the sight of the grey One Man storming up the Cheltenham hill – his nemesis for so long – to win the Queen Mother Champion Chase. Trainer Gordon Richards was forced to deal with endless questions about the horse's attitude and courage at Cheltenham in the build-up to the race, but the simple fact is that One Man did not stay the Gold Cup trip. At the two-mile distance of the Queen Mother Champion Chase, One Man proved what a force he was, showing all his athleticism and exuberance to win in faultless style under Brian Harding. Entering the winner's enclosure, One Man enjoyed the sort of reception a horse of his ability truly deserved, and it left owner John Hales and

Richards extremely proud. With his status as a champion finally realised, fate dealt a cruel blow, as One Man was tragically killed at Aintree three weeks later.

Two huge reputations came through with flying colours on Wednesday. Firstly, the giant, Ferdy Murphy-trained French Holly stormed away from his rivals to take the Royal & SunAlliance Novices' Hurdle, and then Florida Pearl – considered by many to be a future Gold Cup winner – proved too strong for the highly regarded, David Nicholson-trained Escartefigue in the novice's Gold Cup. With the joy of Florida Pearl's win fresh in his mind, trainer Willie Mullins then sent out yet another winner of the Champion Bumper in the shape of Alexander Banquet, who beat a whole host

The giant French Holly on his way to victory in the
Royal & SunAlliance Novices' Hurdle.

Escartefigue returns after defeat to Florida Pearl in the
Royal & SunAlliance Chase.

of future chasing stars such as Frantic Tan, King's Road and Paris Pike.

After a fine third in the previous year's race, Dorans Pride was made favourite for the Gold Cup. The most consistent of horses, Dorans Pride had only been defeated three times in thirteen chases and, on his latest run, had captured the Irish Hennessy. The problem for Dorans Pride though was that the ground was faster than ideal, as it had been in 1997.

One of Dorans Pride's rivals from his novice days was the Paul Nicholls-trained See More Business. The muscular bay had, at times, tarnished his lofty reputation with careless jumping. But in his second season of chasing, See More Business had flashed glimpses of his undoubted potential, by first claiming the King George – albeit aided by some lacklustre finishing from the Martin Pipe-trained Challenger Du Luc – and then, having made a serious blunder four out, recovering to power up the Cheltenham hill in January to stake his claim as a serious Gold Cup horse. The latter win had proved his ability to handle Cheltenham, and he entered the race with the supreme confidence of his trainer.

The drying ground was certainly not going to inconvenience two of the lesser fancied horses, Cool Dawn and Strong Promise. Cool Dawn, a former hunter-chaser, had enjoyed a fruitful season, winning three times at Ascot, and had clearly benefited since jockey Andrew Thornton had taken over the riding duties from the horse's owner, Dido Harding. The well-built Strong Promise had disappointed when favourite for the previous year's Queen Mother Champion Chase, but it had never really been determined as to what distance the horse preferred. Trained by Geoff Hubbard, Strong Promise was a class act on his day, and he entered the race as a distinctly plausible dark horse.

With a competitive field of seventeen, including the Hennessy winner Suny Bay and the winner of both the

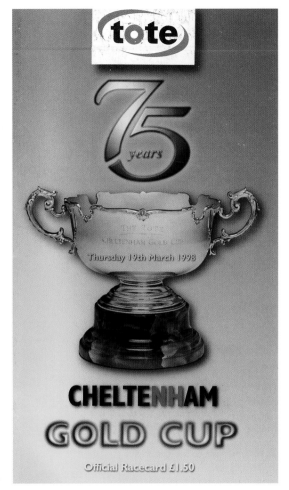

1998 Racecard.

Murphy's and Tripleprint Gold Cups, Senor El Betrutti (both grey horses) facing the starter, the race began with much anticipation and excitement.

As Cool Dawn led the field on their way, the big group of runners settled down in to a comfortable rhythm and the opening series of fences sailed by without incident. However, at the seventh fence, Cyborgo sustained an injury and Tony McCoy quickly decided to pull-up the former Stayers' Hurdle winner. In doing so, Cyborgo, who was

Dorans Pride (7, sheepskin noseband) joins the leaders early on in the Gold Cup. Far right is Rough Quest, second right is Yorkshire Gale and far left is Couldn't Be Better (5).

Andrew Thornton shows the crowd that Cool Dawn is the true hero of the Gold Cup.

positioned in the centre of the field, had to drift out to the right, and unfortunately he carried with him the outsider Indian Tracker and the hotly-fancied See More Business.

With the complexion of the race thus altered, Cool Dawn bounded on in front, relishing the ground and, despite an error at the fifteenth, the horse was still right there in the lead at the third last with Dorans Pride and the dangerous-looking Strong Promise his nearest pursuers, while Suny Bay, Senor El Betrutti and Go Ballistic all started to fade away.

The favourite lost some ground after battering the third last, and the race then developed into a battle between Cool

Dawn and Strong Promise. Norman Williamson had given Strong Promise a marvellously patient ride and looked to be getting the upper hand on Thornton and Cool Dawn as the pair met the last. However, after drifting over to the stand side, it was Cool Dawn that rallied the stronger, and the horse got up to win by a couple of lengths from Strong Promise, with the staying-on Dorans Pride a brave head away in third.

Obviously, Paul Nicholls was extremely disappointed over the way See More Business had exited the race, but it was simply bad luck, and happily Cyborgo – although in grave danger for a number of weeks – survived his ordeal and

1998 TOTE GOLD CUP RESULT

FATE – HORSE	AGE/WEIGHT	JOCKEY	ODDS
1st – COOL DAWN	10-12-0	A. THORNTON	25/1
2nd – STRONG PROMISE	7-12-0	N. WILLIAMSON	14/1
3rd – DORANS PRIDE	9-12-0	R. DUNWOODY	9/4*
4th – Senor El Betrutti	9-12-0	C. Llewellyn	33/1
5th – Suny Bay	9-12-0	G. Bradley	9/1
6th – Simply Dashing	7-12-0	L. Wyer	33/1
7th – Challenger Du Luc	8-12-0	C. Maude	20/1
8th – Barton Bank	12-12-0	A. Maguire	33/1
9th – Strath Royal	12-12-0	M. Brennan	100/1
10th – Yorkshire Gale	12-12-0	L. Aspell	100/1
11th – Go Ballistic	9-12-0	C. O'Dwyer	12/1
Carried Out – Indian Tracker	8-12-0	J. Lower	150/1
Carried Out – See More Business	8-12-0	T. J. Murphy	11/2
Fell – Rough Quest	12-12-0	M. A. Fitzgerald	14/1
Pulled Up – Addington Boy	10-12-0	B. Harding	12/1
Pulled Up – Couldn't Be Better	11-12-0	D. Gallagher	33/1
Pulled Up – Cyborgo	8-12-0	A.P. McCoy	10/1

19 March 1998
Going – Good (Good to Soft in places)
Winner – £148,962
Time – 6mins 39. 5secs
17 Ran

Cool Dawn — Brown gelding by Over The River – Aran Tour
Strong Promise — Bay or brown gelding by Strong Gale – Let's Compromise
Dorans Pride — Chestnut gelding by Orchestra – Marians Pride

Winner bred by John C. McCarthy
Winner trained by R.H. Alner at Blandford, Dorset.

OTHER 1998 FESTIVAL RESULTS

Race	Horse	Jockey	Odds
Citroen Supreme Novices' Hurdle	French Ballerina	G. Bradley	10/1
Guinness Arkle Ch Trophy Chase	Champleve	A.P. McCoy	13/2
Smurfit Champion Hurdle	Istabraq	C. Swan	3/1
William Hill Nat Hunt Hcap Chase	Unguided Missile	P. Carberry	10/1
Fulke Walwyn – Kim Muir Chase	In Truth	Mr S. Durack	20/1
Unicoin Homes G Card Hcap Hur F	Unsinkable Boxer	A.P. McCoy	5/2
Royal & SunAlliance Novices' Hurdle	French Holly	A. Thornton	2/1
Queen Mother Champion Chase	One Man	B. Harding	7/2
Coral Cup Handicap Hurdle	Top Cees	B. Fenton	11/1
Royal & SunAlliance Chase	Florida Pearl	R. Dunwoody	11/8
National Hunt Chase	Wandering Light	Mr R. Wakley	10/1
Mildmay Of Flete Handicap Chase	Super Coin	N. Williamson	7/1
Weatherbys Champion Bumper	Alexander Banquet	Mr R. Walsh	9/1
Elite Racing Club Triumph Hurdle	Upgrade	C. Llewellyn	14/1
Bonusprint Stayers' Hurdle	Princeful	R. Farrant	16/1
Christies Foxhunter Chase Ch Cup	Earthmover	Mr J. Tizzard	3/1
Cheltenham Grand Annual Chase	Edredon Bleu	A.P. McCoy	7/2
Cathcart Challenge Cup Chase	Cyfor Malta	A.P. McCoy	9/4
Vincent O'Brien County Hurdle	Blowing Wind	A.P. McCoy	15/8

eventually raced again. For See More Business too, there would be another day.

Though Cool Dawn had caused a shock by winning at 25/1, the manner of his success could not be faulted, as he had barely seen another horse in the race and had displayed battling prowess in fending off Strong Promise when that rival appeared poised to strike gold. He had been brilliantly ridden by Andrew Thornton, who was capping off a fine individual season that had included winning the King George with See More Business, as well as French Holly's success the day before.

Cool Dawn was trained in Dorset by Robert Alner. The trainer had ridden Domason to win the 1970 Foxhunters' and, before this Gold Cup, his most notable training feat had been sending out the first and second in the previous season's Whitbread Gold Cup through Harwell Lad and Flyer's Nap. Earlier in the season, Alner had told Dido Harding that if Cool Dawn – a very powerful horse and formerly something of a tearaway – was to reach the top of the game, she would have to be replaced by a top, professional jockey. In came Thornton, and the rest, as they say, is history!

1999

SEE MORE BUSINESS

There was no doubting that, with two Festival wins already behind him, Istabraq had rightly earned himself a reputation as an extremely good hurdler. Twelve months previously, he had equalled a record in the Champion Hurdle by winning by an easy twelve lengths. On this occasion, his trainer, Aiden O'Brien, reported the horse to be bigger, stronger and quicker than ever. It was no surprise that he started one of the all-time hottest favourites for the Champion Hurdle, as he attempted to follow up his 1998 triumph. For Istabraq, the race itself transpired like clockwork, as he was casually brought through the field by Charlie Swan before being unleashed to collar the long-time leader French Holly at the last, then saunter up the hill to win by a very comfortable three-and-a-half lengths. Istabraq's stablemate, Theatreworld, though never in a position to win, ran on late to be second for a remarkable third year in a row. After the race, there was a feeling that Istabraq was a very special horse, and could well be the next hurdler to join the greats that had won the Champion Hurdle three times.

Earlier on Tuesday, the Cheltenham crowd were treated to a scintillating performance by a horse that would one day win a Champion Hurdle of his own, Hors La Loi III. The horse was having his first run for his new trainer, Martin Pipe, after his owner Paul Green switched him from the French stable of Francois Doumen. Hors La Loi III showed that he possessed electrifying finishing speed, as he disposed of the fancied J.P. McManus-owned pair of Joe Mac and Cardinal Hill to win the Supreme Novices' Hurdle.

There was no shortage of fine performances on Wednesday, not to mention some explosive, nail-biting finishes. Barton was just one of a number of horses on the day that displayed an enormous amount of future potential, as the huge chestnut destroyed his rivals in the Royal & SunAlliance Novices' Hurdle under Lorcan Wyer. Equally impressive was the similarly strapping Monsignor – a horse destined to be Barton's successor in the race – in the Champion Bumper, the powerful gelding causing a 50/1 surprise.

The Istabraq connection – Charlie Swan, J.P. McManus and Aiden O'Brien.

The grey Call Equiname is sandwiched between Edredon Bleu (left) and Direct Route heading for the line in an epic Queen Mother Champion Chase.

The fragile grey horse, Call Equiname, trained by Paul Nicholls, was to come out best in a three-way battle for the Queen Mother Champion Chase. The brittle chaser with legs of glass, who was rarely seen on a racecourse, was given a wonderfully patient ride by Mick Fitzgerald as he got the better of the favourite Edredon Bleu and the northern-raider Direct Route after jumping the last. It was developing into a

fine Festival for Nicholls, who the day before had taken the Arkle Chase with the game Flagship Uberalles. The week would only get better for the Somerset-based trainer.

The horse with one of the biggest reputations entering the 1999 Festival was the Irish novice chaser, Nick Dundee, trained by Edward O'Grady. The horse had been impressive in his races so far and had very nearly been allowed to take

The much-hyped Nick Dundee (right) studies a fence next to Ardent Scout before the Royal & SunAlliance Chase.

his chance in the Gold Cup, but connections eventually opted for the Royal & SunAlliance Chase. Ridden by Norman Williamson, the horse was backed as if defeat was out of the question, but this race was to provide the Festival with perhaps its saddest moment of the meeting. Absolutely cantering, Nick Dundee had pulled well clear of the field with the Noel Chance-trained Looks Like Trouble, as the pair approached the tricky third last – a fence taken on a downhill slant. It was here that fate intervened with a bitter twist, as Nick Dundee put down on Williamson and tumbled out of the race, to a chorus of groans from the crowd.

The situation got worse though: as Nick Dundee struggled to get to his feet, it appeared that the horse had broken his leg. The quick-thinking Williamson swiftly grabbed hold of the horse to prevent further damage. Most people in the stands, this writer included, had moments earlier believed they were witnessing a future Gold Cup winner, so

effortlessly and powerfully had Nick Dundee swooned down the hill, but the pleasure turned to horror as the dreaded green screens were erected around the stricken warrior. Fortunately, Nick Dundee survived this ordeal but faced a lengthy spell on the sidelines. Against the odds, the brave horse returned to racing over a year later with an emotional win in Ireland, although as his career progressed it was clear he was nowhere near as good as before, with numerous falls ruining his confidence. Nick Dundee had certainly looked a mighty machine before his injury, yet sadly he joins the likes of Buona Notte, Killiney and Paul Nicholls' potential-packed youngster See More Indians as great-looking horses that were cut down before proving their metal at Gold Cup level. From this story though, another picture was painted, for twelve months after Nick Dundee's mishap the horse that eventually won that race, Looks Like

After the disappointment of the day before, many believed Williamson would gain sweet compensation courtesy of the 'find of the year' in the Gold Cup itself. His mount was an ex-hunter-chaser, the grey Teeton Mill – a brilliant jumper trained by Venetia Williams. Teeton Mill had won the Badger Beer Chase at Wincanton earlier in the season before leaping into the Gold Cup picture with a crushing defeat of a strong field in the Hennessy at Newbury. An easy win in the King George only enhanced his blossoming reputation, although on his latest start Teeton Mill ran, and won, over a much shorter trip – leading some to question his ability to see out the Gold Cup distance.

The top two novice chasers from the previous season, the much-hyped Irish bay Florida Pearl and the similar looking Escartefigue, both made the line-up. Florida Pearl had only run twice during the season, falling in the Ericsson Chase at Leopardstown before winning the Irish Hennessy in unconvincing manner from Escartefigue. Although he had a

Teeton Mill goes to post for the Gold Cup.

1999 TOTE GOLD CUP RESULT

FATE – HORSE	AGE/WEIGHT	JOCKEY	ODDS
1st – SEE MORE BUSINESS	9-12-0	M. A. FITZGERALD	16/1
2nd – GO BALLISTIC	10-12-0	A. DOBBIN	66/1
3rd – FLORIDA PEARL	7-12-0	R. DUNWOODY	5/2*
4th – Double Thriller	9-12-0	J. Tizzard	9/1
5th – Addington Boy	11-12-0	A. Maguire	66/1
6th – Simply Dashing	8-12-0	L. Wyer	20/1
7th – Escartefigue	7-12-0	R. Johnson	11/1
8th – Dorans Pride	10-12-0	P. Carberry	11/2
9th – Senor El Betrutti	10-12-0	C. Llewellyn	50/1
Pulled Up – Unsinkable Boxer	10-12-0	A. P. McCoy	14/1
Pulled Up – Suny Bay	10-12-0	G. Bradley	14/1
Pulled Up – Teeton Mill	10-12-0	N. Williamson	7/2

18 March 1999
Going – Good to Soft (Good in places)
Winner – £149,600
Time – 6mins 41. 90secs
12 Ran

See More Business	Bay gelding by Seymour Hicks – Miss Redlands
Go Ballistic	Brown gelding by Celtic Cone – National Clover
Florida Pearl	Bay gelding by Florida Son – Ice Pearl

Winner bred by Ian Bryant
Winner trained by P.F. Nicholls at Ditcheat, Somerset.

OTHER 1999 FESTIVAL RESULTS

Citroen Supreme Novices' Hurdle	Hors La Loi III	A.P. McCoy	9/2
Guinness Arkle Ch Trophy Chase	Flagship Uberalles	J. Tizzard	11/1
Smurfit Champion Hurdle	Istabraq	C. Swan	4/9
William Hill Nat Hunt Hcap Chase	Betty's Boy	N. Williamson	25/1
Fulke Walwyn – Kim Muir Chase	Celtic Giant	Mr B. Gibson	20/1
Stakis Casino Final Handicap Hurdle	Generosa	N. Williamson	12/1
Royal & SunAlliance Novices' Hurdle	Barton	L. Wyer	2/1
Queen Mother Champion Chase	Call Equiname	M. A. Fitzgerald	7/2
Coral Cup Handicap Hurdle	Khayrawani	F.M. Berry	16/1
Royal & SunAlliance Chase	Looks Like Trouble	P. Carberry	16/1
National Hunt Chase	Deejaydee	Mr A. Martin	13/2
Mildmay Of Flete Handicap Chase	Majadou	A.P. McCoy	7/4
Weatherbys Champion Bumper	Monsignor	B. Powell	50/1
Elite Racing Club Triumph Hurdle	Katarino	M.A. Fitzgerald	11/4
Bonusprint Stayers' Hurdle	Anzum	R. Johnson	40/1
Christies Foxhunter Chase Ch Cup	Castle Mane	Mr B. Pollock	9/2
Cheltenham Grand Annual Chase	Space Trucker	J.R. Barry	7/2
Cathcart Challenge Cup Chase	Stormyfairweather	M.A. Fitzgerald	9/1
Vincent O'Brien County Hurdle	Sir Talbot	T.J. Murphy	10/1

high cruising speed, there were definitely worries over the horse's stamina. Even so, Florida Pearl's tall reputation saw him sent off the 5/2 favourite. Escartefigue had looked a potentially great horse when winning at Aintree as a novice, but his campaign this time had been without victory, and the Gold Cup was to prove the start of a frustrating spell for the horse that David Nicholson had previously described as potentially the best he had trained.

The unlucky horse of the 1998 running, See More Business, was another who had suffered a disappointing season. Paul Nicholls had explained that the horse had become lazy at home, and the result was to have blinkers fitted for the first time in the Gold Cup in an attempt to rekindle his enthusiasm. Even so, See More Business was not even the most fancied horse from his own stable, with that honour going to Double Thriller – a former hunter star related to the classy Double Silk. Double Thriller had caught the eye when winning two recent races at Wincanton.

With the 1998 winner Cool Dawn absent thanks to softer ground, and with former champion Imperial Call and the exciting Pipe youngster Cyfor Malta – a winner over the big Aintree fences at the tender age of five – ruled out with injuries, it was a field of twelve that faced the starter. Senor El Betrutti made the early running with Dorans Pride, but soon Double Thriller jumped to the front and began to take them along at a strong pace.

At the seventh fence, Teeton Mill made an uncharacteristically bad mistake, but the grey continued. Unfortunately, it

See More Business (8) and Go Ballistic are locked together at the last in the Gold Cup.

would later transpire that Teeton Mill had slipped a tendon from his off-hind hock and was pulled-up two fences later. Not only was he out of the Gold Cup, but the injury was sadly severe enough to bring a premature end to his career.

As the second circuit progressed, Double Thriller kept up the pace and, by the third last, a group of four had swept clear of the remainder. As well as the leader, Florida Pearl, See More Business and the outsider Go Ballistic were still in contention. Florida Pearl had not been jumping fluently, however, and try as he might he could not stay with Go Ballistic and See More Business as those two stormed clear towards the final two fences.

Tony Dobbin on Go Ballistic had really got his horse motoring in the closing stages, but Mick Fitzgerald on See More Business had timed his run to perfection. As the pair flew the last together, it was the Nicholls runner that

delivered the tough finishing power he had shown during the previous season and See More Business was able to hold the gallant bid of the unconsidered Go Ballistic by a length, with the slightly disappointing Florida Pearl back in third.

The blinkers had clearly worked a treat for the winner and Nicholls had finally been rewarded for his defiant belief that See More Business could win a Gold Cup. The horse had been so unlucky in the previous year's race, but those bitter memories were all swept aside for the jubilant connections as they proudly led their hero into the winner's enclosure. See More Business was jointly owned by Paul Barber and John Keighley (Barber's brother, Richard, provided Nicholls with many horses to train through his involvement in the point-to-point field).

The win emphasised in striking fashion what a force Nicholls had become as a trainer. The Gold Cup, together with the victories for Flagship Uberalles and Call Equiname, were his first Festival successes. The trainer's biggest wins as a jockey came aboard Broadheath and Playschool, who both won Hennessys in the 1980s, while he had learned his trade as a trainer under David Barons and was part of the team that sent out Seagram to win the 1991 Grand National.

Fitzgerald, brother-in-law to the trainer, had enjoyed a wonderful Festival. As well as See More Business and Call Equiname, the jockey also captured the Triumph Hurdle on Katarino and the Cathcart Chase aboard Stormyfairweather.

Hindsight is a wonderful tool, but See More Business could well have been going for a Gold Cup hat-trick the following season if he had received better luck in the 1998 race. His progress in the 2000 campaign was most impressive, with blinkers proving a magical medicine in terms of curing his laziness and former jumping worries. By the time the next Gold Cup rolled around, See More Business would be the hot favourite.

2000

Norman Williamson is all smiles after the big chestnut
Monsignor had crushed his opposition.

LOOKS LIKE TROUBLE

Rumours were rampant on the eve of the 2000 Cheltenham Festival that all was not well with the dual Champion Hurdler Istabraq. Apparently, the now imperious Irish superstar had bled from the nostrils on his arrival at the course. Even when Istabraq was cantering to the start, there were those doubting the wellbeing of a horse trying to become the fifth in history to win a third Champion Hurdle – they need not have worried. Istabraq was simply brilliant, as Charlie Swan played the now customary Istabraq tactics: holding the horse up and bringing him carefully through the field before sending him powerfully clear at the final flight. It seemed an almost routine win for Istabraq, as he stormed up his favourite hill to win from Hors La Loi III and the bold youngster Blue Royal. Not surprisingly, a fantastic reception awaited the horse in the winners' enclosure as he officially joined the hurdling greats. It is tough to say where Istabraq ranks among classic hurdlers – some believe he is the best ever – but the one thing about him, despite a plain distaste for heavy ground, was that he made winning, particularly at Cheltenham, look ridiculously easy. With no signs of decline, there appeared little reason why Istabraq could not win an unprecedented fourth Champion Hurdle in twelve months time.

Edredon Bleu (left) and Direct Route prepare to fight to the line in the Queen Mother Champion Chase.

Istabraq aside, the opening day of the Festival saw favourites beaten left, right and centre. The darling of the novice hurdling division in Ireland, Youlneverwalkalone, a horse with a high cruising speed but untested in a battle, was the first hot-pot to be sunk, after he was beaten in the Supreme Novices' Hurdle by the Noel Meade-trained Sausalito Bay and runner-up Best Mate, trained by Henrietta Knight. Then, in the following Arkle Chase, Mick Fitzgerald guided the exciting looking Tiutchev to a highly impressive win, eclipsing his higher-touted rivals, Bellator and Decoupage. It was a particularly good day for Fitzgerald and trainer Nicky Henderson as, later on, their reward for hours of perseverance with the former suspect jumper Marlborough was a win for the much-improved chaser in

François Doumen leads his jubilant son Thierry in following Snow Drop's Triumph Hurdle success.

the William Hill National Hunt Handicap Chase – where the horse came through strongly to beat the subsequent Whitbread Gold Cup winner Beau.

There was no doubting most people's idea of the Festival banker was the hugely exciting, seventeen-hand chestnut Monsignor in the Royal & SunAlliance Novices' Hurdle. Similar to other much-hyped favourites for the race in recent years – such as Istabraq, French Holly and Barton – Monsignor did not let his followers down and the Mark Pitman-trained machine simply galloped his rivals into submission in the manner of a horse with a significant future.

If anyone had ever questioned the brilliance of Tony McCoy, then the finish to the Queen Mother Champion Chase would surely have overturned their objections. With Howard Johnson's charge, Direct Route, looking every inch the winner over the final fence, McCoy gathered his mount

Edredon Bleu and refused to accept defeat, eventually squeaking his horse past Direct Route in the shadow of the post. Edredon Bleu has been a super warrior over the course of his career, but one has to wonder whether any other jockey would have got the same response out of the horse as McCoy did on this occasion. Edredon Bleu was trained by Henrietta Knight and she had more cause to smile later in the day as Lord Noelie, aided by ground that was becoming faster by the minute, took the Royal & SunAlliance Chase.

Since his thrilling Gold Cup win of the year before, See More Business had gone from strength to strength. He had proved beyond doubt that he was worthy of his Gold Cup crown by winning all three of his races during the season, including a second King George victory. It was no surprise he started a short-priced favourite, even on supposedly unfavourable fast ground, yet it was worth noting that only five horses had won the King George and the Gold Cup in the same season, with Desert Orchid the most recent in 1989.

Florida Pearl was back for a second attempt at the race having somewhat disappointed his followers twelve months before. The horse had run far more regularly in the current season, winning three times – including an aggressive, front-running display in the recent Irish Hennessy. With Richard Dunwoody now retired, it was Paul Carberry that took the mount on Florida Pearl. Carberry was a more-than-capable replacement, and the talented Irishman – son of L'Escargot's regular jockey, Tommy – had won the previous year's Grand National aboard Bobbyjo, trained by his father.

If See More Business had a tough assignment in breaking the King George/Gold Cup hoodoo, then Looks Like Trouble, from Noel Chance's yard, had an even tougher nut to crack. Only three horses prior to Garrison Savannah in 1991 – Arkle, Ten Up and Master Smudge – had ever won the Gold Cup having won the (now named) Royal &

Gloria Victis courageously leads the Gold Cup field at half way.

SunAlliance Chase the year before, yet this was the group Looks Like Trouble would be joining if he was to reign supreme at Cheltenham. The talented chaser had progressed well out of novice company, with his only disappointing run occuring when he pulled-up in the King George. Strangely, on the insistence of owner Tim Collins, this was enough to have Norman Williamson 'jocked-off', with the rapidly progressing Richard Johnson elected to ride the horse.

Ironically, it was Johnson who had ridden the real 'wild card' of the race, in what has since been described as one of the best chasing performances ever seen from a novice. The horse in question was the Martin Pipe-trained and Terry Neill-owned Gloria Victis, and the race that had so many bubbling was the season's Racing Post Chase at Kempton. There, the six-year-old Gloria Victis, a spring-heeled athlete with gallons of heart, had destroyed some lofty reputations –

including the likes of Marlborough, the future Grand National winner Red Marauder, and the highly-regarded Mary Reveley-trained Brother Of Iris – with a pulsating show of front-running and lightning-quick jumping. It may have been the result of what had happened to Nick Dundee at the previous Festival, but after much deliberation, connections plumped to send Gloria Victis for the Gold Cup, rather than the novice version.

With the likes of the Hennessy winner Ever Blessed, former Gold Cup runners-up Strong Promise and Go Ballistic, and the tough, young Irish chestnut Rince Ri in the field, the 2000 Gold Cup was always going to be a hot affair. After the French raider Snow Drop had won the Triumph Hurdle under Thierry Doumen for his father François, and Nicky Henderson's Bacchanal had defeated the game Irish hero Limestone Lad in the Stayers' Hurdle, the scene was set for the Blue Riband.

It was the novice Gloria Victis that bounded zestfully out in front and, although the youngster consistently showed a strong tendency to jump right, he was still in control and running his heart out as the heat was turned up on the second circuit.

All the key characters were still involved as the race entered its latter stages, but it was the third last where the drama began to intensify. First, See More Business suddenly started to tire and drop away, drawing gasps from the packed crowds as he did so, while, as the field took the fence, Rince Ri, who had run a bold race, unshipped his jockey Ruby Walsh.

This left Gloria Victis frantically holding on in front, although both Florida Pearl and Looks Like Trouble were starting to appear behind. However, a dark arrow was about to be fired from the sky, cutting down the gamest of players in the harshest way. Jumping the second last under pressure from his rivals, Gloria Victis crumpled to the floor and out of the race. The horse got up but, tragically, the damage had

Looks Like Trouble has the edge on Florida Pearl at the last in the Gold Cup.

been done. Given painkillers and led away in a horse ambulance, the dreaded news emerged an hour after the race. Gloria Victis had fractured a near-fore canon bone, and although everything was done to try and save him, there was no alternative but to have him put down. Lanzarote, Ten Plus, Cherrykino – the list of talented horses killed in the great race is choking to read, yet the feeling surrounding the demise of Gloria Victis was that this was a horse that could

truly have been special. He had only just emerged as a force on the chasing scene, but he had arrived with such a burst and just bolstered his name with a fine Gold Cup showing before tragedy struck. Connections were devastated, Pipe and McCoy unashamedly tearful. The gods of racing had blessed the pair in their recent achievements, but here was a black moment – and it would not be the last for the pair at Cheltenham.

2000 TOTE GOLD CUP RESULT

FATE – HORSE	AGE/WEIGHT	JOCKEY	ODDS
1st – LOOKS LIKE TROUBLE	8-12-0	R. JOHNSON	9/2
2nd – FLORIDA PEARL	8-12-0	P. CARBERRY	9/2
3rd – STRONG PROMISE	9-12-0	R. THORNTON	20/1
4th – See More Business	10-12-0	M.A. Fitzgerald	9/4*
5th – Lake Kariba	9-12-0	N. Williamson	150/1
6th – Dorans Pride	11-12-0	P. G. Hourigan	40/1
Fell – Gloria Victis	6-12-0	A.P. McCoy	13/2
Pulled Up – Go Ballistic	11-12-0	A. Dobbin	16/1
Pulled Up – The Last Fling	10-12-0	S. Durack	16/1
Pulled Up – Ever Blessed	8-12-0	T.J. Murphy	14/1
Unseated Rider – Tullymurry Toff	9-12-0	G. Lee	100/1
Unseated Rider – Rince Ri	7-12-0	R. Walsh	33/1

16 March 2000
Going – Good to Firm (Good in places)
Winner – £162,400
Time – 6mins 30. 30secs
12 Ran

Looks Like Trouble — Bay gelding by Zaffaran – Lavengaddy
Florida Pearl — Bay gelding by Florida Son – Ice Pearl
Strong Promise — Bay or brown gelding by Strong Gale – Lets Compromise

Winner bred by Stephen Reel
Winner trained by N.T. Chance at Upper Lambourn, Berks.

OTHER 2000 FESTIVAL RESULTS

Capel Cure Sharp Sup Nov Hur.	Sausalito Bay	P. Carberry	14/1
Irish Independent Arkle Chase	Tiutchev	M. A. Fitzgerald	8/1
Smurfit Champion Hurdle	Istabraq	C. Swan	8/15
Will Hill Nat Hunt Hcap Chase	Marlborough	M.A. Fitzgerald	11/2
Fulke Walwyn – Kim Muir Chase	Honey Mount	Mr R. Walford	8/1
Ladbroke Casinos F Hcap Hurdle	Rubhahunish	C. Llewellyn	8/1
Royal & SunAlliance Nov Hurdle	Monsignor	N. Williamson	5/4
Queen Mother Champion Chase	Edredon Bleu	A.P. McCoy	7/2
Coral Cup Handicap Hurdle	What's Up Boys	Mr P. Flynn	33/1
Royal & SunAlliance Chase	Lord Noelie	J. Culloty	9/2
National Hunt Chase	Relaxation	Mr M. Bradburne	8/1
Mildmay Of Flete Hcap Chase	Dark Stranger	R. Johnson	14/1
Weatherbys Champion Bumper	Joe Cullen	C. Swan	14/1
Elite Racing Club Triumph Hurdle	Snow Drop	T. Doumen	7/1
Bonusprint Stayers' Hurdle	Bacchanal	M.A. Fitzgerald	11/2
Christies Foxhunter Chase Ch Cup	Cavalero	Mr A. Charles-Jones	16/1
Cheltenham Grand Annual Chase	Samakaan	N. Williamson	9/2
Cathcart Challenge Cup Chase	Stormyfairweather	M.A. Fitzgerald	11/2
Vincent O'Brien County Hurdle	Master Tern	A. Dobbin	9/2

As the Irish raised their encouragement in trying to magnetize Florida Pearl home, it was Johnson and Looks Like Trouble that suddenly found another gear. Taking the last fence in full flight, they tore up the run-in, even drifting towards the stand side en route to a highly impressive victory. Florida Pearl had been outdone again, but had run his race in second, with Strong Promise third ahead of the favourite See More Business.

Looks Like Trouble had never really received the credit he had deserved after winning at the Festival the year before, with so much attention focusing on the fall of Nick Dundee.

But here was a champion with youth, speed and class and he had only made one mistake during the race; at the business end he had finished in grand style to see off a very strong field.

Noel Chance had now saddled three Festival winners from seven runners, including the two Gold Cups, while the win for Richard Johnson made up for losing the ride he had once possessed aboard Mr Mulligan before the 1997 race.

Perhaps though, this Gold Cup, more than any other before it, showed the two sides to National Hunt racing. Thrilling, beautiful and combative one minute, dark, bitter and tragic the next.

2002

BEST MATE

The 2001 Cheltenham Festival was lost entirely to the devastating foot and mouth disease that had swept the country at the beginning of the year. It appeared at first as though Cheltenham would be able to go ahead, but as the Festival drew near a case was discovered close to the racecourse, meaning there was no alternative but to cancel the meeting. Although the outcome left countless people disappointed, it only paled in comparison to the gutting the country's farming community had suffered to their livelihoods, with a sickening amount of livestock ruined. The images of the smouldering, mountain-like pyres of dead carcases are still fresh in many-a-mind, and are a stark reminder of just how brutal foot and mouth can become. On the racing front, the real shame that accompanied the loss of the 2001 Festival was Istabraq being denied the chance to bid for an unprecedented fourth Champion Hurdle title. The horse looked more than capable of fulfilling the dream – but he would have to wait. There may well have been a new star too in the Gold Cup, as the blossoming talent of First Gold took the season's King George in mighty fashion, and with Looks Like Trouble sidelined through injury, the French gem First Gold was many people's choice to take the Blue Riband.

So it was with perhaps the greatest ever pre-Cheltenham anticipation that awaited the 2002 Festival, and it was not long before the Irish were back with a bang! The big bay mare Like A Butterfly was owned by J.P. McManus and ridden by the King of hurdle races, Charlie Swan, and the horse had constructed a monster reputation in Ireland. But when fellow Irish-raider, the less fancied Adamant Approach, came swinging through at the final hurdle in the opening Supreme Novices' Hurdle, the hot-pot looked cooked. However, Adamant Approach took a crashing fall, and this gave Like A Butterfly and Swan every impetus they needed to steam up the hill and hold the challenge of Westender – ridden by A.P. McCoy – to win, receiving thunderous Irish cheers as they did so. It was a stunning way to start the Festival, and served as a resounding 'welcome back' to the greatest meeting in National Hunt racing.

In contrast, the Champion Hurdle had as many downs as ups. Istabraq was there, but he looked on edge, uneasy. He

Despite every precaution, the 2001 Festival was lost to foot and mouth.

Like A Butterfly capitalizes on the fall of Adamant Approach in
the Supreme Novices' Hurdle.

was going for the record, but many wondered if the sands of time had finally caught him up. Out the back early on, Istabraq seemed to be struggling, and almost inevitably, the three-time hero was pulled-up passing the stands. As soon as he had exited the battle, Istabraq received a unanimous round of applause from the packed crowd; it was a surreal moment as the race had only just got going, but it was a moment the great champion fully deserved. As it transpired, Istabraq had pulled muscles in his back and would soon be

retired. The focus of the race then switched largely to the big grey horse, the rapidly improved Valiramix, representing Pipe and McCoy. Valiramix seemed to be travelling majestically when tragedy struck on the run to two out. The grey clipped the heels of Answar and flopped strangely to the turf. It was the most freakish of accidents, but sadly, Valiramix had broken a shoulder and would be put down. It was heart-breaking for McCoy in particular, having suffered through the demise of Gloria Victis two years before. Both that horse and

Dean Gallagher salutes the heavens as Hors La Loi III
enters the winner's enclosure.

Valiramix and Tony McCoy parade before the
Champion Hurdle.

Valiramix surely would have been champions, and the grey's
death justifiably left McCoy broken. The race saw Hors La Loi
III cap off the promise he had shown at previous Festivals, as
he finished strongest up the hill to win under Dean Gallagher
from Marble Arch and Bilboa. The winner was, on this
occasion, trained by James Fanshawe, who had tasted
success in the 1992 race with Royal Gait.

Flagship Uberalles, owned by American Michael
Krysztofiak, despite running a race of snatches, was the
horse that took Wednesday's Queen Mother Champion
Chase, but the top two-mile performance of the meeting
looked to have come a day earlier when the Jessica
Harrington-trained Moscow Flyer delivered a scintillating
display to win the Arkle Chase.

Another chaser of immense promise emerged from the
Royal & SunAlliance Chase in the form of Hussard Collonges,

a big bay gelding considered a natural successor to his trainer
Peter Beaumont's former Gold Cup winner, Jodami.

The finish of the meeting came in Thursday's Stayers'
Hurdle. The François Doumen-trained Baracouda, a
supremely talented horse that liked to be held up in his
races, seemed to have an awful lot to do to catch the gifted
giant Bannow Bay. But by the final flight, Thierry Doumen
had got Baracouda within striking distance, and as the
French hope powered up the hill to win in cheeky style, the
relief was commonplace among the hoards that had made
Baracouda the week's banker. Many people have criticised
young Thierry Doumen over the years, but whether he timed
Baracouda's run to perfection or not, he certainly showed
the utmost faith in what was clearly an outstanding horse.

It would be hard to find a more competitive Gold Cup
field than the eighteen-strong bunch that lined-up for the
2002 renewal. Virtually every runner had a fair chance of
winning, such was the high quality of those taking part. It
was worth considering the third biggest outsider in the field
was See More Business, the 1999 winner! This Gold Cup
was going to take some serious winning.

With First Gold sadly missing through injury, the favourite
was the most recent winner, Looks Like Trouble; injured the
season before but a horse that had won his only race of the
season in good style. He was strongly challenged in the
market by Nicky Henderson's Bacchanal, a tough stayer that
had won a recognised Gold Cup trial, the Aon Chase at
Newbury, most recently. Bacchanal and the smart big brown
chaser Marlborough were Henderson's first Gold Cup
runners since Raffi Nelson ran in 1981. The worry for the
fancied Bacchanal was that the ground appeared too fast for
him, even though it was officially good.

The Irish sent six worthy challengers. The group was
headed by Florida Pearl, who had won himself a much-

2002 TOTE GOLD CUP RESULT

FATE – HORSE	AGE/WEIGHT	JOCKEY	ODDS
1st – BEST MATE	7-12-0	J. CULLOTY	7/1
2nd – COMMANCHE COURT	9-12-0	R. WALSH	25/1
3rd – SEE MORE BUSINESS	12-12-0	J. TIZZARD	40/1
4th –Marlborough	10-12-0	D. Gallagher	12/1
5th – What's Up Boys	8-12-0	P. Flynn	33/1
6th – Alexander Banquet	9-12-0	B.J. Geraghty	12/1
7th – Moscow Express	10-12-0	J.R. Barry	66/1
8th – Cyfor Malta	9-12-0	R. Greene	25/1
9th – Foxchapel King	9-12-0	D.J. Casey	12/1
10th – Lord Noelie	9-12-0	Richard Guest	16/1
11th – Florida Pearl	10-12-0	C. O'Dwyer	10/1
12th – Bacchanal	8-12-0	M.A. Fitzgerald	6/1
13th – Looks Like Trouble	10-12-0	R. Johnson	9/2*
Fell – Sackville	9-12-0	J.L. Cullen	33/1
Pulled Up – Go Ballistic	13-12-0	C. Llewellyn	66/1
Pulled Up – Shooting Light	9-12-0	A.P. McCoy	10/1
Pulled Up – Behrajan	7-12-0	N. Williamson	11/1
Pulled Up – Shotgun Willy	8-12-0	T.J. Murphy	25/1

14 March 2002
Going – Good (Good to Soft in places)
Winner –£174,000
Time – 6mins 50. 10secs
18 Ran

Best Mate	Bay gelding by Un Desperado – Katday
Commanche Court	Chestnut horse by Commanche Run – Sorceress
See More Business	Bay gelding by Seymour Hicks – Miss Redlands

Winner bred by Jacques Van't Hart
Winner trained by Miss H.C. Knight at Wantage, Oxon.

OTHER 2002 FESTIVAL RESULTS

Gerrard Supreme Novices' Hurdle	Like A Butterfly	C. Swan	7/4
Irish Independent Arkle Chase	Moscow Flyer	B.J. Geraghty	11/2
Smurfit Champion Hurdle	Hors La Loi III	D. Gallagher	10/1
William Hill Nat Hunt Hcap Chase	Frenchman's Creek	P. Carberry	8/1
Fulke Walwyn – Kim Muir Chase	The Bushkeeper	Mr D. Crosse	9/2
Pertemps Final Handicap Hurdle	Freetown	A. Dobbin	20/1
Royal & SunAlliance Nov Hurdle	Galileo	J.M. Maguire	12/1
Queen Mother Champion Chase	Flagship Uberalles	R. Johnson	7/4
Coral Eurobet Cup Hcap Hurdle	Ilnamar	R. Greene	25/1
Royal & SunAlliance Chase	Hussard Collonges	R. Garritty	33/1
National Hunt Chase	Rith Dubh	Mr J.T. McNamara	10/1
Mildmay Of Flete Handicap Chase	Blowing Wind	R. Walsh	25/1
Weatherbys Champion Bumper	Pizarro	J.P. Spencer	14/1
JCB Triumph Hurdle	Scolardy	C. Swan	16/1
Bonusprint Stayers' Hurdle	Baracouda	T. Doumen	13/8
Christies Foxhunter Chase Ch Cup	Last Option	Mrs F. Needham	20/1
Cheltenham Grand Annual Chase	Fadoudal Du Cochet	D. J. Casey	6/1
Cathcart Challenge Cup Chase	Royal Auclair	A.P. McCoy	2/1
Vincent O'Brien County Hurdle	Rooster Booster	R. Johnson	8/1

coveted big race in England earlier in the season by taking the King George. There were those that still believed the Gold Cup trip to be beyond Willie Mullins' chaser, and many preferred his stablemate Alexander Banquet or the fast-improving Foxchapel King from Mouse Morris' yard. Ted Walsh too sent forward an interesting contender in the former Triumph Hurdle and Irish National winner Commanche Court, a horse expected to love the ground.

The latest horse to try and break Martin Pipe's Gold Cup hoodoo was the blinkered Shooting Light, who had won the season's Thomas Pink Gold Cup – formerly the Mackeson and Murphys – while the baby of the race, Best Mate, had long been held in high regard by his trainer Henrietta Knight, and Best Mate positively radiated health in the bustling pre-race paddock.

After a two-year absence, the roars went up as the Gold Cup field were sent on their way. The defending champion Looks Like Trouble was among the first to show, as he led a whole band of top-class chasers. See More Business took a handy position, with the likes of Florida Pearl, Bacchanal

A kiss for Henrietta after Best Mate's Gold Cup win.

going best of all, and suddenly, the horse began to accelerate rapidly on the inside rail as the leading trio pulled clear approaching the last two fences.

As Culloty charged his mount in to the lead at the last, Best Mate responded with a magnificent jump, and the young horse powered up the hill to defeat the brave Commanche Court by a length-and-three-quarters. See More Business had again illustrated his love of Cheltenham by taking third, with Marlborough coming home alone in fourth. Looks Like Trouble finished last of the thirteen that completed and was dismounted quickly by Richard Johnson after the race. Unfortunately, the injury-prone chaser had damaged himself again, and shortly, he too would be retired.

The young Best Mate had fulfilled the potential he undoubtedly had, and looked somewhat special doing it, there was just something about him. His trainer made no secret of the fact she thought the world of him, despite being notoriously afraid of watching him in his races through worry! Knight is married to former champion jockey Terry Biddlecombe, and the pair train many horses for Best Mate's owner Jim Lewis. Lewis, an avid Aston Villa fan, also proudly owned Edredon Bleu, the 2000 Queen Mother Champion Chase winner.

Winning jockey Jim Culloty – who would crown an incredible season by winning the Grand National on Bindaree a few weeks later – always appeared in complete control on Best Mate, and the horse jumped superbly all the way round, dispelling all fears that he may not have the necessary Gold Cup stamina. Indeed, it appeared Best Mate might only have scratched the surface of his potential, as he was very lightly raced prior to the win, and possessed both size and scope. There had been many false dawns in the hunt for the next great chaser, but as the crowds left Cheltenham on that March day, many whispered the name tentatively; Arkle? Time will tell.

and Foxchapel King in close attention. Early on, Best Mate, Commanche Court, Cyfor Malta and Marlborough were towards the rear.

Looks Like Trouble, although continuing to lead, was not jumping with great fluency and he made mistakes at the tenth and thirteenth fences with awkward leaps. Not so See More Business, who was clearly enjoying his fourth Gold Cup bid and was running as well as ever.

The pattern of the race began to change at the third last. Many of the perceived big guns, such as Bacchanal and Shooting Light, had failed to get in to the race, and Florida Pearl too began to go backwards. It was here that Looks Like Trouble started to weaken drastically, and it was one of the largely unconsidered Irish horses, Commanche Court, ridden by Ted's son Ruby, that arrived to dispute the lead with See More Business.

But having made steady progress from the seventeenth fence, it was Best Mate and jockey Jim Culloty that were

2003

BEST MATE

Since the previous year's Cheltenham Festival, the Queen Mother, so long a stalwart of National Hunt racing and a wonderful ambassador for the sport, had sadly passed away. The Queen Mother had been a regular at the Festival for many years, and her annual appearance brought joy and excitement to the thousands that gathered for a glimpse of the lifelong racing enthusiast upon her arrivals at Prestbury Park. In her absence, Her Majesty The Queen was present at the 2003 Cheltenham Festival on Gold Cup day. It was her first visit to the home of National Hunt racing since Silver Fame had won the Gold Cup back in 1951. Not surprisingly, her appearance garnered a huge wave of attention, and among her duties were to unveil a bronze statue of her late mother, and to present the Gold Cup to the connections of the winning horse, whoever it may be.

Perhaps fittingly then, the 2003 Gold Cup was the setting for an attempt to break a thirty-two year hoodoo. Best Mate had fulfilled his youthful promise by taking the 2002 Blue Riband, and had progressed in to a stronger, more respected individual in the current campaign. The chance was there for him to become the first horse to retain his crown since

L'Escargot in 1971. If he could do this, his place among the greats of the race would be assured, so infrequent was his task in hand realised. Since L'Escargot's successful follow-up, thirteen horses had tried and failed to defend their crown, with The Dikler in 1974 and Jodami in 1994 coming the closest with second places. Could Best Mate be the one to break the trend?

The first three races on Tuesday were taken in most convincing fashions by their victors. The Irish were off to a flyer when Back In Front simply destroyed his opponents in the Supreme Novices' Hurdle under Norman Williamson, in the style of a future Champion Hurdler. The win came for trainer Edward O'Grady, who ironically had claimed the same race twenty-five years earlier with the brilliant but ill-fated Golden Cygnet. O'Grady explained that he would be disappointed if Back In Front did not progress in to a serious Champion Hurdle prospect the following season.

2003 Racecard.

Arkle winner Azertyuiop, jockey Ruby Walsh and trainer Paul Nicholls in the trilby. On the far right is owner John Hales.

Rooster Booster is home in the Champion Hurdle.

After the Paul Nicholls-trained Azertyuiop had jumped imperiously to make a mockery of the Arkle field – giving owner John Hales of One Man fame an emotional return to the winner's enclosure – the scene was set for a competitive looking Champion Hurdle. The favourite was the classy seven-year-old Rhinestone Cowboy, trained by Jonjo O'Neill, and a horse unbeaten over hurdles. Indeed, Rhinestone Cowboy's only ever defeat had come in the roughhouse Champion Bumper of 2002, narrowly beaten by a hot fancy for the imminent Royal & SunAlliance Novices' Hurdle in Pizarro; that same Bumper had unearthed exciting novices Back In Front and Iris's Gift. For O'Neill, the worry for his youngster was inexperience, and he publicly preferred his other entry, the much improved front runner Intersky Falcon, owned by, amongst others, former England football captain Alan Shearer. O'Neill's worries were to come to fruition, as Rhinestone Cowboy made early errors, while Intersky Falcon set a hot pace. However, the race was

to belong to trainer Philip Hobbs' tough and much improved Rooster Booster, as the big grey travelled like a dream before tanking up the hill to dismantle his opposition under Richard Johnson. Rooster Booster had ended a frustrating run of narrow misses the season before by winning the 2002 County Hurdle, and he had now won five from five in this campaign. Westender ran a bold race to take second, while Rhinestone Cowboy could never threaten and came third.

The Queen Mother Champion Chase was won in emphatic style by the brilliant Moscow Flyer. Deemed by many the banker of the meeting, Jessica Harrington's charge followed up the promise of his Arkle win the year before by delivering a super display. Moscow Flyer joined the likes of Remittance Man, Klairon Davis and Flagship Uberalles as horses that in recent years had graduated from Arkle triumph to the pinnacle of the two-mile chasing tree. The unlucky horse of the race was Latalomne, who parted company with jockey Vinnie Keane two fences out when travelling well for

The hugely talented Moscow Flyer claims the Queen
Mother Champion Chase.

Baracouda leads the grey Iris's Gift and Limestone Lad at
the last in the Stayers'.

the second year in succession. However, the winner was excellent and proved the highlight of an outstanding Festival for Barry Geraghty, who would take the jockey's title with five wins.

Possibly the race of the meeting came in Thursday's Stayers' Hurdle, where the outstanding Baracouda retained his crown. Envisioned as a battle between Baracouda and the Irish darling Limestone Lad, it was the big grey novice Iris's Gift that moved sweetly down the hill for the final time with serious intent. But between the final two obstacles, Thierry Doumen – well criticised over his riding of Baracouda during the season – had the champion perfectly poised and he battled up the hill to hold the ultra-game Iris's Gift, with Limestone Lad back in third. Despite the defeat of Iris's Gift, together with those of his hotly fancied trio

Rhinestone Cowboy, Keen Leader (Royal & SunAlliance Chase) and Coolnagorna (Royal & SunAlliance Novices' Hurdle) over the three days, Jonjo O'Neill showed what a force he was becoming as a trainer by still registering three winners at the Festival courtesy of Inching Closer (Pertemps Final Handicap Hurdle), Sudden Shock (National Hunt Chase) and Spectroscope (Triumph Hurdle).

The word from Henrietta Knight and husband Terry Biddlecombe was that Best Mate was a stronger, better horse than in 2002. He had appeared a decent champion then and was now the hot favourite to join the elite group consisting of Easter Hero, Golden Miller, Cottage Rake, Arkle and L'Escargot, as multiple Gold Cup winners. Best Mate had won both races during the season, including a battling defeat of Marlborough in the King George. He looked an absolute picture in the pre-race paddock, and with the ground – officially good, good to soft in places – in his favour, there was a feeling that history was soon to be made. Best Mate carried sackloads of confidence into the race, and he was to start as the 13/8 favourite.

Before the 2002 Gold Cup, Best Mate was viewed as the young pretender harnessed with potential greatness. That role on this occasion was filled by the exciting Irish novice Beef Or Salmon. The horse arrived at Cheltenham with a tall reputation having won all four of his races during the season, including two high-class performances when picking off some very good horses at Leopardstown. Beef Or Salmon was held in the highest regard by his trainer Michael Hourigan, who readily passed over the Royal & SunAlliance Chase for a crack at the Blue Riband. A victory would also be a dream conclusion for jockey Timmy Murphy, who had spent some time in prison earlier in the season. Against the young Irish chestnut though was a distinct lack of experience coupled with a lack of the soft ground he had grown accustomed to.

Two interesting eight-year-olds lined-up for their first Gold Cup bids in the forms of Hussard Collonges and Best Mate's stablemate Chives. Both had been very consistent during the season without winning and were also considered to be ideal types for the Grand National, with jumping and staying their calling cards. However, two horses that had risen to prominence with eyecatching wins on their latest starts were Behrajan and Valley Henry. The tough stayer Behrajan had galloped his rivals into the ground when taking the Pillar Chase at Cheltenham in January while Paul Nicholls' young hope Valley Henry had looked a star when taking Newbury's Aon Chase, yet for some reason, had previously struggled at Cheltenham.

An immense crowd settled down to watch the latest renewal of chasing's Blue Riband, and the champion and favourite was quickly settled towards the rear by Jim Culloty, as rank outsider Modulor – having his first run for Martin Pipe – took the field along.

Also being held up at the back was Beef Or Salmon, but the Irish challenger was soon to discover the pressures of competing at Gold Cup level. Misjudging the third, Beef Or Salmon came down, leaving gasps rippling around the shocked crowd. Although the horse was unscathed, the day would only get worse for Hourigan, who lost his veteran ex-Gold Cup runner Dorans Pride to a broken leg in the Foxhunter Chase, won by the promising youngster Kingscliff.

As the field chugged on, it was Behrajan and the 1999 hero See More Business – enjoying an Indian Summer in his thirteenth year – that now led, but for much of the first circuit, the likes of Marlborough and the 2002 runner-up Commanche Court were struggling to go the pace. Even though he was prominent early on, Hussard Collonges was running an untypical race, unable to lie up with the leaders, and as the second circuit commenced, he too was struggling badly.

As the race progressed, there was a feeling of inevitability about the destiny of this Gold Cup, as Best Mate began to move stylishly through the pack. His stablemate Chives was running his usual bold and honest race, and it was he that led at the seventeenth. As they reached the top of the hill, Valley Henry was throwing down his challenge, having travelled supremely for much of the way.

But Valley Henry, Chives and the rest simply had no answer to the champion once Culloty sent Best Mate on from the second last. The response the horse gave served to illustrate what a powerful, classy performer he had matured in to. To a chorus of cheers, Best Mate surged clear and thundered up the finishing hill to claim his place in the elite group of winners. The giant chestnut Truckers Tavern, trained

2003 TOTE GOLD CUP RESULT

FATE – HORSE	AGE/WEIGHT	JOCKEY	ODDS
1st – BEST MATE	8-12-0	J. CULLOTY	13/8*
2nd – TRUCKERS TAVERN	8-12-0	D. N. RUSSELL	33/1
3rd – HARBOUR PILOT	8-12-0	P. CARBERRY	40/1
4th – Valley Henry	8-12-0	B.J. Geraghty	14/1
5th – Behrajan	8-12-0	R. Johnson	14/1
6th – Commanche Court	10-12-0	R. Walsh	8/1
7th – Chives	8-12-0	Richard Guest	25/1
8th – See More Business	13-12-0	J. Tizzard	16/1
9th – You're Agoodun	11-12-0	A.P. McCoy	50/1
10th – Colonel Braxton	8-12-0	K.A. Kelly	33/1
11th – Marlborough	11-12-0	M.A. Fitzgerald	20/1
12th – Modulor	11-12-0	R. Greene	200/1
Fell – Beef Or Salmon	7-12-0	T.J. Murphy	5/1
Pulled Up – First Gold	10-12-0	T. Doumen	33/1
Pulled Up – Hussard Collonges	8-12-0	R. Garritty	8/1

13 March 2003
Going – Good (Good to Soft in places)
Winner – £203,000
Time – 6mins 39secs
15 Ran

Best Mate	Bay gelding by Un Desperado – Katday
Truckers Tavern	Chestnut gelding by Phardante – Sweet Tulip
Harbour Pilot	Bay gelding by Be My Native – Las Cancellas

Winner bred by Jacques Van't Hart
Winner trained by Miss H.C. Knight at Wantage, Oxon.

OTHER 2003 FESTIVAL RESULTS

Gerrard Wealth Man Sup Nov Hur	Back In Front	N. Williamson	3/1
Irish Independent Arkle Chase	Azertyuiop	R. Walsh	5/4
Smurfit Champion Hurdle	Rooster Booster	R. Johnson	9/2
William Hill Nat Hunt Hcap Chase	Youlneverwalkalone	B.J. Geraghty	7/1
Fulke Walwyn – Kim Muir Chase	Royal Predica	Mr S. McHugh	33/1
Pertemps Final Handicap Hurdle	Inching Closer	B.J. Geraghty	6/1
Royal & SunAlliance Novices' Hurdle	Hardy Eustace	K.A. Kelly	6/1
Royal & SunAlliance Chase	One Knight	R. Johnson	15/2
Queen Mother Champion Chase	Moscow Flyer	B.J. Geraghty	7/4
Coral Cup Handicap Hurdle	Xenophon	M.A. Fitzgerald	4/1
National Hunt Chase	Sudden Shock	Mr D.W. Cullen	25/1
Mildmay Of Flete Handicap Chase	Young Spartacus	R. Johnson	16/1
Weatherbys Champion Bumper	Liberman	A.P. McCoy	2/1
JCB Triumph Hurdle	Spectroscope	B.J. Geraghty	20/1
Bonusprint Stayers' Hurdle	Baracouda	T. Doumen	9/4
Christies Foxhunter Chase Ch Cup	Kingscliff	Mr R. Young	11/4
Cheltenham Grand Annual Chase	Palarshan	M. Bradburne	8/1
Cathcart Challenge Cup Chase	La Landiere	R. Johnson	5/4
Vincent O'Brien County Hurdle	Spirit Leader	B.J. Geraghty	10/1

by Ferdy Murphy, came out of the clouds to finish second, with the Irish outsider Harbour Pilot staying on late to snatch third from the gallant Valley Henry.

Only Master Oats had bettered Best Mate's victory margin in recent years, and this performance stamped a huge mark of superiority on the champion's shoulders, with no trace of an error to be found in his round. Jubilant trainer Henrietta Knight had once likened Best Mate to Arkle, and with no obvious challengers – with the possible exceptions of a more experienced Beef Or Salmon or, should they go chasing, Baracouda and the big grey Iris's Gift – to threaten his crown, Best Mate, still only eight, continues to draw frequent comparisons with the most celebrated of champions. This was the day Best Mate was marked as a great horse. A third, highly achievable win, would elevate the strapping bay in to the class of Himself and five-time champion Golden Miller. Barring injury, that dream could surely become reality.